GENBA KANRI

For Joe Grieve, Walter H. Hudson, Kikuo Endo,
Colin O'Neil and Bob and Pat Hodgson, who always
made a special effort to teach things as they are.

GENBA KANRI

Edward Handyside

Gower

Published by
Gower Publishing Limited
Gower House
Croft Road
Aldershot
Hampshire GU11 3HR
England

Gower
Old Post Road
Brookfield
Vermont 05036
USA

Edward Handyside has asserted his right under the Copyright, Designs and Patents Act 1988 to be identified as the author of this work.

British Library Cataloguing in Publication Data
Handyside, Edward J.
  Genba Kanri : the disciplines of real relationships in the
  workplace
  I. Production management
  I. Title.
  658.5

ISBN 0 566 07898 8

Library of Congress Cataloging-in-Publication Data
Handyside, Edward J., 1958–
    Genba Kanri : the disciplines of real leadership and continuous
  improvement in the workplace / Edward J. Handyside.
      p.   cm.
    Includes bibliographial references and index.
    ISBN 0–566–07898–8 (hardback)
    1. Industrial management. 2. Manufactures—Management.
  3. Leadership. I. Title.
  HD31.H3128 1997   97–14929
  658. 4'092—dc21   CIP

Typeset in Great Britain by Bournemouth Colour Press, Parkstone, Dorset and printed in Great Britain by Hartnoll Limited, Bodmin.

Contents

Figures and Tables

FIGURES

TABLES

Preface

In 1989 I attended a conference in Britain on 'Strategies for Human Resource Development'. The UK economy was then at its most buoyant for some considerable time and the conference was conducted in an atmosphere of optimism and self-satisfaction. Many of the discussions concerned the attraction and retention of employees in a competitive and shrinking labour market where companies were struggling to hire, in particular, skilled workers, school leavers and graduates. The phrase 'demographic time bomb' was on everyone's lips. Most of the nationwide initiatives current in Britain with regard to vocational training were conceived at this time and against this background. (Few at the conference anticipated that the problem would resolve itself in the worst of circumstances within 18 months.) High-sounding epithets abounded in the conference hall. Virtually every company was launching some type of 'total quality management' programme. Yet it was clear from their systems, their procedures, their employment practices, their organisational structures and above all from the roles and responsibilities assigned to their people that nothing much was actually changing; that all we were experiencing was a transient nudge forward as a result of a cyclic economic upturn, coupled with the demise, during the 1980s, of some of the more pernicious restrictive practices of organised labour.

One of the first speakers to address the conference was an American called Tom Furtado, who clearly found himself out of step with the ebullient and self-congratulatory atmosphere which prevailed. He fired a few warning shots about the underlying industrial strength of the Asia–Pacific Rim and drew the conclusion, from the conference agenda, that the anticipated debates would be much the same as were taking place in his own country. Whilst recognising the validity of discussions concerning change strategies, competence-based learning routes and career paths to management, the role of professional qualifications, problems of skill transferability, the need to forge links between education and business and the like, he expressed the desire that these debates be conducted and concluded with some urgency so that, having identified form and framework, we might at last tackle the crucial issue of *content* – and thereby start to rebuild our industrial capability.

Alas for Mr Furtado and all those who shared his frustrations and concern for the future of Western industry! Despite the fact that the economic cycle has made a full revolution since the conference, the fulcrum of the debate has still not shifted. *Content*, you see, is fraught with difficulty. It is hard to discuss content without causing antagonism and irritation. Content is subjective. In seeking to define and perhaps to prescribe a better way, it cannot help but implicitly criticise what already exists. This is particularly difficult during those times when we are inclined to be satisfied with our achievements.

Mr Furtado's address was given a tepid response. It was not what delegates wanted to hear. The chairman of the session, a high-ranking human resources development (HRD) strategist from a Western motor manufacturing company, could not help but deliver a mild rebuke when summing up the discussion. He expressed the view that there really was too much of an inclination towards 'donning sackcloth and ashes' and that, in Britain, industry was 'doing really rather well'. Three years later, in the face of a serious worldwide recession which was particularly damaging to the European car market, that same chairman's company started to work a three-day week, drastically reduced its prices to barely profitable levels in order to move stock and started to plan compulsory redundancies. Meanwhile, the car company for which I had been working at the time of the conference, operating within the same restricted market, was working significant amounts of overtime and regularly expanding its recruitment programme and manufacturing volumes to meet increased demand for its products.

This book, therefore, is unashamedly about *content*. It makes no apologies for taking a subjective approach in endeavouring to identify how manufacturing companies *ought to be managed*; how, in broad terms, they *need to be structured*; the disciplines and business practices which *must* be adopted; the systems and procedures for the management of people and processes which are most conducive to high levels of quality and productivity; and, in particular, identifying the roles and responsibilities which *people need to adopt to make this happen*. In writing it, therefore, I am aware that it is not likely to find favour with everyone.

Content is provocative, controversial and lacking in humility. I can only therefore request the forbearance of those whose sensibilities I may well offend in one area or another, be they from the disciplines of engineering, personnel, quality assurance or whatever. It may be that there are those who are achieving excellent results and are working to principles totally at odds with those contained in this book. There may be others who already value and are pursuing the principles set out here. In both cases, I wish such people well and hope that they are nevertheless challenged and stimulated in some way by what I have written. For my part I am content to take refuge in the sound Northumbrian wisdom often voiced by my grandfather: 'If ye've huffed naebody, ye've said nowt'.

Nevertheless I assure readers that, however they finally determine the worth of this volume, it has been compiled in good faith and in accordance with practical experience. I have found these disciplines to work. They work within the structure and culture of the industrial West. They work for so-called 'greenfield sites' and in long-established traditional factories. They work irrespective of product, process or level of technology. They work in highly unionised and in non-unionised environments. They work in large and small companies. They work because they emphasise the *management of the process* and the institutionalisation of continuous improvement in the day-to-day activity of each person in the organisation. For in every manufacturing company, the true wellspring of improvement and profitability lies within the manufacturing process itself.

Edward J. Handyside

Acknowledgements

I am grateful to all those who, consciously or otherwise, have contributed in some way to the ideas contained in these pages. They include: S. Ando, Doreen Bewick, John Burton, Nino Caja, Brian Carolin, Jim Cowan, John Cushnaghan, Arthur David, Chris Davies, Don Dees, Peter Dobbs, Colin Dodge, Alan Downie, Vic Edwards, Paul Elliot, Gunter Finke, Michael Frye, Tony Hammock, Jim Harvey, Werner Hoffmeyer, T. Iizuka, Masaaki Imai, Stan James, Yukio Kakiuchi, K. Kikuchihara, M. Kodama, Yuji Komiyama, Quentin Kopp, Otto Meikus, Lutz Meiller, Steve Milner, Stan Osborne, Bob Reay, Brian Rhodes, Dave Robson, Hamilton Rockliffe, Y. Shibuya, John Smart, Geoff Smith, Terry Smith, Angela Spowart, Brian Tweedy, Bran Walker, Dennis Ware, Jack Watts, Peter Wickens and the first supervisor I ever worked with, the late Greta Woodfine.

The pages themselves have been made possible by the support and encouragement of Malcolm Stern at Gower, the timely advice of my agent Mandy Little and the efforts of Solveig Gardner Servian and Elizabeth Teague to make this a much better book than it otherwise would have been. I am also grateful for the invaluable help of my colleagues Jim Turner, David Redpath, Tim Waddington and Graham Gordon-Hart who not only made contributions and gave feedback but also had to work so much harder to mind the shop while I gazed out of windows.

Special thanks must go to Gillian Stocker, who typed the manuscript innumerable times and with infinite patience, and also to my wife Julie and to my family for putting up with my strange work pattern and barely tolerable behaviour – especially that which I have sought to excuse by the writing of this book.

E.J.H.

Glossary

Check and repair operator A team member, near the end of a production zone, whose assignment, in part or whole, consists of ensuring that no defective products leave the zone and who works for the production team by supplying process and fault data, chiefly for internal consumption.

Conventional companies Non- *Genba Kanri* (q.v.) companies. Companies who may perhaps have introduced new 'Japanese' or 'world-class' manufacturing techniques but whose core business practices and assumptions about managing productive work are still those of the 1950s and 1960s.

Customer Any individual, team or function downstream which expects a product or service and can express its needs in terms of quality, cost and delivery. The term 'commercial client' is used to refer to customers in the traditional sense of the word. Other customers are referred to as 'internal customers' or 'downstream processes'.

Fast changeovers: (see **SMED**)

First Line Manager (FLM) The leader and manager of a production team. Common job titles are supervisor, foreman, team manager, cell manager or even team leader. The First Line Manager is the very focus and fulcrum of *Genba Kanri* (q.v.). He or she has a very comprehensive range of operational responsibilities and the knowledge and authority to carry them out. The term GK FLM is used to denote those who perform such a role in a GK company.

Five C activity Steps for achieving and maintaining a well ordered workplace in the interests of quality, safety and efficiency. Originally 'Five S' system from five Japanese words: *seiri* (neatness), *seiton* (order), *seiso* (cleanliness), *seiketsu* (purity) and *shitsuke* (discipline). The Five Cs are: clear out, configure, clean and check, conformity, custom and habit (see Appendix II).

Four Principles of Motion Economy Simple industrial engineering maxims for removing waste from any physical activity. The four principles are:

1. Reduce the number of motions
2. Perform motions simultaneously
3. Shorten motion distances
4. Make motions easier.

(See Appendix I.)

Genba Kanri A production management doctrine based on Western management traditions but now mainly (though not exclusively) practised by Japanese-owned companies. It emphasises a disciplined approach to managing processes and the institution of direct leadership in the workplace.

GK companies Companies who consciously or otherwise reflect **Genba Kanri** principles in their core business practices and management assumptions. Most are still Japanese or Japanese-owned companies but there is nothing inherently Japanese about **Genba Kanri**.

Help lamps Common devices in GK assembly operations where there is a conveyor line. Flashing lights and alarm buzzers are activated by line workers experiencing difficulties to summon help from **FLMs** (q.v.), **Team Leaders** (q.v.) or other team members. Should help not be forthcoming or should the problem be more serious, or a threat to safety, all workers have the means and authority to stop the conveyor.

Inputs The three factors of production: man, machine and materials. These may be the resources of the production zone or provided as the **outputs** (q.v.) of upstream suppliers.

Kaizen Japanese word for continuous improvement – usually implies small-scale, incremental improvements requiring minimal or zero capital spend. **Genba Kanri** demands that **kaizen** should be seen as:

- *doing*, not suggesting;
- a normal part of the job, a habitual way of life in the company and not just a series of special events.

Kanban Merely a device – usually a ticket or slip – which triggers delivery of an optimal quantity of raw materials, parts or part processed products as and when required by the downsteam process: nothing more or other than this, despite widespread misuse of the term.

Lean manufacturing *Not* merely manufacturing 'just-in-time' or introducing *kanban* systems, but taking an approach which is centred upon meeting the true needs of downstream customers at minimal cost and consumption of resources. Requires a level of awareness and ways of measuring performance which *make waste visible*.

Manufacturing capability   The extent to which manufacturing companies can regularly increase the value ratio of outputs over inputs, or can make more with the same or the same with less. It also refers to the speed and frequency with which they can rotate the improvement cycle of Plan, Do, Check and Action.

Output   One of three characteristics of a marketable commodity, in terms of quality, cost or delivery. *Not* production volume. Key outputs for the *internal* customer chain are quality and delivery.

Overproduction   Producing more than the quantity required by the commercial client or downstream process, usually for no better reason than to keep workers and machines fully occupied and fulfil the demands of performance measures that are rarely relevant to the commercial world that we now inhabit. Overproduction is the biggest cause of waste in conventional firms and the most difficult to identify and remove.

Planned preventive maintenance   An approach which emphasises *avoiding* breakdowns by regular planned activity rather than fixing them. The same approach is used in servicing cars. Requires careful recording of machine histories, for example, to predict the failure of parts and renew or refurbish them before breakdown. PPM activity can be carried out by maintenance personnel, production team members or, most commonly, a combination of both according to the complexity of and time required for the task.

Poka yoke (**'mistake proofing'**)   An approach which uses simple *low-cost* jigs and devices to eliminate process errors. There are three levels of effectiveness, listed here in reverse order:
3. Devices which prevent *receipt* of non-conforming product
2. Devices which prevent *shipment* or passing on of non-conforming product
1. Devices which prevent *manufacture* of non-conforming product.

Post-shift review   Attended by the production management team (FLMs) of a specific unit and key representatives of supplier functions. It is conducted by the **Second Line Manager** and usually lasts between 15 and 40 minutes. Its purpose is to assess the performance of the plant or unit during the shift, highlight problems and establish actions to solve them.

Pre-hire The practice of bringing new production workers on board two or three weeks in advance of proportionate production volume to allow for training and the acquisition of specific operational skills. Usually they are introduced to the workplace a few at a time and in a controlled way against a production volume which is gradually increasing. Pre-hire is basic common sense which is rarely acted on.

Pre-shift briefing Attended by all members of production and support teams at the start of every production shift. It is conducted by the FLM and typically lasts for five minutes. Its purpose is to give specific feedback on team performance and explain anticipated problems, actions and priorities for the forthcoming shift.

Production zone The clearly defined process, product and geographical domain of the production FLM and his or her team, including all the equipment, materials and production processes therein. All upstream zones are supplier zones; all downstream zones are customer zones.

Second Line Manager The First Line Manager's boss. Job titles such as: shift manager, unit manager, production manager, general foreman (common in Japan), senior supervisor (Nissan UK), superintendent (Ford). In a small company this may be the works or operations manager, production or manufacturing director or even the managing director (MD) or chief executive officer (CEO).

SMED (single-minute exchange of die) Simple disciplines which dramatically reduce the time required to change over or reset a machine (**fast changeovers**). Developed by the Japanese industrial engineer, Shigeo Shingo, their real contribution is made within the context of a lean manufacturing discipline. The goal is not so much marginally to increase available running time but to facilitate more frequent changeovers and smaller batch quantities. The four tools of SMED – elimination, conversion, combination and reduction – are machine-specific applications of the **Four Principles of Motion Economy** (q.v.).

Standard Operation The best currently available method (in all its necessary practical detail) for achieving quality, cost and delivery as specified and for sustaining safe working practices. In GK organisations the main responsibility for prescribing this rests with the production FLM; the Standard Operation is forever changing in pursuit of improved performance.

Standard times Classically defined as the time required to perform a standard operation, by standard workers, using standard effort, in standard conditions. In GK organisations, these times are usually determined using work factor tables or other synthetic means with very little added in the way of contingency allowances for local conditions. It is the FLM's job to achieve and maintain optimised working conditions. Standard times are used for budgeting, planning and tendering purposes. In GK organisations they are also starting-points, targets for production FLMs and their teams to improve on. Where standard times are used as a formal or tacitly understood contract between the company and its workforce, they become **work standards**.

Team Leader   The most common job title for the GK FLM's deputy, understudy and 'strong right arm'. *Not* the leader of the team (that is the FLM). The term is actually a Japanese title which happens to use English words. It really should have been rendered as 'leading hand' or 'lead operator'. In a GK company there may be one or more Team Leaders in the FLM's team. Their main functions are:

- to deputise for the FLM where necessary;
- to carry out much of the on-the-job (Standard Operation) training in the team;
- to provide a first response to problems such as breakdowns, quality problems and material shortages, or to give immediate support to any team member encountering difficulties.

Total productive maintenance (TPM)   There are various interpretations of TPM. GK disciplines identify the following as necessary components:

- emphasis on **planned preventive maintenance** (PPM) actions which *prevent* rather than fix breakdowns;
- the majority of simple, short duration, cyclical maintenance activities are undertaken by the machine operator or equipment user on a planned and monitored basis;
- a flexible approach to providing specialist maintenance support. Maintenance team members are 'technicians' or 'maintenance staff', not 'electricians', 'fitters', 'millwrights' and so on; each must do what their skills allow in the service of their customers.

Waste   Any activity or the consumption of any resource which does not add value, that is, makes no contribution to satisfying the wants of customers.

Work standard   A quota or 'rate for the job' (for example, the number of units per hour or time taken to perform a given job to earn a wage). Usually a feature of an 'hourly-paid' rather than a 'salaried' position. Condemned by Deming in his eleventh principle as a serious impediment to the progress of Western companies, they do not feature in GK organisations.

Part I
The Need for Continuous Improvement

1 Manufacturing Capability

Fortunae rota volvitur: descendo minoratus;
Alter in altum tollitur, nimis exultatus;
Rex sedet in vertice – caveat ruinam!
Nam sub axe legimus Hecubam reginam.

(The wheel of fortune spins: one man is abased by its descent, the other is carried aloft; all too exalted sits the king at the top – let him beware ruin! For beneath the wheel we read that Hecuba is queen.)

Fortuna Imperatrix Mundi (Luck, Empress of the World)
Carmina Burana: A thirteenth-century collection of Bavarian songs

RECLAIMING OUR HERITAGE

Even for manufacturing companies, manufacturing strength is not everything. Innovative design, shrewd marketing, financial acumen and commercial enterprise are all important too. For the greater part of the 1990s General Motors, not Toyota, Honda or Nissan, was the world's most profitable motor manufacturer. But then GM are not so fond as to imagine themselves to be as capable as these rivals when it comes to performance in the factory. Nor do they incline towards complacency about the situation, for they know that markets wax and wane, that customer preferences change, and that for any company the next 'design pig' may be just around the corner. Navigating turbulent financial and commercial seas is far less nerve-racking when the corporate hull is founded on a sturdy keel of superior manufacturing capability.

Superior manufacturing capability is, not exclusively, but *predominantly* still enjoyed by Japanese-owned companies and increasingly those from other countries of the Asia–Pacific Rim. Statements of the fact tend to either depress or simply bore Western managers, depending on the phase of the economic cycle in which they are made, but that select band of companies that possess superior manufacturing capability know that it runs like a steel rod through their business, providing an inner reinforcement which is itself immune to the ravages of slump or recession.

3

That competitive edge springs not from low wages, high technology, wartime devastation, Shinto-Buddhism, the team-building characteristics of the medieval rice harvest, a diet of raw fish or even a greater range of manufacturing tools and techniques. It comes from *discipline* and *tenacity* and from a superior level of skill in managing the manufacturing process.

In spite of the language of the term, *Genba Kanri* is not a Japanese phenomenon; rather it is one geared towards the demands of international competition and slow growth. Though a mixture of foresight and historical chance brought it to prominence in Japan, hence giving it a Japanese label, it is derived from the best traditions of *Western* management. That is why, in developing the discourse and after describing some of the background to the subject, I take the simple expedient of referring to it as 'GK' and the companies that follow its principles as not Japanese companies but 'GK companies'. GK is available to all and a threat to all who do not possess it. To adopt and foster GK disciplines is simply to come to terms with the modern industrial world.

Genba Kanri is not a shop window of goods on display. It is not simply a presentation box whose contents vary in accordance with what the purveyors of Japanese tools and techniques have 'on special offer' this month. It is a fully integrated and strategic approach and must be regarded as such. All its component elements are indispensable if its full benefits are to be realised.

This emphasis is not spawned by insensitivity towards the differences between companies in terms of their size, processes, products or demography. For a company to benefit fully from *Genba Kanri* there must be scope for modifying these elements, both in their actual shape and format and in the manner in which they are introduced. But the elements *must be there* in one form or another.

The past two decades have witnessed a procession of writers, consultants and Western manufacturing managers undertaking 'the Cook's tour' of Japanese manufacturing plants, all of them in search of the Grail of manufacturing competitiveness. What have they seen? They have seen quality circles, they have seen morning callisthenics, statistical process control (SPC) charts and company uniforms. They have seen 'fishbone diagrams' and Pareto graphs of performance displayed in production areas. They have seen the trucks of suppliers delivering materials directly to the production lines on the hour. They have heard workers singing the 'company song'.

Some have noted the mere trappings of Japanese culture. Others have brought back useful tools and approaches for Western consumption. Very few have had the opportunity, by working closely with production workers and foremen on the shop floor, fully to understand the disciplines and concepts which underpin the application of these tools. Outside this context few of them, therefore, have had much of an impact, in terms of significantly transforming the performance of Western manufacturing companies.

Moreover, those concepts and principles which have been grasped to a greater or lesser extent are seldom put across in an integrated way. Books and articles have been written, severally and specifically, about 'lean manufacturing', statistical process control, total quality management, *poka yoke* (mistake-proofing devices), total productive maintenance, Taguchi techniques, quality function deployment, seven statistical tools, quick changeovers, visual management, the 5S approach to workplace organisation, just-in-time and *kanban*, simultaneous engineering, one-piece flow methods, cellular manufacturing and many, many others.

Few if any of such publications have faithfully described how all these techniques and principles are, in effect, branches of the same tree; and how these various aspects work together and mutually reinforce one another in order to bring about world-beating standards of manufacturing performance. The relative failure of Western companies to make full use of 'Japanese' techniques stems from the fact that such techniques are based on very different assumptions about how manufacturing ought to be managed. If these assumptions are not changed, then the benefits of the techniques will inevitably be diluted. For the last 20 years, we have been trying to pour new wine into old wineskins.

Furthermore, certain key items are missing. Ironically, these tend to be just those things which the Japanese take for granted as being an integral part of the *Western* management tradition. For they are concerned mainly with *how work is managed*. They are principles which would easily be recognised in the West by those of our grandparents who worked in industry; but their currency has been debased over the years in pursuit of a systemised and stand-off approach to managing manufacturing operations. What has happened here is that, in various ways, we have overturned many of the sound principles held by previous generations – principles which we in the West have successfully transported to the East and then neglected. It has been observed that 'the Japanese practise what *we* preach'. It is rather that the Japanese have practised, improved and refined principles that we, having taught them, have ourselves virtually forgotten.

Hence, what is advocated in these pages is not the worship and mindless adoption of all things Japanese, irrespective of whether they are applicable and transferable to our own situation. Rather their purpose is to argue for the reclamation of our own manufacturing heritage.

If the Japanese were to credit one individual with their manufacturing success, it would surely be the late Dr W. Edwards Deming, a name known by every Japanese high-school pupil and yet, until fairly recently, largely unknown in his own country. Deming was an American who, during the 1950s, together with his compatriot Joseph M. Juran and others, travelled to Japan to teach the Japanese about quality. Deming regarded himself first and foremost as a statistician. He learned statistics from an Englishman, Ronald Aylmer Fisher, at University College, London. Fisher was later knighted in recognition of his work in developing practical applications for statistical methods. He also pioneered a statistical approach to the design of experiments. Much of this work has since been adapted and defined by the Japanese quality assurance practitioner, Genichi Taguchi, and we now know them not as 'Fisher techniques' but as 'Taguchi techniques'.

Eiji Toyoda and Taiichi Ohno, the Toyota executives who developed the Toyota manufacturing system, which includes just-in-time, quick changeover techniques and a vigorous approach both to the elimination of non-value-added activity and to constant application of continuous process improvement, had no qualms about attributing many of their early inspirations to Henry Ford.[1] The late Shigeo Shingo, Japan's most renowned industrial engineer, who not only contributed to Toyota's success but was influential in revitalising Japan's steel and shipbuilding industries, decided to embark on his chosen vocation after reading an early Japanese translation of Frederick Taylor's *Scientific Management*. Konosuke Matsushita, founder of Matsushita Electrical Industrial Co., Ltd, first learned about quality management in 1948 from Homer Sarasohn, a member of General Douglas MacArthur's staff.

The training within industry (TWI) movement started in the US at the end of World War II and quickly became a major government-driven programme, there and in Britain, swiftly to rebuild the industrial skills lost to a generation of fighting men. TWI became an important tool for the Japanese in establishing a thorough approach to on-the-job training and process management and remains the bedrock of their work management discipline today, 40 years after it was dismissed in the West as too slow, too time-consuming and too detailed for pursuing the benefits of the postwar boom. It was quickly forgotten about and now we marvel at the Japanese passion for detail and meticulousness which we mistakenly attribute to their genes or to their culture.

At the start of the 1980s, at the age of 22, I embarked on a career in manufacturing. The terms 'total quality control', 'right first time' and 'building in quality' were whispered by managers as the latest things that the Japanese were up to. But Armand Feigenbaum, an American, was the first to use these words and advocate their disciplines in the year before I was born.[2]

While in Japan, I and my colleagues were constantly receiving gifts and courtesies from Nissan veterans, who wished to recognise and return hospitalities they had enjoyed in Britain during the mid-1950s. They were there to learn how to build motor vehicles.

I would suggest, therefore, to those who have experienced some discomfort at the thought of having to swallow 'the Japanese way of doing things' that, if we wish to survive and prosper, we should not be too proud to learn from our competitors in the same way that our competitors were not too proud to learn from us, particularly when much of the learning in question consists primarily of principles which have originated for the most part in Western Europe and in the US.

REMOTE CONTROL MANAGEMENT

The decline of these principles in the West can largely be attributed to the era of the fast growth economy of the 1950s and 1960s, to the years when Western manufacturers 'never had it so good'.[3] The left-hand column of Table 1.1 lists

Fast growth economy: 1950s & 1960s	Slow growth economy: mid-1970s & onwards
• Local markets and suppliers	• Global markets and suppliers
• Demand exceeds supply	• Supply exceeds demand
• Economies of scale	• *Real* cost reduction
• Emphasis on technical innovation	• Emphasis on process improvement
• Reliance on technical specialists	• Reliance on *all* employees
• Specialised labour and management	• Maximised flexibility
• Product quality relatively unimportant	• Product quality of prime importance
• Product 'pushed' by the upstream supplier	• Product 'pulled' by the downstream customer
• In-process stockpiling before bottlenecks	• Minimising inventories and throughput times
• Big batches – long production runs	• Small batches – more changeovers
• Keep machines running and ensure workers have enough work to do	• Making the right things in the right quantities at the right time
• Emphasis on being *efficient*	• Emphasis on being *effective*
• Emphasis on reducing the need to manage	• Emphasis on sound management disciplines
• Management by remote control	• *Leadership* at the front line

Table 1.1   The changed demands of manufacturing

some of the economic features of that era, together with the assumptions about manufacturing management which accompanied it.

This was a time when there was a unique and unparalleled demand for manufactured goods; when ordinary families were acquiring or aspiring to acquire their first motor cars, television sets and refrigerators; when, if we wanted to enhance our revenues, all we needed to do was invest in the technology which would enable us to make more and attain the benefits of economies of scale. How, at the time, the Japanese must have yearned to exploit these opportunities! But, with neither the capital nor the natural resources to compete in this climate, they could only cling faithfully to the precepts of thorough process management taught to them by Western texts and advisers and rely on their one substantial resource: their people.

When, in the early 1970s, the climate started to change, this approach started to pay remarkable dividends. Supply now exceeded demand, and sound manufacturing disciplines, untended and unwanted in their countries of origin, proved to be of inestimable value when seeking to enhance product quality and reduce actual costs – factors of relative unimportance in a fast-growth economy but vital in a slow-growth economy.

In addition to neglecting the very disciplines taught to their latter-day competitors, Western companies set about supplanting direct leadership in the workplace with management by remote control. Partly in response to real or perceived industrial relations problems, partly out of laziness during the fat years, systems and procedures were created which ostensibly made the job of management easier but which, with the onset of the lean years, destroyed the initiative and flexibility of their workforces and stifled their ability to identify and seize opportunities for process improvements.

The rise of remote control management brought with it a sustained retreat from the obligations of managing work. This is not a reference to surveillance or to any perceived need to oversee people – there is still far too much of that – but to the observation, control and sustained improvement of manufacturing processes, to the disciplines which assure the highest standards of quality and productivity in factories worldwide. Yet in virtually every conventional company that I have visited over the past few years, one feature stands out more than any other: *there is simply an absence of real production management*. Yes, there are people *called* 'production managers', supervisors, team leaders. They run themselves ragged chasing resources and seeking emergency fixes for problems but *they do not manage production*. They usually lack the time, the interest and the understanding to observe, maintain and improve the manufacturing process: the work itself.

It is not merely that disruptions and crises are inherent in Western factories, for it is in the very nature of production operations that there are always unforeseen problems; nor is it that Western managers lack proactive skills. The deficiency runs much deeper than that: they are firefighters because, quite simply, they are given nothing better to do. Nothing further is expected of them. The observation and study of productive work is a lost art and production management is a lost profession.

I confess to deliberate provocation in this discourse, but, if anyone working in conventional manufacturing companies would challenge the veracity of these assertions, let them go down into the factory and observe work, in all its detail: watch one worker perform a job six or seven times. If they can observe the activity for which, as managers, they are nominally responsible, without discomfort or without causing anxiety or suspicion on the part of the person performing the job, then I agree to withdraw the provocation. But why, even after the infusion of new approaches in the 1980s and 1990s, and even during times of relative prosperity, when we are often dismissive and disparaging towards things Japanese, do we still find that most of the production management tools and techniques, for which we seem to retain an insatiable appetite, still come predominantly from Japan? Why so few from Europe or North America? The fact is that virtually all stem from a tradition of managing productive work and a detailed focus on *production methods*. And though that tradition originated in the West, it has long since expired.

This is why these tools and techniques never give full value in conventional organisations. It is why even many of the biggest and most prestigious of Western companies (including virtually all the West's indigenous car makers), who have openly sought to benefit from 'Japanese' approaches, cannot walk the talk. In spite of considerable investment in expensive training and in the production of big, fat, glossy in-house manuals for just-in-time, TPM and the rest, they lack the necessary business practices and fundamental assumptions about production to secure the full benefits. They lack a coherent and compatible *doctrine* of manufacturing management.

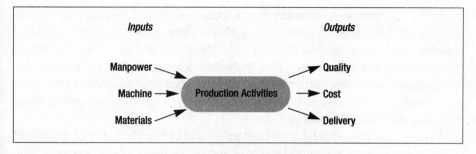

Figure 1.1   Manufacturing capability

OF INPUTS AND OUTPUTS

Having used the term 'manufacturing capability' it is appropriate to introduce a model of what it entails (Figure 1.1). Profitable manufacture, as a concept, is very simple: we only served to make it complicated during the 'never had it so good' years, when sophisticated management systems were introduced to ease our lives as managers and relieve ourselves of the burden of having to manage the work directly. We are simply engaged in converting inputs into outputs. The inputs are often called the 'three factors of production' or the 'three Ms': manpower, machinery and materials.[4]

By a series of production activities which we describe, sometimes rather flatteringly, as methods or processes, we convert our inputs into outputs. These outputs need to be *marketable commodities*. Products become marketable only when they have the characteristics of quality, cost and delivery time. All three are aspects of quality. The label 'quality' in Figure 1.1 refers to the product's functional or visual attractions (often uninspiringly described as 'fitness for purpose'). But competitive pricing and availability are equally important. Quality and cost are inseparable in the perception of prospective customers, who will invariably evaluate the one in terms of the other. Together all three comprise the factors which combine to please. When aggregated, they give the perceived value of the product and service in the market.

Clearly, profitability is determined by ensuring that the value of outputs exceeds the value of inputs. There is nothing new or clever in this. It is the first requirement for the owners or directors of any business and is as old as commerce itself. At times in history this, of itself, has been sufficient. When we wanted to increase our profits, all we needed to do was improve our access to the market and enlarge our capacity for supplying it, without necessarily changing the ratio of the value of outputs and inputs; without enhancing our manufacturing capability.

However, when we consider the demands of modern, internationally competitive manufacturing, in what is now a predominantly slow-growth economy where market demand is strictly limited, there are two further imperatives. We must *continually* strive to increase the value of the outputs and reduce the value

9

of the inputs: improved manufacturing capability is now a prerequisite of long-term survival. What is more, we must do this at a rate, in terms of both speed and volume, which surpasses the achievements of our competitors, who are naturally endeavouring to do the same. This, in bottom-line terms, is what enables GK manufacturers to outperform so many of their conventional competitors. They can recognise and respond to opportunities for improvement *faster, more frequently* and *in greater volume*.

They are able to do this because their entire workforce, the entire population of their organisation, is aware of the model and of the need for improvement. The imperatives are no longer regarded as the preserve of senior managers and of technical specialists. Improvement is everybody's job. All are responsible not only for carrying out their everyday allotted tasks as part of the conversion activity but also for improving the ratio of outputs over inputs; for constantly finding the means of improving quality and shortening lead times at no commensurate increase in cost, or reducing the cost of manpower, equipment and materials without any detrimental effects on the supply of quality goods or services.

There is a new unwritten job description at work in such companies. It is the only job description with profitable consequences, the only one capable of reducing costs or adding real value to products and services. It is simple and universal. It applies to everyone, irrespective of seniority, professional discipline or functional role:

> Your job is to partake in the transformation of resources into marketable commodities and also to strive constantly for the means to reduce consumption of the former and increase the value of the latter: to find means of making more with the same or the same with less.

It is often said that workers in Japanese companies work not harder, but *smarter* than their counterparts in most Western factories. They do not work smarter because they *are* smarter. They work smarter because they are allowed, encouraged and, above all, *expected* by their employers to work smarter. Their systems, procedures and management assumptions lend themselves to making changes and improvements easily, whereas those of most Western organisations conspire to make them prohibitively difficult and tediously slow. This, in a nutshell, is the real fundamental reason for Japanese manufacturing supremacy. What follows is an explanation of the doctrine, assumptions and mechanisms which make such success possible.

NOTES

1. Ohno published his book on just-in-time in Japan in 1986 (Tokyo: Diamond Inc). When it was translated into English for US publication two years later, he elected to give it the subtitle 'For Today and Tomorrow', directly alluding to the title of a book co-authored by Henry Ford. It is worth pondering how many of Ohno's American readers either knew or would find it significant

that Ford had written such a book. See T. Ohno and S. Mito(1988), *Just-In-Time For Today and Tomorrow*, Cambridge, Mass.: Productivity Press; and H. Ford and S. Crowther (1926), *Today and Tomorrow*, New York: Doubleday and Co. Ltd.

2. A.V. Feigenbaum (1957), 'Total Quality Control', *Industrial Quality Control*, May; and (1961) *Total Quality Control: Engineering and Management*, New York: McGraw-Hill.

3. Clearly indicative of a transatlantic feeling of contentment, though the statement 'You've never had it so good' is famously attributed in Britain to Harold Macmillan in 1957, it was originally a slogan in the US presidential election campaign of 1952.

4. Some people like to add money and/or management to our list of resources, because they also start with an 'M' and because they like to complicate things. Putting the exigencies of cash flow to one side I assume, for the purposes of a pure manufacturing model, that we only spend on manpower, machinery and materials. If in a given organisation we have the good fortune to regard our managers as a resource rather than a constraint, then I am content to include them under the banner of manpower.

2 *Kaizen* and the Improvement Cycle

> *We have to understand that the world can only be grasped by an action, not by contemplation ... The most powerful drive in the ascent of man is his pleasure in his own skill. He loves to do what he does well and, having done it well, he loves to do it better.*
>
> Jacob Bronowski, *The Ascent of Man*

KAIZEN DEFINED

The word *kaizen* and its association with continuous improvement are now fairly familiar to Western managers. The term was popularised by Professor Masaaki Imai in 1986. Imai defines his subject thus:

> When applied to the workplace KAIZEN means continuing improvement involving everyone – managers and workers alike.[1]

Taiichi Ohno, former Vice President of Toyota, defines it as follows:

> Operational Improvement (Kaizen) means coming up with better methods using existing equipment. The important thing is to think of new work methods, not to make new tools or equipment.[2]

However, since a number of common misunderstandings about *kaizen* have given rise to debilitating problems for companies seeking to reap its benefits, three aspects require particular emphasis.

First, *kaizen* is not a specific application or technique. It is not a new word for suggestion schemes, a more fashionable term for quality circles or 'improvement teams', or a tool or methodology for problem solving. It is a unifying concept for all that needs to be done to bring about a situation where the whole organisation engages in the quest for improvement.

Second, *kaizen* is about *doing*, not suggesting. It is easy to suggest that others *do*. The difficult part is translating ideas into timely and effective action. The contribution to Japanese industrial performance of systematised small-group activities and suggestion schemes has been greatly exaggerated. They may make a unique contribution in terms of the education and development of employees, to morale and to achieving synergistic solutions. But these constitute the icing on Japan's continuous improvement cake. They are not the cake itself. There is certainly room for suggestions within the overall scope of improvement activity. They are particularly appropriate for ideas which would involve a change in the characteristics of the product (these need the consent of the commercial customer); for ideas which imply significant spending on new tools or equipment (outwith Ohno's definition of *kaizen* in any case), or ideas which apply to the activities of other people or other functional groups within the organisation (we need their consent and full involvement). But *the cake* consists chiefly of those small improvements which can and should be quickly and easily implemented by people in respect of their own activity or that of their own work team, and these generally comprise more than 80 per cent of improvement opportunities in manufacturing businesses. We only *suggest* when we are not permitted to *do*. The word 'empowerment' has become something of a cliché in organisations. It often seems that there are now many 'empowered' people in companies who cannot actually do anything.

Third, my own definition of *kaizen* would be 'continuous improvement *as a habitual way of life* in the organisation'. Very few companies have managed to achieve this but in the world's best-performing factories, improvement is an everyday part of business, a normal part of the job for everyone. It is something we do between 8.00 a.m. and 5.00 p.m. – or whatever our production shift hours happen to be. It is not something for special occasions, for discrete training events, for lunchtimes or after hours, or for special management weekends. Nor is it for those times when the weather is fine, when we have no absences, when the machines are all running perfectly, when there are no material shortages or quality problems (which is to say, virtually never).

MAINTENANCE AND IMPROVEMENT; INNOVATION AND *KAIZEN*

Imai uses a very simple and lucid model in which all managed activity, in any business, East or West, falls into two categories: *maintenance* and *improvement*.

Maintenance comprises all actions undertaken to ensure that any aspect of our performance is in line with what we currently expect it to be. It therefore includes all manufacturing activity, all administration and all management action geared towards the realisation of current budgeted expectations. So, for example, should we expect to produce 250 units per shift with a workforce of 100 direct staff; should we be achieving a right-first-time ratio of 95 per cent in terms of conformance to existing quality standards; should we be accustomed to unplanned employee absence of 5 per cent of available working days; should we expect to lose no more than 10 per cent of production time to machine breakdowns: in all these cases maintenance consists of all the actions which need to be taken to ensure that these business assumptions are realised and that there is no deterioration in our performance.

Improvement activity, of course, comprises those actions taken to enhance this performance: to produce 280 units per shift without increasing the workforce; to increase our right-first-time ratio to 98 per cent; to find ways of reducing our absentee figure to 3 per cent or less; or to reduce breakdowns to 5 per cent of production and below.

Maintenance and improvement are parallel activities in organisations. There is always a need for both consolidation and advancement. There are current expected performance standards which need to be upheld and there must always be a search for new methods, new technologies, more efficient equipment, better or more inexpensive materials, and so forth.

In this way, progressive company performance is a helix of maintenance and improvement actions (Figure 2.1), reflecting the fact that, at any given moment, some actions are being taken in order to preserve existing standards of performance while others are being taken to improve that performance. In the best companies, everyone in the organisation will have a component of maintenance and a component of improvement in their jobs. Naturally, the proportions of time and effort devoted to maintenance and to improvement will, for all practical purposes, be largely determined by level of seniority in the organisation.

Top managers are expected to spend most of their time on matters relating to improvement: taking a strategic view of the operation and keeping a watchful eye on the demands of the market and the strengths of competitors; being concerned with what will be happening in two, five, ten years' time rather than with the

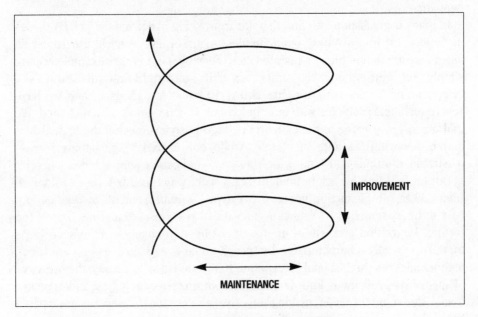

Figure 2.1   **Maintenance and improvement**

operating details of today. On the other hand, we would expect the maintenance–improvement ratio to be reversed when we consider direct workers, simply because direct production work is maintenance activity and of a nature which precludes the availability of much discretionary time. Nevertheless the contribution of the direct workers' improvement component should never be underestimated. After all, how many senior managers do we have in our organisations: 5? 10? 20? 50? – depending upon the size of the company. And how many workers: 70? 250? 1000? 10000? 50000? When we look at middle management and 'supervisory' levels, those at which we would also expect to find most of our technical specialists, we might naturally expect time and effort spent on maintenance and improvement to be fairly evenly distributed.

These assumptions seem at first to be fairly obvious and self-evident, except that virtually all of us who have had any significant experience in manufacturing recognise that this is simply not how things are in established Western companies.

There, even at the very top level of management, the bulk of time and effort is spent on maintenance activity and not on improvement. Once we get below middle management level, opportunities for people to engage in improvement activities virtually disappear. Maintenance activity is *the only activity* for the vast majority of people in the organisation.

What is happening is that, generally, people eventually perform the jobs of those who work for them, one level down from the jobs that they are actually paid to do. This is not a very healthy environment in which to work, but the biggest indictment is the amount of effort for improvement which is lost. Why does this happen?

In many organisations we find that, far from being in a situation which enables us to look for improvement opportunities, many of us are having to spend an inordinate amount of time on maintenance. To exploit our earlier example, we are simply not getting our 250 units per shift, our right-first-time ratio is a disappointing 80 per cent, absenteeism is 10 per cent and rising and we have severe technical problems with our equipment, which we had not anticipated. We find ourselves *reacting* to the situation by vigorously overseeing the endeavours of our subordinates and, of course, while our current expectations remain frustrated, thoughts and actions for improvement become something of a luxury.

But there is another more fundamental aspect which needs to be considered. Imai makes the distinction between two types of improvement: *innovation* and *kaizen*. Improvement in Western organisations is almost exclusively that of the former. Innovation consists of improvement by step changes, significant leaps forward, usually characterised by revolutionary new processes, advanced technologies and high capital investment. Innovation is, of necessity, the preserve of specialists proficiently knowledgeable about these technologies, and of senior management in terms of making investment decisions based on anticipated payback.

Technical innovation is, *and always has been*, a Western and not a Japanese obsession. In Britain, this has been the case ever since Prime Minister Harold Wilson made his famous 'white heat of technology' speech in the early 1960s. In fact, our apparent inability to see improved performance as attainable by any means other than investment in 'state-of-the-art' equipment is what often savagely limits our ability to improve. We see scope for significant improvement simply in terms of our ability to procure sufficient capital investment. This is particularly crippling during those periods of the economic cycle when we feel the effects of overseas competition most acutely. For then, in the wake of trade imbalances and with the onset of high interest rates and severe credit restrictions, many Western manufacturers find themselves impaled on a vicious trident of reduced domestic demand, intense overseas competition and macroeconomic austerity.

There is very little difference between manufacturing technologies across the developed world. Technical innovation is vital; but what we have today our competitors will have tomorrow – and vice versa. Technology is a *leveller*, a base entry requirement, the 'ante' in a poker game. *Real* competitive edge belongs to companies who can most effectively harness and exploit the creativity and initiative of their whole workforce to overlay the base technology with a myriad of performance enhancements to achieve a critical margin of competitiveness.

I sometimes draw an analogy between two gunfighters facing each other on the street of a frontier town. Assuming that they possess weapons of comparable performance in terms of their accuracy and velocity, then victory will go to the one who has done whatever is required to give himself 'something extra'. Perhaps it is skill and practice. Perhaps he has removed the trigger guard or greased the holster to provide a vital half-second advantage. Perhaps he has developed a stance which makes him a smaller target. The difference may be minimal; but at the end of the contest, one of the combatants will lie bleeding in the dust while the other stands victorious.

In 1991, Triumph, flagship of Britain's once mighty motorcycle industry, annihilated by Japanese imports in the 1960s and 1970s, restarted commercial manufacture after lying comatose for more than ten years. John Burton, a former colleague of mine, was appointed its first manufacturing director. His brief was to ensure that the company's manufacturing doctrine incorporated *kaizen, Genba Kanri* and all that was best in modern competitive manufacturing principles, a task for which he was admirably qualified. I visited him just under a year later and had the opportunity to tour Triumph's plant, established on a 'greenfield site' in Hinckley, Leicestershire. He was able to demonstrate how he lacked nothing in terms of the financial commitment of Triumph's chairman and proprietor, evident from the 'state-of-the-art' equipment installed throughout the facility. But he confessed that one slight problem he had encountered was to convince his newly hired supervisors and Team Leaders that high technology was far from the 'be all and end all' of securing competitive advantage. He finally succeeded in driving the point home by wangling an opportunity to take them on a visit to the Kawasaki works, just outside Osaka. There, they witnessed a machine which had been commissioned in the late 1950s, still fully operational and machining engine parts for one of Kawasaki's leading, high-volume motor cycles. True, the machine had not remained unchanged throughout the intervening decades. Parts had been added and functions had been modified to maintain and improve its performance, but, apart from these enhancements, the essence of the machine remained.

Kaizen improvements are small improvements which, in a gradual and incremental way, build upon existing processes and technologies. *Kaizen* can involve everyone in the organisation since all are capable of finding simple but effective means of improving their own and their team's performance. *Kaizen* improvements entail little or no capital spending but, by their very nature, each one of them seen in isolation makes a minute contribution to the bottom line. *Kaizen* therefore requires a high volume of such improvements to have a significant impact.

It should be emphasised that innovation and *kaizen* are *not* competing alternatives. Neither one nor the other is sufficient to give an organisation a competitive edge in world markets. *Kaizen* is the superstructure which, when added to the capabilities of shared technologies, makes the crucial difference.

If we purchase and install a robotic spot-welding line, then that is *innovation*. When the operator ensures that the robots are kept clean and well lubricated, and that worn parts are replaced to minimise the potential for breakdowns, then that is *maintenance*. When the same operator re-programs the robot to perform a more efficient sequence of motions between spot-welds in order to shorten the machine cycle and reduce the amount of wear and tear on moving parts, then that is *kaizen*.

The acquisition of a more energy-efficient furnace for the smelting and casting of aluminium components is *innovation*. When a supervisor ensures that the furnace operator is carrying out his work in accordance with established process parameters and safe working practices, that is *maintenance*. When the supervisor and operator together experiment with alternative stacking methods for the aluminium ingots inside the furnace until they find one which melts the ingots and reaches the specified temperature in the fastest time, and also further reduces the energy consumption of the new furnace by an additional 50 per cent, then that is *kaizen*.

On an assembly line, ensuring that tools, parts and materials are laid out in a neat and orderly fashion is *maintenance*. *Changing* the layout of materials to allow a more efficient sequence of assembly operations, which reduces the time required to perform a job by 20 seconds on every unit produced, is *kaizen*.

When we use inspection to ensure that dimensionally out-of-tolerance items from an injection-moulding machine do not reach the customer, or the next process, then that is *maintenance*. When we use control charts, 'fishbone' diagrams or 'Taguchi techniques' to *solve* problems, so that all parts produced are much closer to the nominal value and therefore well within the limits defined by the quality standard, then that is *kaizen*.

FACTORING *KAIZEN* INTO THE BUSINESS

The spate of Japanese tools and techniques which have become well known in the West during the past ten to fifteen years, such as just-in-time, *kanban*, statistical process control (SPC), *poka yoke*, quality circles and Taguchi methods are all included by Imai under the umbrella of *kaizen*, since all are examples of approaches which do not rely on new technologies and capital spending but achieve results by enhancing the performance of existing technologies. The fact that these have come from Japan is further evidence of the lack of a *kaizen* way of thinking in the West, by whatever name we might call it. Innovation and workforce exhortation have customarily been the only weapons in the Western arsenal of improvement. In most Western manufacturing companies, improvement is considered only to come from these sources: the judicious expenditure of capital on new technology; urging the workforce to greater efforts; and persuading, threatening, bribing or educating people to work harder or be more diligent, cooperative or conscientious in their endeavours. Rarely is much consideration given to the wealth of improvement opportunities afforded by simple changes to the manufacturing process. Between the watershed events of innovative improvements nothing much changes.

Of course, some will argue that this is not so. Every Western manager can recall occasions where problems have been solved by managers or workers or where an ingenious idea has made an excellent contribution to company performance. But this is not the same thing. These tend to be memorable and exceptional events. They are not the norm. We cannot claim that, in most Western companies, continuous improvement is a habitual way of life as it is in GK organisations where it amounts to a constant, never-ending and systematic onslaught on every aspect of operations. In these companies, the improvement of existing processes is always regarded as the first option and as the richest seam of improvement potential. There, the pressures on management are invariably for *kaizen*, which is *expected* to be a significant contributor to company competitiveness – so much so that this assumption is heavily *factored into* future expenditure budgets and manpower projections. In pulling together a five- or ten-year budget plan, the management of these organisations not only consider the calculated payback of any improvements in technology but also assume *additional*, across-the-board reductions of cost in the order of 10, 15 or 20 per cent per annum, which they *expect* will be funded by *kaizen* improvements of one sort or another. What are these improvements? Right now, no one knows. *But they will come*, as they always do in a GK company.

Let us suppose that a company expects a significant increase in market demand for its products next year. It calculates that the additional volume, using current processes and technologies, will require another 70 workers. The calculated contribution from the imminent implementation of automation brings this requirement down to 60 workers. But it is now further assumed that the volume and value of *kaizen* improvements over the next year will, by that time, have yielded an additional improvement of 10 per cent in terms of productivity alone. The company's hiring plan now calls, not for 70 or 60 new recruits a year from now, but for only 54 – and 49 the year after and so on. Similar assumptions will be made for every other aspect of cost in the business. Against this background then, for all managers in the organisation, continuous improvement becomes not an option – but an imperative.

Before turning to examples which quantify the contribution made by *kaizen* to the success of world-class companies, there is one further conceptual model which needs to be fully understood. It complements Figures 1.2 and 2.1 and, like them, will be a constant and recurring reference point for subsequent chapters on the practical implementation of GK principles.

THE IMPROVEMENT CYCLE

If anyone were to ask a Japanese manager to identify Deming's most significant contribution to Japan's industrial regeneration my guess is that it would not be statistical process control (SPC) but the model shown in Figure 2.2.

This is sometimes called the 'improvement cycle', the 'management cycle' or

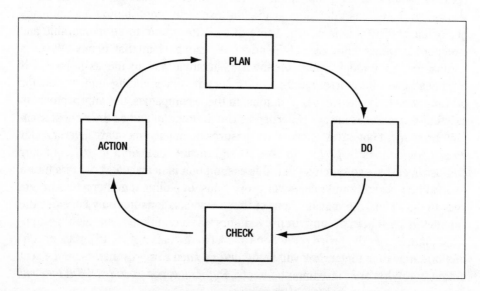

Figure 2.2 **The Deming/Shewhart cycle**

simply the 'PDCA cycle'. It is popularly known as the Deming wheel, although Deming himself constantly attributed it to his own mentor, Walter A. Shewhart. An unfortunate consequence of the essential simplicity of this model is that we often gloss over it without understanding its full meaning and value. I confess to being as culpable as any in this. For the six years I spent at Nissan everyone ate, drank and slept PDCA. For the last three of those years I was responsible for Nissan's workshop management (*Genba Kanri*) programmes and, therefore, for teaching the concept to others. But it was not until I again found myself in conventional factories that I could truly grasp its full significance and power.

This is a practical model of continuous improvement, which needs to be woven into the very fabric of how we conduct our daily operational activity. Sadly, though, we seem too often to debase it to the level of some business school mnemonic – a cheap and cheerful *aide mémoire* for 'time management'. So, once more from the top ...

First of all, a simple explanation for those not already familiar with the model and who may find the distinction between DO and ACTION elusive. Our physical activity is in the DO stage of the cycle. This could be a production shift, a production or engineering trial of new methods, processes or equipment, or an experiment of some kind – all of which are activities from which we should expect to learn. ACTION is the *corrective* action or countermeasure stage. (I suspect that the only reason we don't call it either of these is that this would give us two Cs in our model.)

Figure 2.2 shows a true cycle, a closed loop as indicated by the arrows. This means two things. First, it tells us that we can start wherever we like. If we were setting up a new facility or launching a new product then we would no doubt start at the PLAN stage. Most of the time, however, we are dealing with an existing product or facility, a current schedule and order book and current problems. We are concerned with what is happening right now in our factories and the extent to which events are meeting our hopes and expectations. Therefore it is usually appropriate to begin at the CHECK stage.[3] What were the outcomes of our day's production, our trial or experiment? What were the problems? What were the causes? What do we now need to address as part of the ACTION stage? How do we PLAN our next shift, our next trial? How do we firm up and *standardise* the corrective actions we have taken to ensure that their expected benefits are secured?

Second, the closed loop means that we never actually arrive at our destination. There is always scope for further improvement. We are never satisfied with current performance. We shall always strive for better methods, better quality, shorter lead times, reduced costs, more effective use of manpower, machinery and materials.

I have sometimes heard the PDCA cycle explained in a way that suggests that its whole purpose is to illustrate the importance of proper planning. But if that is all we want to do then Figure 2.3 is probably more effective at conveying this.

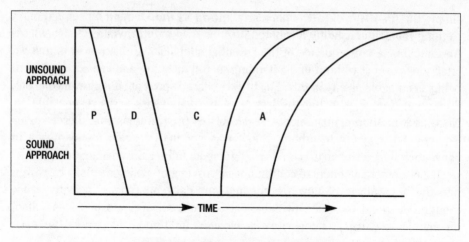

Figure 2.3   PDCA: the importance of planning

When we skimp on the PLAN stage we reap the consequences in terms of a greater number of problems and the need to spend much more time at the CHECK and ACTION stages. A more generous proportion of time and effort devoted to planning is rewarded by fewer problems and much shorter CHECK and ACTION stages, shortening the time spent overall.

However, there is a danger that we lose sight of the cycle as a whole. There is a misleading and simplistic misuse of the model which runs as follows. Western managers are inherently impatient and short-sighted. They never plan adequately and get themselves into all kinds of trouble as a result. (It is even wickedly suggested that, since the ability to put out fires is such an admired trait in Western business, managers deliberately light them in order to display their swashbuckling prowess at extinguishing them.[4]) Japanese managers, on the other hand, are by nature patient, quiet, contemplative people and, moreover, the seniority system for promotion does not require them to flap around like Red Adair to get noticed.[5] Faced with a given project, the Japanese manager adopts the lotus position and plans, and plans again in meticulous detail. As a consequence there are no problems at all and everything goes like clockwork. Thus, there is a generic psychological and cultural impediment which affects most managers in Western companies which must somehow be overcome if those companies are to make progress. This is what the PDCA cycle supposedly tells us.

But this is nonsense. The cycle actually demonstrates how all four of its component actions are of equal importance and must be carried out in due sequence. The complexities of modern manufacturing mean that there are always problems and always will be problems. These are our opportunities for improvement, provided we can capture them. The whole cycle is needed to do this.

In my own experience of Western companies there is often no shortage of managerial time and effort devoted to planning, conjecturing, considering, speculating. Contrary to the aforementioned stereotype it is often an affinity for the DO stage that is lacking. Nobody seems keen to go into the factory and *try something* which will either confirm or eliminate possible causes or solutions. Often uncomfortable and expensive mistakes in production are not the consequence of insufficient planning, but the lack of a small controlled trial to confirm the effectiveness of the plan. Others PLAN and DO but do not adequately check the outcome and therefore fail to learn sufficiently from the trial. Increasingly I find organisations who PLAN, DO *and* CHECK. Even the smallest companies now, fully exploiting the power of low-cost information technology, demonstrate their capability quickly and easily to spew out a volume of data of which, a couple of decades ago, a government department would have been proud: pages and pages of information on costs, time analysis, machine performance, quality faults, tables, multi-coloured graphics and so on. But often it seems nobody has either the time or inclination to study the information, much less take any appropriate ACTION.

The PDCA cycle reminds us that there is no point in a plan without a trial, no point in a trial without checking the result and no point in a check without taking action on the outcomes. Usually the nub of these problems is that the responsibility for the various sectors of the cycle is separately allocated to specific groups in the organisation. Those who make the plan are not those who will be responsible for carrying it out. Those who check the results and produce the data are not expected to do anything other than circulate them, and it is often not clear who, if anyone at all, is responsible for taking swift and appropriate action.

All organisations engaged in trying to improve performance are making their way around the cycle as best they can, whether they are aware of it or not. Each turn of the wheel brings its crop of improvements. It is a natural consequence of the human psyche (and has parallels with Kolb's learning cycle, which summarises the development of learning through experience[6]). But those companies who make full and *conscious* use of PDCA, teaching it to all their employees and fully integrating it into their way of doing business – their way of managing operations and production processes – achieve a competitive edge by turning the wheel faster and more frequently than their rivals. They maximise the capacity for discovering potential improvements and at the same time reduce to a minimum the time required to effect appropriate action.

The contribution of PDCA can be clearly understood when it is linked to our earlier model of maintenance and improvement, as in Figure 2.4. Turning the PDCA cycle is our means both of ensuring that our current performance is maintained and of propelling us forward to higher levels of performance. As such it is inextricably linked to the concept of standardisation, which will be discussed in forthcoming chapters. The cycle's function resembles both the motor which takes us skyward at the beginning of a roller-coaster ride and the safety dogs which click into place behind us to prevent our rolling backwards.

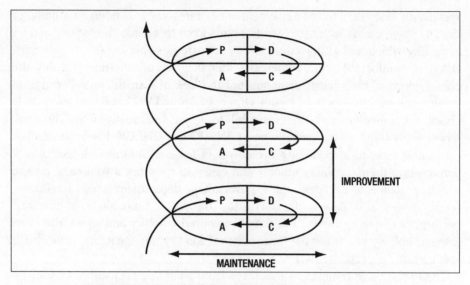

Figure 2.4   Continuous improvement and the Deming/Shewhart cycle

THE POWER OF *KAIZEN*

The devastating and relentless power of continuous and habitual improvements in the manufacturing process can scarcely be overstated. The following is an illustrative example. (I choose a car company, not so much to reflect my own background as the fact that motor vehicles are products with which everyone can identify and of whose costs all of us have a reasonable appreciation.) Figure 2.5 shows the dramatic effect of a simple mean contribution to reduced unit costs by each employee of one penny.

Naturally, we shall also benefit in the years to come from those improvements already made together with a continued cumulative monthly yield of £300 000 while continuous improvement still enables our employees to reduce our costs by a measly penny per vehicle.[7]

There are no items of capital investment, no wonders of 'state-of-the-art' manufacturing technology that in my experience can give such a return. But in fact, 'return' is a misnomer, for we are not talking about capital investment. There has been no expenditure of any significance to achieve these benefits. Furthermore, these cost reductions are *additional* to whatever innovative, centrally planned, capital-intensive projects have been carried out during the same period.

Let us supplement this conceptual model with a real automotive example. The British-built Nissan Bluebird had its production launch in June 1986 at its factory in the North-East of England. By this time, virtually all the early problems associated with the introduction of new motor vehicles had been ironed out

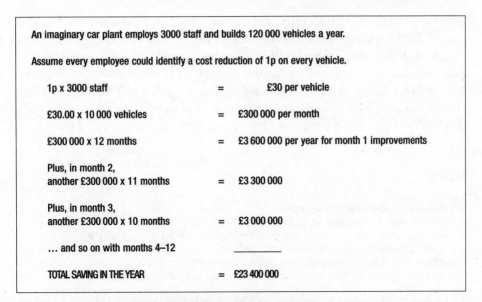

An imaginary car plant employs 3000 staff and builds 120 000 vehicles a year.

Assume every employee could identify a cost reduction of 1p on every vehicle.

1p x 3000 staff	=	£30 per vehicle
£30.00 x 10 000 vehicles	=	£300 000 per month
£300 000 x 12 months	=	£3 600 000 per year for month 1 improvements
Plus, in month 2, another £300 000 x 11 months	=	£3 300 000
Plus, in month 3, another £300 000 x 10 months	=	£3 000 000
… and so on with months 4–12		
TOTAL SAVING IN THE YEAR	=	£23 400 000

Figure 2.5 The power of *kaizen*

during its development and trial stages, giving an average, mid-range model, standard labour time of about ten hours through the final assembly[8] plant.

When Bluebird was run out in the autumn of 1989 and efforts were being redirected to Primera, its replacement, this time had reduced to a mere seven hours – a reduction of 30 per cent over less than three-and-a-half years. This was achieved almost entirely by *kaizen*: continuous incremental process improvements, most of which were conceived and executed by the final assembly production teams themselves.[9] Of course, even this is not the whole story. Production-team-generated *kaizen* brought about similar levels of improvement in product quality and its associated costs, the costs of direct and indirect materials, and in the levels of safety and comfort of those building the vehicles. Nor would it seem that *kaizen* is suffering from the law of diminishing returns at the plant. During 1993 Nissan launched a worldwide *kaizen* programme labelled '10–10–10', which called for productivity improvements of 10 per cent in all plants, in each of three successive years. This objective was achieved by the UK plant in 1994, 1995 and 1996.

This simple, quantified productivity improvement is doubly significant when we compare it with what typically characterises established, Western-owned car factories. There, during the production life of a model, standard production times scarcely change at all. When they do they are almost invariably the consequence of automation, the significant redesign of components, or a concerted, management-driven industrial engineering exercise to purge more obvious instances of wasteful practice and consequent overmanning. Reducing standard times at Ford and General Motors plants is an arduous and politically sensitive business, requiring considerable managerial effort and persistence. For this reason Ford maximise their improvement efforts at the trial and development stages, flooding their plants with engineers. Their goal is to grab all the improvement opportunities they can before the launch, when processes and work standards are finalised, recognising that this short period may well be their last chance to do so for all but the most lucrative of possibilities. Clearly *kaizen* is a commodity which some companies are able to exploit and others find elusive.

NOTES

1. Imai, *Kaizen*; see Select bibliography.
2. Ohno, *Workplace Management* (p. 122); see Select bibliography.
3. For this reason some Japanese practitioners refer to the PDCA cycle as CAP-DO.
4. Therefore, most of what is written in management textbooks about how to achieve results with little effort and few problems must be pointless; for when someone behaves in this way they will not be recognised by their boss or colleagues as exemplary managers, but as people with easy jobs.
5. Or rather display behaviour thought to emulate the archetypal firefighter. Red Adair was, by all accounts, a distinctly cool and *un*flappable character.
6. David A. Kolb's experiential learning model is familiar to many practitioners in training and development. The four components of his cycle are: concrete experience, observations and reflections, formation of abstract concepts and generalisations, and testing implications in new situations. See D.A. Kolb, I.M. Rubin and J.M. McIntyre (1971), *Organisational Psychology: An Experiential Approach*, Englewood Cliffs, NJ and London: Prentice-Hall.
7. Clearly, the power of *kaizen* is the product of the multiplying effect of a number of employees and the volume of product to be manufactured. It is not too difficult to draft a similarly revealing schedule for *any* product. Those companies who manufacture relatively low-value, high-volume products may wish to think carefully about the unit of measure. A penny per thousand or a penny per truck-load, for example, might be more appropriate. But the effects will be the same.
8. *Final assembly* comprises the fitting of all components to a painted body shell: engine and transmission, fascia, screens, seats, wiring, fluids, soft trim and all the rest. The car is then started up for the first time, to be driven off the end of the line for test, inspection and shipment. Naturally, this is by far the most labour-intensive part of any motor manufacturing process.
9. During the product life of Bluebird there was scarcely any introduction of automation in final assembly. Capital spending was concentrated on other projects, notably the development of engine assembly and stamping facilities. The only machine I recall appearing during this period was for applying sealer to the tail-lamp clusters. The benefit of this small investment was a more consistent sealer bead: it had little impact in terms of labour saving.

3 'The Trouble with *Kaizen* ...'

He that contemneth small things shall fall by little and little.

Ecclesiasticus 19:1

My first encounter with Professor Imai and with the concept of *kaizen* was at Nissan's Oppama plant near Yokohama in June of 1985, several months before the publication of his influential book on the subject. He addressed an audience of about 35 personnel from Nissan's embryonic British operation, which comprised virtually all its production management team (including the production director, John Cushnaghan, all the original 22 supervisors and a number of managers and staff from engineering and personnel). They were all British and all, at that point, completely unfamiliar with the *kaizen* concept.

Imai's address had a profound effect on those present. All of us had, only weeks and months previously, been working for typical Western manufacturing organisations, either in the established British motor industry or in a variety of non-automotive manufacturing companies in the North-East of England; we were all still in the process of absorbing and making sense of our experiences and unfolding discoveries about Japanese manufacturing. *Kaizen*, as described by Imai, struck an immediate chord by giving a rationale for these experiences, and in echoing our own observations on the shortcomings of the conventional approach with which we were familiar.

The event had far-reaching consequences, not only for the development of the manufacturing philosophy, strategy and subsequent performance of Nissan Motor Manufacturing (UK) Limited, but also for the spread of knowledge about *kaizen* throughout Britain and mainland Europe. Nissan's UK facility was far and away the highest-profile industrial development in Britain during the 1980s. Not only did it attract a phenomenal amount of media attention from its inception, but, once it had started production and once its performance in terms of product quality and productivity became apparent, scores of managers, academics and journalists from dozens of different organisations were all beating a path to its gates. In their search for the Grail of world-beating manufacturing performance, few could avoid learning *something* about the *kaizen* concept, which had become a keystone of Nissan's approach. By the time Imai's book was published in Britain, the phrases 'kaizen' and 'continuous improvement' had already been fully disseminated, though rarely well understood.

Of course, placed in a worldwide context, Nissan's British plant was only one significant example among many. The company had already launched a transplant facility in Smyrna, Tennessee, and established a joint venture with the Spanish company Motor Iberica near Barcelona. Toyota embarked on a partnership with General Motors near Fremont, California,[1] and would soon launch its own facilities in Kentucky and in Derbyshire. Honda did likewise in Marysville, Ohio, and also established a collaborative partnership with Britain's Austin Rover group.

Inward Japanese investment by electronics companies was already well under way: across North America, mainland Europe and Australasia, in the valleys of Wales and along England's M4 corridor. Would-be pilgrims no longer needed to make the trip to Japan in their search for the Grail. Moreover, the evidence was now clear that continuous improvement was not a feature of Eastern culture; it was there for the taking by companies with a Western workforce and Western managers operating within Western economies and Western culture.

For those seeking knowledge without becoming hajjis, there were now other alternatives. Japanese texts became widely available to Western readers, largely due to the efforts of the Japan Management Association and Productivity Press.[2] Following an article in *Business Week* in 1981, Deming had been discovered by his compatriots and the rest of the Western world. US corporations were swift to embrace their new-found octogenarian hero.[3] Making selective choices from his wisdom, the Ford Motor Company enthusiastically embraced statistical process control (SPC) and Ford suppliers worldwide were soon covering their factory walls with control charts to gain the approbation of their clients. The total quality movement was being rejuvenated and popularised by Phillip Crosby.[4] Peters and Waterman made their big splash in 1982,[5] sending out a clarion call for an approach which combined an obsession with pleasing the customer, the institution of leadership in the workplace (another echo of Deming) and the unshackling of workers from the management structures and assumptions that constrained their full contribution to the business.

The late 1980s were a pinnacle of Western enthusiasm, confidence and resolution in terms of businesses seeking to identify and capture the means of using continuous improvement to catch up with and possibly surpass the achievements of their Eastern counterparts. Looking back now, we know that much was achieved but also that much would also ultimately disappoint.

Why?

There are five common difficulties which have been encountered by conventional Western companies seeking to introduce *kaizen* or continuous improvement in recent years – difficulties not found in GK organisations. They have robbed companies of the full benefits of *kaizen* and stem directly from basic assumptions about the management of work which fundamentally differ from those of the GK companies which spawned *kaizen* in the first place. The first three of these difficulties are integrally related.

CONTEMPT FOR SMALL IMPROVEMENTS

For us middle and senior managers, innovation is a passion. We get excited when a new piece of state-of-the-art equipment arrives, and the process of installation and commissioning begins. We see this through to a satisfactory conclusion with almost the same degree of consummate interest that we lavish on the birth and early development of one of our children. Better still, though, when the machine finally does its stuff, we can walk away and forget it. So long as our maintenance people can take care of it and it gives us no problems, we can concentrate on planning our next breakthrough with eager anticipation.

Individual incidences of *kaizen*, however, are less than captivating – not 'sexy', as Professor Imai confesses.[6] Whatever lip-service we may pay to the overall desirability of *kaizen*, if we are honest with ourselves it's hard to be 'turned on' by someone in our factory managing to shave off a few seconds of time here or there, or by cost improvements equating to a few bits of loose change in our pockets. We should sympathise with the hard-pressed manager charged with achieving major financial improvements on budget. It is easy to understand how we fall into a situation where there is institutionalised contempt for small incremental process improvements, a tendency to be dismissive of small problems and impatience with operational details.

The very first time that I used the 'penny per car' model (Figure 2.5) at a public seminar, most of my audience were impressed with the scale of contribution involved. However, one company chairman, seated at the back of the hall, looked up from his pocket calculator and beamed in triumph. 'Your figures *sound* impressive,' he said, 'but I have just worked out the percentage improvement that a penny per car represents of what I would imagine to be the approximate costs of a motor vehicle. In percentage terms it really is very low, and,' he proclaimed with an air of finality, 'I have to tell you that, in my company, I would not regard such improvements as being worthy of the time of any of my managers!'

Whatever lip-service has been paid to the virtue of continuous improvement, we actually despise the value and contribution of small incremental improvements. At the heart of our problems lies that same assumption that such improvements necessarily involve the expenditure of management time.

MANAGING *KAIZEN* AS INNOVATION

Imai attributes the difficulty of Western managers in appreciating the contribution of small improvements to differences between the judgemental characteristics of Western and Japanese managers. The former are 'results-oriented' and have little concern or patience with the process. Japanese managers have a greater tendency to be involved with the process and will be particularly attentive to the *efforts* of people to improve, recognising that positive results will surely follow.[7]

There is something to be said for this but there is a simpler, more practical and more fundamental explanation. Imai's own model provides the key by dividing all management activity into maintenance, innovation and *kaizen*. Because there is no long-standing tradition of *kaizen* management in the West, and because we understand *kaizen* and innovation both to be aspects of improvement, it is natural to assume that we manage *kaizen* as innovation, the part of improvement with which we are familiar, rather than as maintenance. In fact, maintenance provides a better example: we are quite good at delegating responsibility for maintenance in our companies. It is improvement which has always been the problem.

The innovative tradition carries with it an expectation of management involvement with the evaluative process of improvement. This is entirely appropriate, since innovation is characterised by specialised technical knowledge and significant capital spend. We have to make sure that we have closely examined all the available options, and that there will be sufficient payback over a reasonable timescale. We need to subject our ideas to a cost–benefit analysis. But this is far from true of *kaizen*, which is defined as small, incremental process improvements involving little or no investment. Thus it is not so much an issue of redefining the evaluative criteria for *kaizen* but of questioning the involvement of middle and senior management in evaluation *at all*.

The innovation-centred way of thinking is clearly apparent when managers so often ask of *kaizen*: 'How do we measure it?' or 'How do we evaluate potential *kaizen* improvements to determine whether or not they are worthwhile?' The only way to measure *kaizen* is in terms of its long-term aggregated effects on the business. *Kaizen* must be managed. It must be promoted. A climate must be generated in which it can flourish. But it is wholly impractical to expect individual *kaizen* improvements to be subjected to management evaluation before the event.

LOW-VALUE/HIGH-VOLUME OPPORTUNITIES FOR IMPROVEMENT

The preceding difficulties give rise to one of the most seemingly intractable problems now facing organisations. Fifteen to twenty years ago the issue was how to get our people to contribute their ideas for improved company performance. Now the burning question is: 'How as an organisation do we cope when they do?' The problem arises from the presumption of a management evaluation process for small improvements – improvements which must of course be coming thick and fast to significantly affect the bottom line. Unfortunately, this high volume of small improvements must pass through a wicket gate of restrictive and time-consuming management controls and limited evaluative resources. All potential improvements must compete with one another to be worthy of these resources. Those improvements whose expected contribution is prejudged not even to be worth evaluating simply will not happen. Symptoms of this problem can be seen in many organisations where there are complex and sophisticated priority rating systems for even the most trivial problems with the most obvious solutions. Often there is as much management effort spent in logging and categorising potential improvements as there is in pursuing them.

Let us look back at our model of the power of *kaizen* (Figure 2.5). Appealing though this may be, another perspective can make it daunting and intimidating. *This company is executing 3000* kaizen *improvements per month*. Even if we regard the penny saving as an average – some employees may fail to contribute at all and others may make a more valuable contribution – that could still mean 1000 improvements per month. This is what we have to be capable of implementing to achieve this kind of result. And, as we have seen in our Nissan example, such results *are* typical of GK companies. This illustrates the extent to which we have to make it easy to introduce improvements, and why assumptions based on workers suggesting and management and technical specialists evaluating and executing are not feasible for *kaizen* in the true sense. Such an approach raises the value threshold of potential improvements prohibitively: they must at least be judged, by the would-be initiator, to be worth the time and administrative hassle involved. Production managers and supervisors, struggling with day-to-day problems of schedules and failing resources, lack the time and energy to pursue them.

Consider the supervisor arriving at work at the start of the shift. He or she expects two team members to be absent, but finds there are four. After two hours it is apparent that a crucial item of equipment has broken down; there are also some serious delays on materials for one of the other processes. When the stuff finally arrives it is defective. Some of the necessary engineering documentation has not yet arrived and the worker is making do with an old issue document with some hand-written amendments. The quality assurance auditor has spotted this and is calling for the work to be stopped. The supervisor is already starting to lose hope of making schedule. However, things could be worse – somebody might come up with an idea for improvement.

In such circumstances it is not too difficult to guess the outcome, especially if this idea means filling out a form for submission to the production manager, to engineering, to a suggestions facilitator or to an improvements committee for evaluation and approval. Furthermore, technical resources and process control systems are often barely capable of reacting to the frequency of external, commercially imposed changes – much less of responding to internally generated ideas for improvement. In such circumstances, the very last thing engineers want is for a suggestion sheet or '*Kaizen* Request Form' to be landing on their desks, especially if the likely improvement is of moderate or low value.

This is the problem of the ubiquitous wooden box. After the initial enthusiasm which accompanies the company's latest suggestion scheme, workers become disheartened and finally cynical when their contributions are not followed up. The flood of improvement ideas soon dries to a trickle.

SECURING THE FRUITS OF *KAIZEN*

'OK', acknowledges the Western production director. 'Doing, not suggesting. I understand. Spontaneous worker-generated improvements – right? Well *we* have those. If that's a big piece of what *kaizen* amounts to, then our people have been practising *kaizen* for years! People improve their jobs around here all the time. But who benefits? Not me and not the company. We put somebody on a job that should take an hour or a minute. After a week, by working out a better method and by slickening up the job they can do it in 50 minutes or 50 seconds. Who does this new-found 10 minutes per hour or 10 seconds per minute belong to? Not the rest of us, it seems. They give themselves an extra coffee or cigarette break or simply slow down and relax – mentally compose a symphony or think about tonight's football. We don't achieve any productivity increase from this at all. What I want to know is: how do I harvest this kind of improvement on the bottom line? All right, I can always send in an industrial engineer with a stopwatch and a shrewd eye and have him retime the job and increase the work quota. But it's a bloody business and isn't this the kind of thing we need to get away from, according to Deming and others? It hardly constitutes true worker involvement in the improvement process, does it? And this takes me back to the earlier problem. If I want to realise something like the "penny per vehicle" model, I'll have to hire two dozen IEs just to retime jobs.'

PRODUCTIVITY AND PHYSICAL EFFORT

Kaizen is about making jobs easier. The easiest methods are not only the safest and most comfortable, but also the quickest, most efficient and most conducive to high levels of quality. Productivity-related *kaizen* takes the strain, effort and awkwardness out of work: the bending, walking, stretching, reaching, fumbling and double handling. But the clichés about working 'smarter – not harder' are often not reflected in the way that we pay people or even in the way we measure productivity in companies. Sometimes this is not a matter of what we do now, but rather a legacy of how we have behaved in the past, which makes it difficult to purge this association from the minds of workers and managers alike.

My colleague, Jim Turner, once visited an automotive supplier based in South Wales. The company had moved from piecework to 'measured day work' almost ten years before. He watched a man producing pressed parts from steel blanks using two small power presses (Figure 3.1).

The presses were situated some 20 metres apart. The operator would load the first press with a stack of blanks and start a machine cycle. He then walked across to the second machine and loaded a similar stack of blanks. By now the first machine had completed its cycle and was ready for a new stack. The first machine would, therefore, stand idle while the operator walked between the machines. By the time the first machine was reloaded, the second machine was ready and idle ... and so on.

Not surprisingly, Jim suggested that the two machines be brought much closer together in order to reduce significantly the walking time of the operator and increase substantially the production volume from both presses. The managers of the plant, who accompanied Jim on his tour, made quick enquiries of the site maintenance crew, who concluded that there would be minimal time and cost involved in resiting one of the machines. The idea was also discussed with the operator. Jim expected some degree of enthusiasm, given that the operator could no doubt expect to make a considerable saving in sweat and shoe leather. However, he was astonished by the degree of antipathy encountered from that quarter.

The operator took the view that the proposed improvement would mean he produced more product. If he was producing more product then he must be working harder. If he was to work harder then he should be paid more money. The plant managers then explained to the operator that an optimally agreed level of output could be established whereby output was increased for the benefit of the company, and yet the amount of work and physical effort involved would still be significantly reduced. Try as they might, they could not dislodge from the mind of the operator that, by contributing to increased output in the interests of the company, he must somehow be working harder. As far as we are aware, neither of the presses has yet been moved and the operator presumably continues to notch up something in the region of eight miles of unnecessary walking per shift.

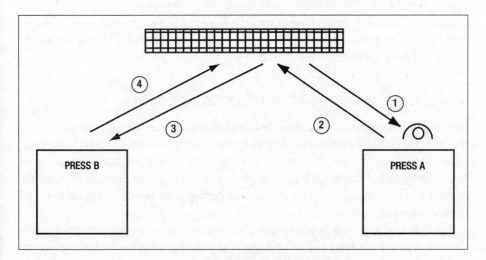

Figure 3.1   Feeding two power presses

KAIZEN AND RE-ENGINEERING

The problems of *kaizen* and of organisations seeking to improve their performance through continuous improvement became increasingly apparent by the end of the 1980s. Though few were openly disputing the wisdom and appropriateness of the pursuit, there was a growing undercurrent of discontent and frustration. For every company which secured real and worthwhile benefits, another would be disappointed with the achievements, and a third would start to wonder whether the exercise was not simply a time-consuming and unprofitable struggle. Beleaguered managers awaited redemption; they hoped for something, *anything* that would relieve them of the continuous improvement burden, and be sufficiently respectable or fashionable to enable the dogs to be called off. The stage was truly set for the dramatic entrance of business process re-engineering.

The allure and consequent impact of re-engineering in the early 1990s had far less to do with the potency of its central principles than with the strongly implied suggestion that it could and should replace the pursuit of continuous, incremental, process improvement as the means of bridging the competitive gap for Western companies. 'Continuous improvement maybe just isn't our thing', was the message. 'Our strengths have always been in pursuing radical and innovative approaches. This is what we do best and this is what we should be concentrating on if we want to catch up with Japan.'

Of course we now know that efforts to make sufficient progress under the banner of re-engineering have proven no less arduous and no less disappointing in their outcomes than those made under the banners of TQM and continuous improvement. By 1995 surveys and reports were indicating that 70 per cent of re-engineering initiatives had failed. Clearly there have been common underlying problems with all such initiatives, and these will be discussed in the next chapter. But meanwhile, how do we now assess the impact of re-engineering on *kaizen* or continuous improvement? Has the case for the latter been strengthened or weakened by what happened in the 1990s?

RE-ENGINEERING AND *KAIZEN* ARE NOT COMPETING ALTERNATIVES

Re-engineering reminds us that there is no point at all in improving the efficiency and effectiveness of what we do if we are doing the wrong things. Manufacturing capability is only one factor in determining business success and, as acknowledged in Chapter 1, it is only valid once we have established that we are in the right business and that the goods or services we produce will be deemed to be of value in the market.

There is nothing new in the virtue of a radical, scrap-and-rebuild approach to satisfying customer needs. The best applications of innovative technology come from, and have always come from, an equally innovative approach, a 're-engineered' approach, in the new fashionable parlance, to business and in the provision of goods and services to customers.

Automatic cash dispensers, introduced over two decades ago, are a prime example which we all now take for granted. I for one would now find life extremely difficult without the glorious 'hole-in-the-wall' machine. But someone once told me that the automatic cash dispenser was conceived, during a management brainstorming session at Barclays Bank, as exactly that. In considering ways of extending banking service hours to clients, and having made no progress within existing process paradigms about bank opening times and employee working patterns, someone chimed in: 'Why don't we just knock a hole in the wall so that the customers can get at their money?' Of course since then telephone banking and other innovative breakthroughs have changed the face of personal banking even more radically.

Re-engineering is simply the sort of innovation already discussed in our earlier model but applied to business systems, procedures and work arrangements, as opposed to manufacturing technology. As we have seen, innovation and *kaizen* are complementary and not competing approaches. Just as we need to intersperse technical innovation with continuous improvements to fully secure its benefits and to enhance those improvements further, so must we also intersperse any periodic exercises in re-engineering with continuous improvement. How often do we plan to re-engineer our companies? Every ten years? Every five years? Every six months? What happens in between? We need to ensure that the roles and responsibilities operating in our organisation can sustain a company-wide commitment to never-ending improvement, whether the organisation is conducting a re-engineering programme or not.

In basic terms we have identified three key sources of improved company performance:

1. Technological innovation
2. Business systems innovation – 're-engineering'
3. High-volume, high-frequency process improvements – *kaizen*.

All these sources are necessary but of themselves insufficient to meet current worldwide standards in manufacturing. It is a fundamental error to bolster the importance of any one of them at the expense of any other.

We must therefore adopt an attitude and approach which questions our systems and procedures, the shape and orientation of our organisations, and which calls for a far more adventurous and voracious appetite for closing the competitive gap. But the last thing we need is an excuse to either preserve or regress to a bull-at-a-gate approach to process and operations management, characterised by impatience with detail, complacency in the face of 'minor' problems, and contempt for the value and benefits of small incremental improvements. It is not a question of innovative change *versus* incremental improvement. This is a false dichotomy brought on by ignorance of the nature and application of continuous improvement, naivety about the complexity of modern manufacturing operations and perhaps an element of self-delusion.

'Reengineering is new and it has to be done', proclaimed Peter Drucker from the dust cover of Hammer and Champy's book.[8] Who am I to argue? The figure of Peter Drucker has stood like a colossus over virtually every development in Western management thinking over the past 50 years. If anyone should know the difference between strong medicine and snake oil, then it ought to be Drucker.

One of the developments with which Drucker was most closely associated was management by objectives (MBO). For the last 15 years of his life Deming engaged in a passionate and near obsessive onslaught on what he saw as the evils of 'management by objective' and other management assumptions which he claimed were constraining Western companies in the struggle to compete in the modern world. Two days after Deming's death in December 1993, Drucker was among the eminent commentators invited to assess his contribution – around about the same time as his enthusiastic endorsement of re-engineering.

Drucker blamed not management but organised labour for the failure of Western companies to adopt Deming's approach in the postwar decades. He went on to remark that the Japanese had largely moved through and away from Deming's philosophy in their approach and that, in particular, continuous improvement was no longer a significant feature of their strategy.[9] Drucker's comments are a startling revelation to me. I thought that I had spend the greater part of my recent working life in Japanese manufacturing companies. In deferring humbly to Drucker's eminence and erudition, I conclude that I must have been abducted by aliens and become the victim of some spurious memory implant.

THE COMPETITIVE EDGE OF JAPANESE MANUFACTURERS – *KAIZEN*

Any notion that re-engineering can be an adequate substitute in the West for the benefits of continuous incremental improvement is disingenuous. A passion for the pursuit of added value as determined by the needs of customers, coupled with a readiness to discard all activities or company pastimes unrelated to those needs, are, and *always have been*, threads which run through every aspect of Japanese management.

Once, as an undergraduate, I had to write an essay on the nature of material existence: whether we can be sure that objects and substances have any independent being other than as the product of our own senses. I never did have much aptitude or tolerance for the metaphysical or abstract, and I found the subject hard going. In my conclusion I sided with Dr Samuel Johnson, who once expressed his own boredom with a debate on the subject by smashing his bowl on a tavern table to demonstrate the real and physical nature of matter. My tutor, a Fellow of St John's College, Oxford, was very kind about my poor efforts.

'I enjoyed your essay very much', he said, 'but don't ever write anything like that again – especially in the examination schools. You are required to answer the question, not make fun of it. Your paper will be marked by people who have devoted their lives to considering these questions. You can hardly expect to gain their sympathy by implicitly ridiculing their profession.'

In the search for the key to a competitive edge in Western companies, the suggestion that a greater spur in the direction of more technical innovation or more business systems innovation can replace a shortfall in continuous improvement is unsustainable. If the failure of most Western companies to exploit the potential for continuous incremental improvement of the process *is the problem*, then the difficulties which they encounter must be confronted. We cannot run away from or make fun of the question. We must meet the continued need for *kaizen* head on. There is no significant difference between the technologically innovative capabilities East and West. There are no significant differences in the approaches taken by 're-engineering' and the rigorous customer-driven business disciplines already existing in Japan. (Try telling Akio Morita, the president of Sony, that an innovative approach to the market is a particularly Western strength; then watch him smile.) This still leaves intact a competitive margin in favour of Eastern companies *achieved through continuous improvement*. That competitive margin is crucial and must be addressed.

Without the resource of a company-wide approach to finding high-volume, high-frequency improvements in our processes, we are asking our companies to fight with one arm tied behind their backs. Strengthening the muscles of the other arm will never compensate for this disability. No boxer with one arm can outfight another with two.

CORPORATE FAITH IN BIG SOLUTIONS BREEDS COMPLACENCY IN THE ORGANISATION AND DESTROYS THE APPETITE FOR IMPROVEMENT

One of the key differences between technical innovation and 're-engineering', on the one hand, and continuous improvement or *kaizen*, on the other, is that whereas the former are examples of tools used by management to improve company performance, the latter is something which, though management have responsibility for developing and maintaining it, is used primarily by the critical mass of people in the organisation. In this way, re-engineering belongs to the category of those things which are done to or on behalf of people in the organisation, as distinct from those things which people do for themselves.

It has been my own experience that those companies which have been most active in promoting 'all-singing-and-dancing' IT solutions to business and operational problems usually suffer most from apathy and inertia when it comes to taking prompt actions to improve performance.

'Yes, this is a problem, and there may be a few things that we can do to improve things, but why bother? I've heard the computer guys saying that they're putting in a new system in six months' time and the problem will be eliminated.' (Of course it will!) Or even worse: 'I've told the boss what we plan to do to improve the situation, but he's put the skids under it. "What's the point?" he says, "everything will change a few months from now.'"

Even the most drastic and sweeping organisational and structural changes can themselves be superficial if we do not fundamentally alter the way we *think* about manufacture. Boardroom shuffles, the reshaping of departmental structures, and the introduction of new software systems and databases are all in vain unless we change the way we think and give our people a completely new sense of their roles and responsibilities for carrying out work.

I am familiar with one company which possesses a vast array of sophisticated data retrieval and planning systems. It also has a technical support staff that would shame NASA. It has recently undergone an expensive re-engineering programme. As a result, senior managers will be reshuffled, the shape of the organisation will change, new cost centres will be established, and old IT systems and company reporting procedures will be scrapped and others introduced. Even the very name of the company is likely to be 're-engineered'. But this is not at all dissimilar to previous 'radical' changes made in the past. The only difference this time is that, when the 'blue-chip' consulting company sends its usual six-figure invoice, the words 'Re-engineering Programme' will feature in the description of services rendered. However, the company has still shown no signs of changing the way that it manages work, or the key responsibilities of those who, *on the factory floor*, actually produce added value. It refuses to abandon its vain belief that if only it can find the ideal system, the ideal IT solution, then it can make the manufacturing environment a perfect place. This is a lethally seductive myth, a prime example of remote control management and the failure to come to terms with the realities of manufacturing.

The company has a long and proud history. It is given to ascribing its problems to the fact that it has been in existence for over a century. But its problems are those of the 1960s and 1970s, when big and complex was highly fashionable, not those of its illustrious founder, who would undoubtedly be heartbroken at its current predicament. It is no dinosaur. Sadly, it rather resembles a tortoise on its back with its legs in the air. All that remains to seal its fate is that the buzzards gather. They have not done so yet, but it is only a matter of time.

CORPORATE CHANGE AND BUSINESS IMPROVEMENT: CONFUSION OF ENDS AND MEANS

Hammer and Champy's most valuable contribution was in making not the first, but the boldest and most influential challenge to the prevailing wisdom of the 1980s: that corporate change in the interest of improved performance must be prudently wrought on a piecemeal basis – the notion that we can somehow create an oasis in a desert by bringing and pouring out a bucketful of water at a time. For the first time managers questioned the validity of 15 years of tinkering with cultural ambience, cheap psychology and a smug and complacent 'softly, softly' approach to closing the yawning competitive gap between East and West.

Urgent and drastic action is indeed called for, but we need to distinguish clearly between our methodology and our objectives, between improvement *of* the organisation and improvement *in* the organisation. Those unsuccessful initiatives made in the furtherance of 'total quality' or 'continuous improvement' did not fail because of the subject matter, but because of the manner in which they were attempted. It is rather that managers did not sufficiently understand the concepts and underestimated how much they would have to change their ways of working and of managing in order to secure their benefits.

Kaizen is not a means but an *objective* of organisational improvement. For a manufacturing company, one of the key goals of its corporate change programmes, whether labelled as 're-engineering' or not, must be the creation of an organisation which is capable of generating and sustaining continuous incremental improvement in processes and working methods. But *kaizen* is not itself a tool for such a transformation, and neither incremental nor half-hearted corporate progress will bring this about.

NOTES

1. New United Motor Manufacturing, Inc. (NUMMI) was established in 1984. The old GM Fremont plant had shut down in 1982. GM persuaded Toyota to reopen and manage the plant. Eighty per cent of the NUMMI workforce had worked at Fremont under the old regime. By 1986 NUMMI was already outperforming GM plants across a range of performance indicators. See J.P. Womack, D.T. Jones and D. Roos (1990), *The Machine That Changed the World*, New York: Rawson Associates (pp. 82–4).
2. Productivity Press was founded in Cambridge, Massachusetts, in the early 1980s by Norman Bodek.
3. Deming was elected to the US National Academy of Engineers in 1983 and admitted to the Science and Engineering Hall of Fame in 1986. The British Deming Association was founded in November 1987.
4. P.B. Crosby (1979), *Quality is Free*, New York: McGraw-Hill.
5. T.J. Peters and R.H. Waterman Jr (1982), *In Search of Excellence: Lessons from America's Best-Run Companies*, New York: Harper and Row.
6. M. Imai, *Kaizen* (p. 28); see Select bibliography.
7. Imai, *Kaizen* (pp. 16–21).
8. M. Hammer and J. Champy (1993), *Reengineering the Corporation, A Manifesto for Business Revolution*, New York: HarperCollins.
9. John Hillkirk (1993), 'World-famous quality expert dead at 93', *USA Today*, 22 December.

4 Why *Kaizen* Demands Real Change

His 'noontide peace', a study of two dun cows under a walnut tree, was followed by 'a mid-day sanctuary', a study of a walnut tree with two dun cows under it.

Saki (H.H. Munro), *The Stalled Ox*

Notwithstanding the spate of initiatives for 'total quality' and 'continuous improvement' in recent years, very few companies have succeeded in making continuous improvement in quality and efficiency a way of life – a normal part of the operational business. There are several reasons for this, all of which are interrelated.

RELIANCE ON SPECIALISTS

The first reason for failure is dependence on specialists or specialist groups. This diminishes the involvement and denies the ownership of functional managers, causing them to regard company strategies as an occupational hobby: *apart from* the business rather than *a part of* the business.

Over the years I have become an accidental collector of business cards. It always seems somehow disrespectful to throw them away, even in cases where I would be unlikely to meet their donors again. Rather, I have progressively acquired a series of business-card wallets and inserted the cards into them as I empty my pockets. I find that I now possess something of a representative history of British industrial job titles from the early 1980s to the present. The early entries are fairly mundane, workmanlike and commonplace: 'Works Manager', 'Senior Process Engineer', 'Quality Manager', 'Production Director' and so on. Later on, however, the job titles on the cards become altogether more varied and exotic. We find the 'TQM Facilitator', 'the Continuous Improvement Coordinator', 'the *Kaizen* Manager'. For quite some time, the pride of my collection had been given to me by one described as his company's 'Journey to Excellence Manager'.[1]

I wish to make it clear at this point that I have nothing but unreserved admiration for those who, under a variety of intriguing sobriquets, have been appointed standard bearers of continuous improvement in their respective organisations. I have always found these individuals to be energetic, highly motivated and extremely dedicated in their efforts, which, in the better organisations, is no doubt the reason they were appointed in the first place. They almost invariably repay the value of their salary to their companies many times over but are, because of the nature of their task, very unsuccessful at making continuous improvement an accepted part of everyday business, which means that the best of their endeavours will always fall well short of what most companies could achieve.

Irrespective of the amount of support that 'improvement champions' may enjoy from top management or the amount of resources at their disposal, they will always be seen by established line managers as inhabiting a privileged, peripheral and rather perfunctory sphere of activity. What production managers, foremen, and engineers do on a daily basis, in terms of meeting volume quotas, hitting current quality standards and coping with machine breakdowns, sporadic material flow, lack of tooling, rapidly changing customer requirements, absenteeism and so on, is the *real work*, the *real business*. In essence, the *real business* is the maintenance activity of Imai's model. And, although all those people wrestling with the demands of the *real work* may well be very supportive and positively disposed towards the *idea* of 'continuous improvement', *'kaizen'*, 'total quality', 'excellence', or whatever other name the company uses for its programme for employee-generated enhanced performance, there will always be an undercurrent of antipathy when they are approached by specialists whose brief seems to absolve them from the need to worry about the *real work*. I do not envy the jobs of these specialists and I admire their fortitude and perseverance. I have never known a production manager or a foreman pronounce the word 'facilitator' or 'coordinator' without managing to make it sound like 'leper' – or something far worse.

The difficulty is that chief executives who are most convinced of the value of continuous improvement, who are most determined to ensure that it is taken seriously throughout the company and who seek to demonstrate the degree of their commitment by creating a *specialist* of it or a *department* of it, actually undermine their own intentions. The very *separateness* of continuous improvement, which this approach underlines, sows the seeds of its own demise. Meeting current standards, dealing with current problems, surviving shift by shift, is the *normal business*. Improvement becomes something to engage in during lunch breaks, on weekend training courses, or when there are not too many production problems. By making improvement *special* we have diminished rather than enhanced its importance to the organisation.

IMPROVEMENT HIT SQUADS

One large manufacturer located in the North-West of England has demonstrated a particularly vigorous and voracious approach to using specialist squads to secure productivity improvements in the workplace. Since this approach was deployed in the interests of business survival – to pull the plant from the brink of collapse in the face of more productive and cost-effective competition – it could be argued that this is an example of internal specialist-driven improvements being recognised as a normal part of business activity. An experienced and particularly shrewd and discerning production manager was appointed to champion the initiative which was labelled QPI (quality and productivity initiative). Company employees from a variety of different disciplines, predominantly industrial engineers, quality assurance personnel, experienced foremen and HRD staff, were seconded to the QPI programme, ostensibly on a temporary basis. They received a certain amount of formal training, some of which was delivered 'in-house', some delivered externally by consultants. This covered quality tools and techniques, work study and problem solving. Thereafter, their task was to work in small sub-teams in targeted areas of the production line, cooperating, as far as possible, with established production teams in pursuit of improved performance. Production areas were targeted on the basis of an initial premise of a high volume of improvement to be had for the taking and in areas where it was felt there would be minimal opposition to the activity.

However, despite the amount of time and money spent by the company in communicating the purposes and ideals of QPI, few production foremen – much less their groups of production workers – were favourably disposed towards these activities. Responses varied from indifference to outright hostility. This was a plant which had a long history of periodic redundancy in response to just the sort of financial exigency that QPI was now attempting to confront. The company went to great lengths to explain that no lay-offs would ensue from any QPI project. It sweetened the pill still more by introducing a scheme whereby all workers in a group which cooperated with ideas for improvement, whether generated by themselves or by a QPI project team, and which thereby made it possible to reduce the notional direct headcount in that section, would receive a one-off payment amounting to a share of the annual employment costs of the wage saved.

Even so, scarcely any ideas for improvement were actually generated from production groups and most of the achievements of QPI were initiated by the QPI project teams themselves. Furthermore, virtually all these ideas were related to savings in direct labour cost; few were geared towards better product quality or improved standards of operator safety. Moreover, in spite of (or perhaps because of) the company's undertakings on redundancy and its reward package for encouraging a trouble-free introduction of productivity improvements, QPI was given, among many sections of the workforce, a completely different acronym: SAM, 'sack a mate'. (FAB, 'fire a buddy', might be an acceptable North American transcription.)

To judge QPI as a vehicle for the introduction of a concept of continuous improvement, as discussed in Chapter 2, by the criterion of total involvement of all employees in improvement activity as a perpetual and habitual way of life, it must be regarded as a spectacular failure. Nevertheless, as an exercise in reducing direct headcount and in taking many of the steps required to bring the company back from the brink, it was largely effective. It therefore gained the approbation of senior management who, by retrospectively redefining the objectives of QPI as a short-term response to an immediate need, judged it a success.

However, the management of this particular company are under no illusions about the efficacy of this approach as a longer-term means of closing the productivity gap which remains between it and its Japanese rivals. The problem with the approach is that it is simply geared towards the rapid harvesting of a few plump and obvious cherries. Once these have been picked, it becomes progressively more difficult to sustain improvements. And, as these improvements become more difficult to identify and implement, the support and ownership of the production groups themselves becomes ever more critical. Unfortunately, by now the earlier cherry-picking activity has provided line managers, supervisors and production workers alike with further evidence for believing that improvement is not an important or integral part of their job. 'Let the Smart Alecs in QPI find improvements. That's what they're *paid to do.*'

Now there is nothing wrong, as such, in management taking this kind of action, particularly in response to a crisis. But this is not *kaizen* in the sense that we need to understand it because it still projects improvement as something that is done to people rather than something which people do for themselves. This means it is not potent enough to be sustained on a permanent basis. After making the more obvious improvements we find that, when we really need to squeeze the mop hard, our production people are no longer with us.

At its worst, in companies that have not succeeded in giving their employees a sense of employment security and who do not enjoy a trusting relationship with them, such an approach will actually be regarded as threatening. Far from encouraging all employees to find and identify improvement opportunities, it causes them to *conceal* waste and potential for improvement. The best response that can be hoped for in this situation is the passive, non-involvement encountered by the QPI teams. An even more common reaction, however, is just what we would expect when Shylock appears over the horizon, blade in hand, looking for his pound of flesh: everyone instinctively pulls in their stomachs. This is the exact opposite of the sort of mentality we need to encourage in a modern, competitive, 'lean' manufacturing company. (See Chapter 12 on the importance of making waste visible; Chapter 16 on the importance of job security.)

IMPROVEMENT TEAMS

This *separate* approach to attempting continuous improvement in organisations is most marked in companies who seem determined to establish a complete counter-organisation within their company – almost an alternative and parallel universe in which the formal organisation is mirrored by an altogether more benevolent and enlightened structure of informal 'improvement teams'. The best-known example of this is quality circles. The failure of quality circles in virtually every Western company in which they were introduced is now largely beyond dispute. Also, retrospectively, there is now far greater awareness that the contribution made by quality circles in Japan has historically been greatly exaggerated. Nevertheless, the approach remains with us in the guise of a number of different fashionable labels.

Companies wishing to embark on the path of continuous improvement still very often speak of their intentions to 'introduce teams' into their organisation. Why is it that they do not ask a far more pertinent question, namely: Why do our existing functional groups, both in direct production and in indirect areas, not perform effectively as teams? Dare we suggest that the existing functional groups are involved with the *real business* of the company which, as we have discussed, is primarily 'maintenance activity'? Again, improvement is something which we tacitly understand to lie beyond the normal way of doing things and we feel bound, therefore, to build it on completely different foundations. But we cannot expect to make improvement a normal and habitual part of the business by having a *formal* organisation structure for all maintenance activity, including the achievement of quality standards, the achievement of the production schedule, the adherence to safe working practices, and an alternative, *informal* structure for continuous improvement. This diffuse approach is simply not feasible.

Some companies take refuge in the notion of establishing 'cross-functional' or 'multidisciplinary' teams which will meet, on a regular basis, to identify and iron out common problems and establish workable countermeasures as a spur to improved company performance. Cross-functional teams are a well established and well known aspect of Western organisational life. Virtually every Western democracy is governed by a cross-functional team of executives whose ministries are collectively responsible for all aspects of government. A board of executive directors is a cross-functional team. The attendees at a weekly get-together of sales staff, production management, production schedulers and material buyers are working as a cross-functional team. Cross-functional teams, as a natural response to practical problems which affect a number of different functions, are a perfectly practical and respectable institution, *well established* in both Eastern and Western traditions of management. But to '*introduce* cross-functional teams' at every level and in every corner of the organisation on the supposition that this will somehow create a climate conducive to continuous improvement, involving all employees, is to take similar refuge in a would-be alternative organisation structure. I suspect that the real reason for the current level of interest in cross-functional teams is simply symptomatic of diffuse and disparate responsibilities for operations management. Their existence reflects the fact that too often we need to call a committee meeting before we can legitimately take the simplest of actions. When it comes to dealing with cross-functional problems on a day-by-day basis, cross-functional committees are no substitute for *functional* teams with a clear understanding of the needs of downstream customers (see Chapter 9).

CULTURE AND ATTITUDES

We even separate improvement from normal business activity by the very words that we use. Our maintenance vocabulary consists of imperatives which are as hard, solid and tangible as the concrete beds on which our machines rest: words such as *authority, accountability, control, conformity, procedures, parameters, responsibility, requirements, standards, systems, structure.* This is the familiar world of work. But we seem to leave that world behind when we set off in pursuit of continuous improvement. We enter instead an abstract realm, almost spiritual and mystical in the altruistic values which abound: *climate, communication, cooperation, culture, environment, empathy, empowerment, involvement, motivation, ownership, participation, partnership.* These are the words we use when we wish to bring *enlightenment* to our employees. As managers in our companies, we convince ourselves that, if they become so enlightened, and recognise that their interests are our interests, they will vigorously pursue improvements throughout the organisation. We therefore subject our employees to programmes which seek to bring change by way of enlightenment, which seek to invoke profitable behaviours by instilling fresh attitudes.

Of course, the difficulty with these unenduring passions is that they fail to make any significant impact on the real business activity of the company. Moreover, each failing and each abandonment, by fermenting scepticism and cynicism throughout the organisation, serve only to inoculate it against subsequent initiatives. It is rather like trying to start a car with a dying battery. Every time the engine fails to turn over we are aware that our attempt has only served to weaken the battery still further, and that our chances of success diminish with each subsequent endeavour.

Someone once pointed out that organisations are rather like the fashion-conscious at an important social function. The very worst that can befall them is to discover that someone else is wearing the same dress. Of course management consultants are ever ready and willing to supply an unending variety of variously packaged cultural change programmes for fashion-conscious companies.

Cultural change programmes are a boon to management consultancies who know full well that a high proportion of their revenue is earned, not so much in diagnosing the current status and needs of the organisation, as in implementing the programme. A long-drawn-out cultural change programme, aimed at 'gradually changing attitudes' company-wide, is just the ticket when it involves a calendar of repeat interventions and 'workshops'. It is a relatively easy way of making money and provides good business visibility. And when it fails, as it invariably does, there will still be the opportunity of bringing out the same fabric in a new design next year. Companies themselves are not altogether unhappy with the cultural change approach to introducing continuous improvement. For some companies this pursuit is a costly but undemanding option, since it does not impinge on that other realm of *real work* that we discussed earlier. It may be impotent but it is unthreatening. It does not require that companies change the way that the real work is managed; it does not invite them closely to re-examine and, if necessary, change the roles and responsibilities of people in the organisation.

It is our contention here that when we do not change these things we in fact change very little; that all corporate endeavours to achieve a transformation by tweaking cultural and ambient factors are of little consequence. One of the first articles to cast serious doubt on the conventional wisdom of cultural and attitudinally driven change was contributed by Michael Beer, Russell A. Eisenstat and Bert Spector:[2]

> Most change programmes don't work because they are guided by a theory of change that is fundamentally flawed. The common belief is that the place to begin is with the knowledge and attitudes of individuals. Changes in attitudes, the theory goes, lead to changes in individual behaviour. And changes in individual behaviour, repeated by many people, will result in organisational change.
>
> According to this model, change is like a conversion experience. Once people 'get religion', changes in their behaviour will surely follow.
>
> This theory gets the change process exactly backward. In fact, individual behaviour is powerfully shaped by the organisational roles that people play. The most effective way to change behaviour, therefore, is to put people into a new organisational context, which imposes new roles, responsibilities, and relationships on them. This creates a situation that, in a sense, 'forces' new attitudes and behaviours on people.

Since then the popularisation of re-engineering, for all its faults, has further strengthened the cause of those who advocate a radical, root-and-branch shake-up of organisations in order to bring about meaningful and profitable change. But even this comes to nought unless it involves changing the work itself and the responsibilities that people have for carrying it out or managing it. There is nothing new in this thinking. One of my treasured possessions is a video recording made by the BBC of an address given by Frederick Herzberg, who made the following observation as early as 1973:

> Now, in industry we communicate too damn much. Most of the communication is passive communication. The idea is if you tell the worker what it's all about he will be more motivated. So you tell him why he has to be an idiot. We get too much communication ... because we feel we have to tell everybody everything – he really doesn't give a damn. If he's in an idiot job, he doesn't give a damn.[3]

'Cultural noise' is the term used by Herzberg for this kind of communication. Communication is indeed one of those words, like 'empowerment' or even 'quality', that tends to become an organisational mantra. If it is chanted solemnly and often enough, good things are supposed to result. Many will have attended 'residential weekends' at which the company management team locks itself away to expose, confront and resolve the organisation's problems. Many hours of arduous discussion produce flipchart listings of problems, then attributed causes, then causes for those causes. As participants become increasingly tired and look forward to going home, the word 'communication' starts to feature more and more in these listings. 'Isn't it amazing?', someone notices, 'It's all about communication!' Some others nod sagely. ('Communication' is a word revered by sages.) Better communication becomes the common countermeasure for most of the problems. The group parts company in good spirits, resolved to communicate better in future. All problems are instantly solved – at least until Monday.

There has been insufficient emphasis on job roles and responsibilities – too much on 'attitudes', 'communications initiatives', 'awareness raising' and so on. Any corporate initiative for the enhancement of quality and productivity can only succeed when grafted onto the main stream of *daily operational activity*.

We make rather too much of 'culture' in business. The only beneficiaries are those who seek to sell us cheap psychology at inflated prices, while imagined 'cultural' constraints remain the most common excuse for failing to move forward in a positive and practical way. 'Culture' is only a word we use in an attempt to aggregate behaviours. Business and operational practices mostly determine those behaviours. These practices are determined by management and can be changed by management. It is necessary and sufficient only that they have the courage and desire so to do.

A PRIVILEGE OR A DUTY?

Daily operational activity, that which seeks to add value, is determined by the roles and responsibilities that people have and *perceive themselves* to have. If we are serious about instituting continuous improvement and if we truly want to end the conditions in which it is so marginalised that it is no longer regarded as an important part of normal everyday business activity, then all employees must be expected to take part in the quest for improvement *as part of the job for which they are paid*.

Let us consider the now rather infamous words of Konosuke Matsushita, founder of the Matsushita corporation:

> We are going to win and the industrial West is going to lose out: there's nothing much you can do about it, because the reasons for your failure are *within yourselves*.
>
> *Your firms are built on the Taylor model*; even worse, *so are your heads*. With your bosses doing the thinking while the workers wield the screwdrivers, you are convinced deep down that that is the right way to run a business.
>
> For you, the essence of management is getting the ideas out of the heads of bosses into the hands of labour ...
>
> Your *'socially minded bosses'*, often full of good intentions, believe their duty is *to*

protect the people in their firms. We, on the other hand, are realists and consider it our duty *to get our people to defend their firms* which will pay them back a hundred-fold for their dedication. By doing this, we end up by being more social than you.[4]

Apart from a near-contemptuous dismissal of any prospects of Western companies catching up with their Japanese counterparts, what is actually being said here? After all, few Western manufacturers would wish themselves to be thought of as still following doggedly in some of the more unfortunate traditions of 'scientific management', often referred to these days as 'Taylorism'. I think there are two aspects of this extract which demand closer examination.

The key words in this extract are 'convinced deep down'. Matsushita seems to be saying: 'I know of your espoused values; I know of the outward and visible displays you are making; the signals about involvement, participation, empowerment and so on, and I don't believe a word of it – neither do your people and, however much you might try to convince yourselves otherwise, "*deep down*", in your heart of hearts, *neither do you.*' He implies that our innermost managerial feelings in the West are made manifest in our organisational behaviours, in our organisation structures, in our procedures and in our systems, in the roles and responsibilities that we assign to people, and in the way in which we address or fail to address the problems of managing work. Everything else is, as Herzberg has already put it, simply 'cultural noise'.

Later in the extract is an example of this phenomenon. Scientific management required us to believe that the workforce should faithfully carry out instructions and spare themselves the burdensome responsibility of having to think. Gradually over a decade or two we modified our stance, moving from a position of denial to one of indulgent toleration. (This is typified by my feelings when my six-year-old son asks to help mow the lawn or paint the fence. 'Of course you can, son!' I reply, forcing a smile and aware that my cold beer will now have to wait rather longer than I had anticipated.) 'Worker participation' became the new coinage: 'Of course we don't object if members of the workforce have any ideas for improvement.' A decade or two later still, we moved from a position of toleration to one of mild encouragement: 'We would welcome and appreciate any contributions the workforce may have to enable us to improve our business performance.' We are still dealing with various refinements along the development of this particular theme of cultural noise. We are still, in most Western manufacturing companies, far short of the situation to which Matsushita refers, where employee contribution is regarded as a *duty* rather than a *privilege*. We have yet to move from the position of mild encouragement to that of *expectation* and *demand*.

There is a need to purge, once and for all, the notion that managers are paid to think and workers are paid merely to do, from the perspectives of managers and workers alike. Unfortunately, many of the initiatives ostensibly aimed at greater workforce involvement and contribution actually reinforce the old moribund tradition rather than eliminate it – again, because they are seen as *separate from the job* and, therefore, *outside the normal scheme of things*: quality circles, involvement groups, suggestion schemes. This altruistic, paternalistic and ultimately patronising stance must be abandoned if we are to make progress. We need to be able to treat our employees like rational, grown-up human beings and pay them the tribute of *demanding* of them that they contribute with their brains as well as their hands, as part of the job for which we pay them.

THE EMPOWERMENT PARADOX

The third, most specific and compelling reason for the continued failure of many Western manufacturing companies to ensure that the drive for continuous improvement becomes a normal part of the operation, amounts to a *fear of losing control*. This has developed gradually over the past three decades as the demands of international competition have intensified; but it began much earlier. This is the great empowerment dilemma of modern manufacturing. It operates across two dimensions: the first concerns the management of people; the second concerns product and processes (Figure 4.1).

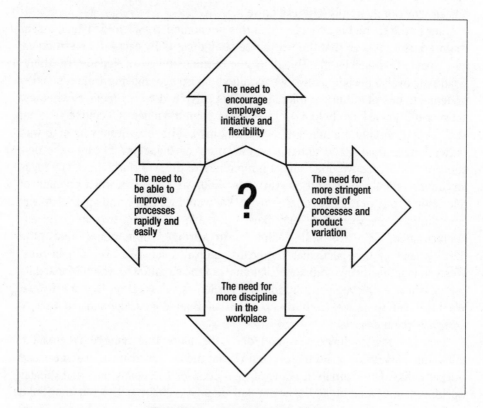

Figure 4.1   **The empowerment paradox**

In the management of people, current conventional wisdom rightly impels us to encourage employee initiative and flexibility if we are to exploit fully the contribution which all our employees must make in pursuit of improved company performance. On the other hand, there is a deep awareness (though often muted by fashion) that much more discipline is needed in the workplace. It appears to us that these are conflicting aspirations. The more we demand discipline in the workplace, the more we are liable to constrict the initiative and flexibility of those who work within it; the more we pursue an open and pliable approach, which encourages initiative and flexibility, the more we develop the feeling, in our bones, that our actions might somehow be conducive to a form of industrial anarchy.

An even greater anxiety is felt when we consider the axis of product and processes. How do we reconcile the demands of more stringent control of processes and product variation, on the one hand, with an apparent requirement to enable people in our organisation to be able to improve, to *change* processes rapidly and easily? If continuous improvement requires that more and more of our staff have a hand in influencing and adapting our methods of manufacture, how does this square not only with our need to build products of consistently high quality, but also our requirements to meet and adhere to the procedural demands of externally certificated systems such as BS 5750 or ISO 9000? We appear to be seeking a compromise which lies somewhere between total mayhem and disorder on the one hand and a stifling, system-driven bureaucracy on the other.

It is no small part of the purpose of this book to contend that this is a false dilemma, brought about by a sustained and historical retreat by management from the task of managing the work that is actually performed. It is merely a symptom of the inadequacy of remote control management, exposed and made manifest by the competitive industrial climate that now prevails in the world. In particular, this retreat has brought about the decline and emasculation of the first level of production management and its crucial responsibilities for both people and processes. This malady has robbed Western manufacturing companies of the lynchpin which once held these seemingly contentious elements together.

NOTES

1. I mentioned this, in a similar context, at a seminar which I conducted in Coventry in 1991. At the morning coffee break I was accosted by one of the attendees, a very senior executive from one of the four or five most prestigious manufacturing groups in Britain. He was not the first to be critical of some of the ideas I was putting forward and he was certainly not the first, nor I suspect the last, to offer 'constructive criticism' of my style of presentation and personal idiosyncrasies. But he did both of these things with a degree of enthusiasm to which I was unaccustomed and for which I was quite unprepared. As he concluded his remarks, and before moving off to refill his coffee cup, I already had the feeling that I had injured this person in some way and that due retribution was being exacted. He handed me his business card which informed me that he was his company's 'Project 2000 Director'.

2. M. Beer, R.A. Eisenstat and B. Spector (1990), 'Why Change Programs Don't Produce Change', *Harvard Business Review*, December.
3. F. Herzberg (1973), 'Jumping for the Jelly Beans', in *Management Classics* (video recording) London: BBC Enterprises.
4. Quoted by a number of authors, including R.T. Pascale (1990), *Managing on the Edge*, New York: Simon and Schuster and London: Penguin Books, and F. Price (1990), *Right Every Time*, Aldershot, Hants: Gower.

Part II
A Creed for a Lost Profession

5 The Penultimate Customer

We know that the tail must wag the dog, for the horse is drawn by the cart;
But the devil whoops, as he whooped of old: 'It's clever, but is it art?'

Rudyard Kipling, *The Conundrum of the Workshops*

We cannot begin to understand *Genba Kanri* without first examining the very different levels of esteem, East and West, for manufacturing itself. The UK affords probably the worst example in the developed world of institutionalised national contempt for the role of manufacturing, but I am assured by production managers in North America and mainland Europe that this malaise is only relatively less virulent in their own countries.

MANUFACTURING AS A NECESSARY EVIL

Those in Britain who work in the manufacturing sector of the economy may well have just cause for anger and frustration at the way it has been scandalously treated by successive governments and the lack of esteem and recognition accorded to it by society as a whole. I am forced to conclude, however, that British manufacturing companies are themselves largely to blame for this situation. If manufacturing is regarded as the poor relation of the British economy, then is this any different from the way in which most of its manufacturing companies treat their manufacturing function? If the 'brightest and best' of our young people generally spurn manufacturing companies in favour of what they presumably see as more lucrative options in government services, finance, the media or the 'professions', do not most of those rare exceptions also shun at all costs anything to do with the actual manufacturing part of manufacturing industry? Most fall over themselves to work in marketing, finance, personnel, engineering (if they really must) but avoid production like the plague and regard the factory as a charnel-house.

We cannot blame our schools, our universities, our careers advisers or our national culture for this condition. These young people have learned their lessons well – from their older siblings and friends and from their parents. They know, as we do, that in most manufacturing companies, with only a few rare exceptions, the production or manufacturing department is a forlorn place which presents few opportunities for career development. In many UK companies manufacturing directors (if they exist) are the worst paid directors on the board, even though they may have responsibility for the overwhelming majority of people in the organisation. The production managers often have significantly lower salaries than line managers in other departments, and there is simply no comparison, either in terms of salary or status, between the production supervisor and the buyer, the accountant, the engineer, the salesperson or the personnel officer.

I like to imagine a situation where six or seven people get together to form the directorship of a new manufacturing company. They set about distributing responsibility for the various company functions and, given that none of the group has any specialised expertise, they decide to exercise their own preferences and cut cards to determine first and last choice. The marketing, finance, personnel and purchasing options are taken up very quickly. I am not so sure about the managing director's post – it may be filled first; it may not, depending upon the temerity or deference of the characters involved. But I would be willing to bet that the person who draws the lowest-value card but one will be the engineering or technical director. After a brief sigh of disappointment, he or she will be consoled, at least, to have avoided the production department.

There are generally two types of production manager in British industry. The first are 'high-flyers' seconded from other, more prestigious disciplines, to build up a portfolio of varied experience in order to progress further up the company hierarchy. They usually move up and on as soon as they get the opportunity, as soon as they can make an impression, or before they get found out. The second type are frequently older and more experienced – at least in the established way of doing things. They may well have risen through the ranks, having been a worker or supervisor, though not necessarily in the same firm. Their next move is retirement or, possibly, if they can manage it, a move to another company.

Manufacturing for most manufacturing companies, is a necessary evil. It would be much more fun if we didn't have to do it at all. Manufacturing *management*, at any level, is something that *somebody* has to do. Companies console themselves, however, with the belief that, fortunately, virtually *anybody* can do it. All that is required is a basic standard of general management skill. A good manager of a technical or commercial function, it is assumed, should be able to manage production easily. The reverse, of course, does not follow. It is not expected that a good production manager *per se* will be similarly comfortable managing the finance, purchasing, personnel or even engineering functions, for these are *professions*, requiring *specialist knowledge*.[1]

Manufacturing in the West, and certainly in the UK, is simply not regarded as a profession. It is scarcely regarded as any kind of discipline at all. Many British manufacturers take pride in describing themselves as 'engineering companies', not only those making heavy, fabricated or bespoke products, but virtually anything which does not adorn the human body or is not consumed by its digestive system. Many companies who *are* looking for some degree of professional standing among their production managers specifically demand engineering qualifications or membership of a chartered engineering body.

If we peruse the prospectuses of our universities and business schools, we may be forgiven for wondering whether manufacturing management exists at all. We find 'paint technology' ... 'polymers' ... 'production control' ... 'textile weaving', and, yes, occasionally something described as 'total quality', the content of which may vary considerably and may or may not be tangentially related to some of the principles contained in this book.

I have tried in vain to identify any other field of human endeavour where the main component of the espoused activity is so nebulous or so generally despised. I wonder how it would be if our armed forces reflected this situation. I imagine that our army commanders would invariably come from administrative and logistical support groups. Nobody in the infantry or cavalry would ever progress beyond a colonel's rank. A handful of officers in engineer units might manage a couple of steps further. The most promising graduates from West Point or Sandhurst and the best new rankers alike would compete to join the Pay Corps or the Catering Corps and only join a fighting regiment or a combat unit as a last resort.

In a Utopian organisation, just as in a Utopian society, each of the individuals and identifiable sub-groups within it would be regarded equally for their unique contribution to the success and well-being of the whole. In the real world of organisations, however, there is usually a power base *somewhere* – one or more groups, departments or disciplinary functions which are felt to 'carry more clout' than others; or are perceived to be the 'hothouses' from which either the leaders of the organisations tend to emerge or in which a period of time for other emerging senior managers is regarded as obligatory.

Some companies self-consciously and deliberately set out to develop such a professional bias and even proclaim it to the outside world, describing themselves as 'design-led', 'sales-led', 'investment-led' and so on. Of course this intended bias may or may not reflect reality. In other organisations, the perceived or actual relative strengths of the various departments and functions have emerged in the course of history and these may change from time to time. My first manufacturing employer was a typical example. The company made a varied range of electronic components using different technologies and had a divisionalised structure, with each of its product families forming a distinct business unit. Virtually all the executive positions in the company were filled by people with technical backgrounds in electronics, process engineering or research and development. Many of these people had long service histories in the company. However, the general managers of the various divisions (the next layer down in the hierarchy) were for the most part accountants and sales people: most were recruited externally and few stayed for long. This pattern reflects a general trend within British industry during the 1970s and 1980s.

A JOURNEY TO THE CENTRE OF THE UNIVERSE

Many of our better-known companies have reputations for particularly influential departments. In the motor industry, for example, it is commonly believed that the Ford Motor Company has very muscular purchasing and HRD functions. In the early 1980s Austin Rover was regarded as having a strong production control emphasis. On the European mainland, engineering departments are particularly powerful, especially among German manufacturers.

Among Japanese manufacturers, however, including their successful transplant operations in the West, there is far greater emphasis on the role and importance of the manufacturing function. This is certainly true of Nissan. If there is a power base at all in the Nissan plant in the North-East of England, then it is to be found in manufacturing: such is the perception of the people who work in that organisation and the company shows every sign of deliberately fostering and reinforcing that perception. Having worked for roughly equal amounts of time within and outside the manufacturing department at Nissan, I can confidently verify this. There, production managers, supervisors and manufacturing staff[2] proudly proclaim that, in their company: 'Production is the centre of the universe.' I have occasionally used a model (Figure 5.1) in public seminars attended by representatives of various professional disciplines from a variety of companies to demonstrate this perception. It is an approximate recollection of a slide used by a Nissan body assembly supervisor as part of a presentation made to visitors.

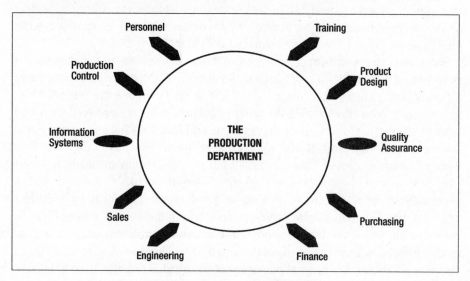

Figure 5.1 'The centre of the universe'

After showing this diagram it is immediately apparent, from the facial reactions of the audience, which are the production managers and which are the representatives of support departments. The most crestfallen or hostile faces of all often turn out to be those of engineers. The model clearly represents a dream to some – a nightmare to others.

But it is not my intention in using this device to belittle the professionalism of *any* discipline or to question its contribution to success of the company: quite the contrary. The following story might shed some light on the concept I am trying to describe. It was related to me by an acquaintance who worked in the personnel department of Komatsu (UK) Ltd during the period when it was establishing its manufacturing facility at Birtley in County Durham, having taken over the aborted US-owned 'Caterpillar' plant which had previously occupied the site.

At that time, each department was assigned a Japanese 'adviser' whose function was to assist British departmental managers in ensuring that the organisation was established along the most propitious lines. A new, young personnel officer had recently joined the company and, before long, he found that he needed to talk to a particular supervisor – about a wages query, a recruitment issue or something of that sort. Having failed to reach the supervisor directly by telephone he then, in all innocence, put out a message on the company public address system requesting the supervisor to report to the personnel office. This drew an immediate response from the Japanese adviser who was at once incredulous and outraged at what he had just heard. He went straight to the personnel officer and instructed him never to do such a thing again. 'This is the Personnel Department,' he explained, 'We do not summon production supervisors to this office. The supervisor is a very busy man. If you need to speak to a supervisor then you go out into the factory and ask to speak to him. *You work for the supervisor,* he does not work for you. *He is your customer.*'

Now it would be wrong to think of this little episode as merely illustrating a very different perspective of the relative esteem of the manufacturing function in Japanese companies – although it certainly does that. There is nothing humble or self-deprecating in the sentiments being expressed here by an individual who, back in Japan, would be a very high-ranking manager indeed in Komatsu's personnel organisation. On the contrary, this is the voice, not of humility, but of intense professional pride, almost to the point of arrogance, by one who judges the performance of his department and profession on the service it gives to its client departments and functions within the organisation. So it is also with every other support department in a Japanese manufacturing company, *including the engineering and technical functions.* The production or manufacturing department, comprising its workforce, its supervisors and managers, and its director is *the penultimate customer* – the *ultimate* customer within the organisation itself.

Of course, people will ask 'What about sales and marketing?' 'What about design?' 'Is not the strength of Japanese industry that it is marketing-led?' (Was not the proud boast of Akio Morita, the president of Sony, that 'We make the things that the world wants to buy?') No one is suggesting otherwise. It is not the function of manufacturing to determine the necessary characteristics of finished products or the volume of supply the market requires. These are determined by customers in the market and relayed to the company via sales, marketing, design and quality assurance. To the manufacturing function these are *givens*, and not subjects for debate. Thereafter, however, in a normal running condition and until we have a different appraisal of market requirements, the battle for quality, cost and delivery is won or lost *in the factory*. Every individual and every group within the organisation is a part of that battle, either directly, as part of the manufacturing department, or indirectly, providing all the logistical support that manufacturing requires. Like our personnel adviser, support functions in Japanese companies take fierce pride in the service they give.

It is commonly remarked that the career of a manager in a Japanese company starts 'where the rubber touches the road'. Where does the rubber touch the road in a manufacturing company? Many are aware that all graduate trainees at Nissan's British plant spend their first two months working on the production line. But this practice is not merely restricted to them. The purchasing department is particularly insistent that *all* its new members undertake a programme of 'production experience'. Irrespective of their seniority or knowledge of either procurement or the motor industry, their purchasing career at Nissan begins with a number of weeks spent working on the production line. This is not an exercise in gratuitous 'beasting'. Bringing humility is not its purpose. New buyers are exposed, above all, to fitting those parts for which they will thereafter be commercially responsible. Not only does this mean that their subsequent transactions with vendors will be conducted with first-hand experience of problems associated with fitting the parts, but they will have built up a good working relationship with supervisors and production teams in whose eyes their professional esteem and individual respect have been greatly enhanced by their earlier experiences.

PRODUCTION AND ENGINEERING

The production department's status as the penultimate customer is as valid in engineering as in any other discipline. The 'institutes' and other professional engineering bodies continually lament the lowly status of their profession in British society and frequently equate this with British industrial decline.[3] But, though I have every sympathy for the sentiment, it misses a more fundamental problem. For what tarnishes the esteem of engineering if it is not the smear of the workshop or factory? It is manufacturing itself which suffers the stigma. Engineers are only tainted by association – an association which some would gladly sever in pursuit of social rehabilitation, even though it might compound the real problem. Engineers in Japan enjoy a degree of professional esteem, both within manufacturing organisations and in Japanese society as a whole, which is the envy of their peers in the West, particularly in Britain. But I cannot emphasise strongly enough that, in Japanese manufacturing organisations, engineering has a very different outlook from that of its Western equivalent, especially in the relationship which it enjoys with manufacturing.

On three separate occasions I have exploited opportunities to learn of the impressions that senior Japanese managers have of the relative strengths and weaknesses of British and Japanese engineers. These impressions have proven most consistent. In general, the British engineer is regarded as more technically knowledgeable than his Japanese counterpart of a similar level of age and experience. When comparing two electronics engineers, for example, or two metallurgists, the Briton will usually be thought to know more about electronics or metallurgy than the Japanese. The Japanese engineer, however, is regarded as having a far more thorough, more methodical and, ultimately, more effective approach to solving production problems, together with a better awareness of the need to develop practical solutions which actually work on the shop floor and a greater affinity for working with production personnel at all levels.

Sadly, when conducting diagnoses in many companies, and especially when making enquiries of production managers, supervisors and production workers, I find that the engineering and technical functions are regarded as no less given over to 'ivory tower' behaviour than their commercial counterparts. They are judged, at best, as no more helpful than any other department and no less disdainful of their obligations to the factory and to those who work in it.

Many companies are now seeking to reduce their product development times. Some have achieved remarkable results. 'Simultaneous engineering' is a common Western term for approaches characterised by greater involvement of production in the trial and development phases. My friend Nino Caja, an Italian quality specialist, once told me how he went to Japan on a study trip to learn about the subject. Nobody in the host companies he visited had any idea what he was talking about: they had no such specific concept and certainly no label for it. This should not surprise us. What is at work in a GK company during the pre-launch activity for a new product is simply its customary relationships between production and engineering, with perhaps a few small procedural bells and whistles attached. There is no special invocation of a high-profile system, just a collaborative partnership between the two functions and the effective use of PDCA. The start of commercial production is not the same watershed event that it is in conventional companies – before which the engineering function jealously guards its ownership of both product and tooling, and after which it largely washes its hands of both. In a GK company, production teams are involved at a much earlier stage of development and the engineering function continues to give specialist support well into the life of products. The 'handover' of responsibility, if there could be said to be one, is sometimes difficult to identify. Both groups are involved in trials, and at every stage of development check the outcomes and find appropriate countermeasures to problems.

'"Vorsprung durch Technik" as they say in Germany' – a land whose manufacturing performance has traditionally been lauded as the epitome of technical excellence, a land where the professional engineer is king. Yet even in Germany there is a growing awareness that the role and performance of its engineering functions must alter in line with current worldwide competitive standards. Wendelin Wiedeking, manager of the once mighty Porsche, being hammered by Japanese competitors for ten years, took the drastic step of introducing a particularly aggressive team of Japanese consultants to its operation in Zuffenhausen, near Stuttgart. Chihiro Nakao, of the consulting firm 'Shin-Gijutsu', relates: 'When I see one of Porsche's fine engineers, I do not say "good morning". I say, "show me your hands". They must be dirty – engineers must always have oily hands.'[4]

The relationship between engineering and manufacturing in GK organisations is characterised both by a perpetual awareness of manufacturing's status as *the customer* and by a climate of mutual support and respect which is lacking in too many conventional companies. This consists of an awareness that manufacturing and engineering are two complementary but fundamentally *distinct and separate* disciplines. This may come as a surprise to many, for whom the words 'manufacturing' and 'engineering' are largely synonymous, or who have difficulty in identifying a specific professional discipline for the manufacturing function at all. Herein lies the crux of the problem.

After all, we can find a concise definition for virtually any professional discipline in a manufacturing company except for manufacturing itself. Engineering is often described as 'finding practical applications for, or solving practical problems using, scientific principles', or words to that effect. A similar summary of the personnel or HRD function might be 'to acquire, motivate, gain the commitment of and retain capable people operating in an effective and efficient organisation in such a way that the company achieves its business goals'. We could continue as far as we wish, visiting every profession in our organisation – quality assurance, production control, finance and the others – finding for each a suitable concise but loftily worded description of its purpose.

And what of manufacturing or production? What of the men and women who engage in production activities as production workers or as managers? Here we seem to be forced back on banalities such as 'making things', 'making products', 'making products or overseeing others who make products'. Very well, we can add high-sounding, qualifying terms about 'quality', 'performance' and the like, but these are generics which we could add to any of the descriptions of other disciplines with equal validity. Our difficulty is that we have long since lost any distinct and clear concept of production, and particularly of production management, as a professional discipline in its own right.

The Japanese, on the other hand, have a very clear view of the professional role of the manufacturing function: to be *responsible for the manufacturing process*, its maintenance and improvement. What can be inferred from this, given that, over the past 50 years, Western companies have gradually taken this responsibility away from the manufacturing function and vested it in 'engineering', 'quality assurance' or a combination of both?

First, it must be apparent that the prevailing manufacturing doctrine of Japanese industry and its central assumptions about the management of productive work differ substantially from those of conventional Western companies, and are much closer to an older Western tradition which subsisted before this key responsibility was transferred. Second, there are very different sets of roles and responsibilities, systems and procedures which pertain to process control and improvement. Third, these affect the exploitation of opportunities for detailed incremental improvements and the greater emphasis placed on the process as the richest vein of such improvements.

NOTES

1. There are always interesting exceptions. The current personnel manager at Nissan's British plant was previously production manager of its body assembly shop. His former background was as an engineer.
2. Nissan's term for production workers.
3. An example appeared in the British national press following BMW's acquisition of the Rover group in January 1994. The author of an article which mourned the passing of the last British-owned, volume car manufacturer saw great significance in the fact that, whereas the Rover executives seated at the negotiating table were all from commercial backgrounds, those representing BMW were all engineers.
4. Reported in an article by John Eisenhammer in the *Independent on Sunday*, 3 July 1994. The article revealed how the first-fruits of Shin-Gijutsu's introduction of Genba Kanri and *kaizen* approaches had already halved the number of in-plant vehicle defects, reduced inventory levels by 44 per cent, the amount of operating space required by 32 per cent and the production hours required to build a Porsche by 33 per cent.

6 Real Management

Oneness generates everything:
When the sage rules in the light of it,
He rules everything.
A wise man never tries to break up the whole.

The Tao Te Ching

I have described how Japanese manufacturers have retained a clear and distinct professional regard for their manufacturing function, centred on that function's responsibility for the manufacturing process, that is, all the events and activities involved in transforming the three factors of production into marketable commodities as described previously in Chapter 1 (see Figure 1.1).

Most Western companies do not have such a clear view of a professional role for the manufacturing function because, over the past few decades, they have systematically farmed out this responsibility to other functions. This has not only diminished the esteem of the production or manufacturing department and all its members, from the manufacturing director to the newest recruit on the production line, but has severely weakened our capacity both for controlling quality and for rapidly and regularly introducing method improvements. Instead, methods and processes are scarcely considered at all in many companies when it comes to searching for the means of securing improved company performance. Since significant and meaningful improvements in performance and profitability must come from the production process itself, far greater recognition and esteem must be accorded to the production functions and those who work in them. They must become the main focus of company activity; they must be seen as the vehicle by which costs are constantly reduced and product quality is continuously enhanced.

WHAT RESPONSIBILITY FOR QUALITY MUST MEAN

So far in this book I have purposely avoided the term 'total quality', or any of its common derivatives, 'TQC (total quality control)' or 'TQM (total quality management)' and shall continue to do so in subsequent chapters. This is not to disregard the contributions of Armand Feigenbaum, Kaoru Ishikawa and others who have used such terminology in the past and whose sterling endeavours in the cause of quality are worthy of admiration. Rather it is to point out that total quality has been so misunderstood in the West. Masaaki Imai clearly experienced and identified this difficulty as early as 1985 when writing his seminal work on *kaizen*.[1] Since then, the terms 'total quality' (and in particular 'TQM') have been overused, abused and misapplied, almost to the point of meaninglessness, by companies, consultants, academics and government officials alike. By the end of the 1980s, it was almost impossible for a company to buy one of its inspectors a new pair of eyeglasses without proudly announcing to the world that it had introduced 'total quality'.

Nevertheless, in spite of the wide variety of interpretations given to the concept, most authors and commentators and, consequently, many Western managers, would agree on the following characteristics of total quality control, both of which have had an undeniable and beneficial impact on Western approaches to quality.

1. MANUFACTURING IS RESPONSIBLE FOR THE QUALITY OF ITS PRODUCTS

No longer is product quality regarded as the preserve of an 'inspection' or 'quality assurance' department. Quality is now regarded as everyone's responsibility. In the 1980s and 1990s scarcely any organisation, in any sector of business or public administration, neglected to attempt to impart this thinking to its employees in some way or another. 'Quality awareness' training has endeavoured to raise the profile of quality and customer satisfaction among existing employees. Company 'mission statements' have been drafted to reflect this simple tenet and these have been emblazoned across reception areas while posters, proudly proclaiming that 'Quality is everyone's business', have adorned factory walls and works' canteens. Company induction and orientation programmes for new employees incorporate this message. 'We are a quality company', recruits are told; 'Quality is important to us'. 'You are all, each of you, responsible for the quality of your own work'. 'Remember, think quality at all times'. Some companies may go to the trouble of giving a practical explanation of just what 'responsibility for quality' means. Others may be justly arraigned for flagrant infringement of Deming's tenth principle.[2]

A heavy engineering plant enjoying a period of business expansion was recruiting skilled machine operators in some numbers for the first time in several years. Simultaneously, it was making strenuous efforts to improve its image and reputation for manufacturing quality products and also to raise the awareness of quality throughout the organisation. It launched an extensive new induction package for its new recruits which covered the first four weeks of employment. The first and last week consisted of formal, off-the-job training and lectures concerning every aspect of the company's business, with a special emphasis on its philosophy about and approach to quality. During the two intervening weeks the recruits received their on-the-job training, learning and practising their new jobs. At the end of the four-week period, they were invited to partake in an 'open forum' to talk freely of their impressions and experiences in their new organisation. A fair number of them were very vocal in expressing the opinion that, as far as quality was concerned, the company's words simply failed to match the music.

'You tell me that I'm working for "a quality company",' stated one, 'but only yesterday, I wasted four hours out of an eight-hour shift because nobody could give me the right tools, the right equipment or the necessary engineering documentation. Later, when I finally got started, I found that I needed a micrometer. I asked my foreman. He told me he didn't have one and sent me to the stores. The man at the hatch told me that all the micrometers were "being used". He sent me to a man at the other end of the factory who he thought might have one. He did; and I took it back with me to use on the job. I found that it was broken. I took it back to the man who had loaned it. "It's broken", I said. "Micrometers are like gold dust around here", he replied. "I find this one does the trick if you stick a little bit of tape on it," he added. "I suppose it depends on what you're using it for." I took the micrometer back with me and managed to find a roll of masking tape. I did the best job I could and hoped it was all right – and you tell me that I'm working for "a quality company".'

Regardless of whether companies have made real strides in transforming their approach to quality or whether they have simply engaged in a rather vacuous espousal of fashionable values, it cannot be denied that few production managers, supervisors or workers today would seek to disown or to pretend ignorance of their nominal responsibility for product quality – however frustrated or embittered some of them may be at perceived organisational failings which prevent this becoming any more than a token responsibility.

2. PRODUCT QUALITY IS DETERMINED BY THE PROCESS

The inspection–selection approach to product quality has now been largely discredited, at least in the thinking of senior managers. We have taken a simple causal principle as old as the gospel parable of the tree and its fruit, and combined this with a more discerning attitude towards the cost implications of making, and possibly shipping, defective products or of delivering an unsatisfactory service. There is now a wider understanding that if good manufacturing processes are designed and adhered to in our factories, then good-quality products and lower manufacturing and service costs will both *inevitably* follow. We are more inclined to regard high quality and low cost as complementary rather than conflicting objectives and are more aware that neither quality nor cost can be described or understood in a meaningful way without a qualifying reference to one another. We recognise that trying to prevent defective products from reaching the customer is far less satisfactory than preventing their manufacture in the first place, and that if we can deploy more of our efforts and resources towards resolving process problems, rather than in dealing with their consequences, then we can not only eliminate or substantially reduce the costs of inspection and repair but also, at the same time, have much more confidence in the quality of product which reaches the commercial customer.

Need we say more? I cannot imagine that anyone reading this book has managed to avoid these simple and universal maxims of total quality control. On the face of it, we in the West could almost be forgiven for supposing that we have just experienced a revolution in our thinking about quality sufficient to transform radically our competitive standing in terms of profitably supplying the world with manufactured products. We know that this is not the case. It is belied by our trade figures; by the national origin of so much of the product range of both commercial and consumer goods available to the customers; by the feeling of so many managers that the fruits and benefits of even our better initiatives in the direction of total quality have somehow fallen short of our expectations; by our sense that somehow, though much improved, the commitment of many people in our organisations to these principles is partial, superficial, short-lived or leaves something to be desired in some other way. Hence the constant search for rejuvenating programmes or means of repackaging existing approaches referred to in Chapter 4. Something is clearly lacking.

What has been missed (or perhaps subconsciously avoided) in most conventional companies is that these two simple maxims, when taken together, are the logical premises of an inescapable conclusion. The formula runs:

1. Manufacturing is responsible for the quality of its products.
2. Product quality is determined by the process.

ergo

3. Manufacturing must be responsible for the process.

'Responsibility for the process' in its true sense requires that holders be *accountable* for any failings in it; this in turn demands that they are able to *influence* it and *make changes to it* in order to redress those failings. In other words, there is a conferred *legitimate ownership* of the process on the holders – in this case the production or manufacturing department.

As we all know, this is not the case in most companies, where such ownership is conferred on engineering functions. *This remains one of the starkest areas of contrast between Japanese and Western companies in terms of how they actually manage their factories,* and yet so few observers and commentators have seen fit even to mention this aspect. The formula can of course be reversed: if manufacturing is not responsible for the process, then neither can it be held responsible for product quality.

Those of us in conventional Western companies, accustomed to the orthodox and prevailing method of pursuing process discipline – that of segregating responsibilities for aspects of manufacturing activity and employing technical functions as tabernacle guards whose ascribed role is to deny unsanctioned changes to the manufacturing process – could possibly argue that manufacturing personnel are responsible for quality in so far as they are expected to adhere to established 'engineering processes'. But can we be satisfied with this narrow and sterile view? There is all the difference in the world between being held responsible for product quality and being required to follow instructions. If we mean the latter, then we should state this clearly and cheerfully consign to the waste bin the posturing that has been the hallmark of so many 'quality awareness' initiatives of the past 15 years.

Further important questions arise, however, concerning the credibility of a limited engineering resource which assumes sufficient political will and practical wherewithal to specify processes *in sufficient detail* to guarantee internationally competitive standards of product quality – even on the assumption that they are rigidly adhered to. Ironically, Western manufacturers are remarkably lax, compared with their Japanese counterparts, when it comes to defining specific processes, providing far more latitude to the individual production worker and consequently allowing for much more process and product variation. Necessarily limited (and often unnecessarily remote) engineering resources are rarely capable of a very precise definition of how the work should be carried out. In many companies the 'process' is not a process at all, but a mere product specification or technical drawing which conveys the required characteristics of the finished article: critical dimensions, tolerances, location of components, polarities, torque settings and so forth. These may or may not be supplemented by a broad statement of an operational sequence or be annotated with one or two 'helpful hints' or 'care points' here and there. In the main, we give workers a general statement of what is required, pray that they can work out the detail for themselves, and expect them to deal with any ambiguities contained therein. We have a name in the West for this imprecise and uncoordinated fumbling and groping forward on the part of someone endeavouring to perform quality work. We call it 'skill'. Yet it would not be recognised as such in GK companies or by our own grandparents' generation.

Let us suppose, however, that we adhere to this concept of responsibility for quality in manufacturing departments, equating it to strict adherence to established processes. Let us also stretch our imagination somewhat to suppose that our technical and engineering functions are able to provide our workers with processes which are beyond reproach in terms of their efficacy, clarity, irremissiveness and detail. What then? There would remain the question of identifying suitable levers for ensuring strict compliance with these processes. Who would be responsible for this on a continual basis? Who would instruct workers in the understanding and practical application of such processes in the first instance? Who is best fitted to make subsequent controlled amendments and alterations to processes in the pursuit of improved performance, in terms of enhanced product quality, cost reduction or reduced delivery time? Only the authors of the processes themselves have sufficient resolve, commitment, enthusiasm and practical understanding to be able to undertake this activity.

We therefore have a simple choice to make. We can recruit a prohibitively expensive battalion of process and industrial engineers – enough, not only to define processes in sufficient detail to cope with the complexities and competitiveness of modern manufacturing, but also to carry out all the monitoring, training and people management duties in the factory – and dispense with production management altogether. Or, within broad established technical parameters, we can entrust the authorship of the detailed processes to our first-line production managers.

Unless manufacturing can be made responsible for the manufacturing process, then, not only is its professional standing seriously weakened, but we are left with a diffuse mechanism for process control which is woefully inadequate in terms of ensuring process stability and consistent quality, and yet at the same time is enough to stifle the drive for the manufacturing-led improvements which characterise Japanese manufacturing performance.

Without responsibility for the process, manufacturing, including manufacturing management:

- can never be held accountable for it;
- can never be held accountable for the quality of the products that come from it;
- will not be *able* to make improvements;
- will not be *interested* in making improvements;
- will often produce and achieve *in spite of* laid-down processes rather than because of them;
- will always be able to pass the buck to engineering whenever there is a problem (whether process-based or not).

TAYLOR'S BEQUEST

Perhaps it is time that Western industrial management re-evaluated the doctrine of scientific management as espoused by Frederick Taylor and his followers and which remains, whether or not we care to acknowledge it, the common legacy of both Japanese and Western approaches to manufacturing. In the West we tend to be rather shame-faced about this part of our inheritance. Decades after his death Taylor has tended to become the sin-eater for all that we perceive to be wrong with Western industry. There are those, however, who still regard Taylor as a much maligned figure, wholly humanistic and benevolent in his aspirations, whose memory has been contaminated by those who misunderstood and misapplied his principles. The jury is still out on scientific management and its creator. Fascinating though the debate may be, it is not my intention here to discuss which elements of scientific management, *as it came to be applied* in the West, should be directly attributed to Taylor and which to organisations that may have clumsily or partially sought to implement his ideas. But there are two main aspects of that legacy which should concern us.

The first is a fervent belief in the systematic and logical analysis of work, the quest to find, establish and stipulate detailed methods of working which remove waste, maximise efficiency and profitability and ultimately make the task of the worker less arduous. Once determined, these methods should be assiduously followed by all who carry out such work.

The second is that managers and technical staff – *professionals* – are, by dint of their knowledge and education, uniquely and exclusively qualified for this role. Only they are sufficiently enlightened and dedicated to the interests of both the company and all those who work in it. Others are dedicated only to an extent determined by self-interest and the desire to increase their earnings. They lack both the skills and motivation required to improve the performance of their own work unassisted. This second aspect, when combined with the first, gave rise to the development of 'piecework', 'productivity bonus' and 'measured day work' schemes, some of which still feature in most factories. This inheritance remains the greatest curse of Western business, the most voracious thief of the benefits to the company of improved working methods.

In the West it is the second aspect which has had the most abiding influence on management assumptions and on organisational behaviour: the belief that managers are paid to think and that workers are paid to do. Yet when we seek to conjure up the worst images of what we call 'Taylorism', it is to the first aspect that we are drawn. The detailed analysis and regulation of work strikes us as mechanistic, impersonal and cold. We think of a regime typified by Charlie Chaplin in *Modern Times*: a place where the old virtues of craftsmanship and pride of work have been submerged in a soulless drudgery where even the need to think has been extinguished. This is why we are reluctant to prescribe methods in meticulous detail and why we shy off from ensuring that detailed, standardised operations are meticulously adhered to. It is as if, by being more tolerant of non-standard working, by being non-prescriptive beyond broad product and process parameters about how work should be done, we can somehow atone for a wider tradition which is generally disrespectful to workers, dismissive of their intellectual contribution and generally lacking in humanity – as if two wrongs can somehow make a right.

But to the Japanese the first aspect is perfectly rational and is a mainstay of their whole approach. After all, how can you achieve consistent standards of product quality with inconsistent working methods? And the growing complexity of products and processes has made the need for meticulousness and detail even more acute. For the Japanese, it is the second aspect of the legacy of scientific management which is so reprehensible and lacking in respect for human dignity. In their approach *all* are invited and expected to join in the quest for better working methods; and the role played by those who will be required to carry them out is of paramount importance. To them is assigned the lion's share of the responsibility for managing, maintaining and improving the manufacturing process.

This is what Matsushita is referring to when he describes the progress 'beyond the Taylor model' (quoted in Chapter 4). Japanese manufacturers are *post-Taylorist* organisations. They have *transcended* the principles of scientific management whereas most Western organisations have struggled in vain to free themselves. In maintaining a rigorous approach to job standardisation and yet overturning a jaundiced and blighted perspective of the aspirations and capabilities of the workforce, Japanese companies have managed to throw out the bathwater and yet keep the baby.

GENBA KANRI: THE 'THREE REALS' OF PRODUCTION

Genba Kanri is the dominant manufacturing doctrine of Japanese companies, including their subsidiary organisations in Europe and North America and a select but increasing number of indigenous Western companies who are now using its principles to achieve internationally competitive levels of performance. It is the foundation on which its better-known offshoot applications, such as JIT, *poka yoke*, TPM and *kanban*, are constructed. It makes clear assumptions about the management of the manufacturing process, which it regards as the source of all real improvement, and consequently also about the roles and responsibilities of manufacturing personnel, particularly its First Line Managers and their key tasks of defining, controlling and improving that process. The very words *Genba Kanri* are themselves laden with assumptions about the role of manufacturing and of how factories should be managed.

Giving a satisfactory and concise translation of *Genba Kanri* into English, however, is not a straightforward task. The very richness of the English language, proffering a specific word for almost every precise application or subtle nuance, poses problems. Like many other languages, Japanese has a much smaller vocabulary than English, and one word can have a variety of precise meanings depending on its context. This can sometimes be advantageous: one word can instantly suggest several mutually supporting connotations in a very vivid and arresting way. *Genba* is such a word. (*Kanri* simply means 'management' . The Japanese often refer to PDCA as the '*Kanri* cycle'.)

Taiichi Ohno, Toyota's influential strategist, known in the West principally for his development of 'just-in-time' concepts and the *kanban* system, was among the first to refer to '*genba*' in 1982.[3] His terminology was translated into English as 'workplace management'. In the Nissan organisation worldwide, its English-speaking population is accustomed to having its manufacturing disciplines described as 'workshop management', and it was these principles and practices that were introduced to my colleagues and myself as newly recruited Nissan production managers and supervisors in Japan in 1985. (Its deeper underlying assumptions and an understanding of how these differed from those of Western companies only gradually emerged in the intervening years.) I have also known *Genba Kanri* to be rendered into English as 'shop floor management'.

But none of these translations does full justice to the meaning and flavour of the original. The *Genba* is indeed the factory, the workplace, the shop floor, but it is much more besides. It is also the everyday Japanese word that would be reflected in English expressions such as the 'front line', the 'sharp end' the 'coal face' and 'on the spot'. The sentiments and values inherent in *Genba Kanri* are thus made clear at the outset. The shop floor is where the *real* battle for quality and productivity is fought, where *real* problems are encountered, where *real* decisions must be taken, where *real management* happens.

Russel Castings Ltd is the last remaining iron foundry in Leicester. Thanks to the forward thinking of its management team and the skill, commitment and energies of its workforce, it not only survived, but prospered throughout the 1991–93 recession. It was during this time that its managers, supervisors and team leaders learned about and started to implement *Genba Kanri* principles. The company, however, wanted its own phraseology, to reflect its unique identity. It had a high proportion of Punjabi speakers among its personnel and it particularly wanted to avoid confusing Japanese expressions. It was not attracted by the conventional 'workplace' or 'workshop management' which were regarded as rather bland. I was most gratified by their eventual choice which had a bold and sanguine ring to it: 'Khas Parbandah': 'Real Management'.

This is a perfect rendition of the spirit and meaning of *Genba Kanri*. '*Gen*' in Japanese means 'real'. The Japanese teach of the 'three reals' of manufacturing (*san gen shogi*) which are as follows.

The first real is *genba*[4] – 'The real place', the factory, the workplace – not a drawing office, a laboratory or an engineer's or manager's desk. The *genba* is, by its very nature, its very *reality*, an imperfect place. The factory may be old. Plant, tools and equipment are not always 'state-of-the-art'. They may not function as well as we would wish. They may be prone to breakdowns and may not always give a consistent result. The *genba* is populated by real human beings, each with their unique faults and virtues. It is the world of things *as they are*, not as designers and engineers would wish them to be. It is the world that we require our production and First Line Managers to manage.

The second real is *genbutsu* – 'The real product', actual parts, raw materials and partly processed units, production parts and materials – not prototypes, models or drawings. Like the *genba*, the *genbutsu* are less than perfect. Whether they come from internal upstream processes or from commercial vendors, they are merely the product of someone else's *genba*. Like the perfect equilateral triangle, perfect parts and materials only exist as a mathematical abstraction. The very best that we can hope for is that they are subject to minimal variation and conform to specification limits which are sufficiently narrow to enable us to perform the best possible job.

Only from a very detailed and intimate understanding of *genba* and *genbutsu* and of the way in which the one affects the other can the third real, *genjitsu* – 'realistic action' – be taken.

There are two implications of this thinking for the roles and responsibilities of both engineers and first-line production managers.

The first is that real and effective engineering work is performed on the factory floor. Engineers work alongside production teams, *their customers*, helping the latter deal with *their* problems. Of course there is scope for problem-solving work in a laboratory, at a desk or in some quiet contemplative corner, but ultimately solutions must be tried, tested and made to work *in the genba*, and this is where design, process and facility engineers are expected to spend most of their time. Thus we can understand the Japanese image of an engineer in a manufacturing company as being, not someone in a lounge suit who rarely visits the place where the product is made but, as in the Porsche example, of someone 'with oily hands'.

The second implication is particularly important. We employ engineers to benefit from their technical expertise, their specialist knowledge of the base manufacturing technology – knowledge of chemical processes, the stresses of metals, the function of electrical components, the composition and characteristics of plastics, paints and adhesives and so forth. That is what we pay them for and rarely, it seems, can we ever afford to have enough of them. However, recalling that 'realistic action' is a function of a very *detailed* and *intimate* understanding of the relationship between the *genba* (real factory and equipment) and *genbutsu* (real product and materials), it becomes clear that the role of production teams in resolving problems and making improvements is vital. Only they possess that understanding. *Genba Kanri*, therefore, requires that first-line production managers are the key operational decision makers in the factory. It demands that operational decisions be taken 'on the spot', *in the genba*. In 90 per cent of cases such decisions will be reached by First Line Managers *unilaterally*, consulting only with members of their own work team or, if there is shift working, with their peers and colleagues on other production shifts. In contrast to the development of remote control management in the West, the decision-making arena *is* the factory floor. The decision maker *is* the First Line Manager. This particularly applies to process management, as summarised in Table 6.1.

WHY *GENBA KANRI* IS ROBUST

The effectiveness of *Genba Kanri* lies in its inherent *robustness*, which is brought about by five main contributing factors.

First, by abandoning any vain pretensions about manufacturing, accepting it for what it is, with all its imperfections, not only is *Genba Kanri* an essentially

Elements of process management	Conventional approach	Genba Kanri approach
1. Underlying assumptions about manufacturing responsibilities	Should be separated and diffuse	Should be combined and mutually reinforcing
2. Mechanism for process control	Denies production ownership	Emphasises production ownership
3. Scope of responsibilities. Geographical/functional	Extended/specialised	Localised/comprehensive
4. Mode of operational decision making	Remote	Direct: on-the-spot
5. Approach to improvements	Relies on production making suggestions	Requires production teams to take action
6. Expected production first response to a problem	Raise a quality-concern report	Identify and execute appropriate countermeasure
7. Process revision	Reaction to a major problem or externally imposed requirement	Constantly – in pursuit of improved performance
8. Esteem for production function	Low	Aims to build strong production department
9. Source of engineering esteem	Knowledge, qualifications, professional status	Standard of service provided to customers
10. Production teams' view of engineers	Prima donnas in ivory towers to whom we enjoy giving problems	Invaluable partners who help us with *our* problems
11. Process author	Process engineer	Production First Line Manager
12. Process instructor	Works trainer or 'skilled' worker	Production First Line Manager
13. Process auditor	Quality assurance engineer or inspector	Production First Line Manager
14. Improvement introduction	Sparse, infrequent and slow	Numerous, frequent and rapid

Table 6.1 Contrasting approaches to process management

practical and realistic approach, but it emphasises at the outset the importance of continuous improvement. For those of us engaged in production management there can be no final victory. We can never approach a point where we are satisfied with current performance or believe that we have fully optimised conditions in the factory. Rather our task is to engage in a constant and relentless struggle for improvement which does not begin to let up until the product nears obsolescence and our energies are redirected to the fresh demands made by the imminent introduction of its replacement. It is pointless to lament our lack of perfect raw materials, perfect state-of-the-art equipment or infallible technical processes. The challenge, to paraphrase Theodore Roosevelt's maxim, is to 'do what you can, with what you have, where you are' – and then, tomorrow, to do a little more, a little better, with the same.

Second, GK places great emphasis on the place where products are actually made and raises the level of esteem and respect for those managers and workers who inhabit it, those who very often make up the bulk of the organisation's membership. Virtually every piece of doctrinal or training literature that I have ever seen that has been produced by Japanese manufacturers and that either deals specifically with GK or simply with general production management disciplines, constantly reiterates the need to 'create a strong production department' or to 'build a strong shop floor'.

Third, GK is robust in the way that a molecular structure is robust. Its resilience is derived from the way in which it exploits *mutually supporting* principles and techniques (many familiar to the West to a greater or lesser extent but invariably introduced there on a piecemeal basis) and particularly in the way it *combines* rather than separates key management responsibilities. It thus brings about real control of manufacturing processes and of quality, coupled with a capability for a lightning-fast response to process problems or to opportunities for improvements in quality, cost and delivery.

Fourth, the combination of these complementary responsibilities, as borne by First Line Managers, creates a situation where most decisions can be and are taken *on the spot*, as, when and where production difficulties or improvement opportunities occur. This is the very antithesis of the 'remote control' approach to manufacturing management prevalent in most companies. *Genba Kanri* uses *personal leadership* as its central drive motor rather than all-embracing systems, regulations and procedures.

Finally, *Genba Kanri* aims to develop a climate of *action* in the factory: where production First Line Managers and their teams do not need to be bribed, cajoled or exhorted to deal with what they regard as their own problems and opportunities for improvement. The elements of this climate are shown in Figure 6.1. None is dispensable. All are bound cohesively together.

The core principles of *Genba Kanri* which need to be invoked to create the conditions for sustained continuous improvement are as follows:

1. First Line Managers *run the operation*.
2. Each First Line Manager's zone of control is treated *like a business*.
3. The downstream process is *the customer*.
4. There are clear and ever more challenging customer-driven performance targets for each and every First Line Manager's team, whose members are never satisfied with current levels of performance.
5. All teams receive specific, quantitative feedback on *their* performance on quality and delivery for *each and every shift*.
6. All activity must add value to products and services or else be discontinued.
7. All procedural or system delays to the swift resolution of problems or the implementation of improvements are eliminated.
8. Deming's cycle, Plan Do Check Action, is imbued into the thinking of all personnel such that process management is seen as the continual alternating application of standardisation and improvement.
9. The production First Line Manager is responsible for establishing, instructing, monitoring and revising the process: the Standard Operation.

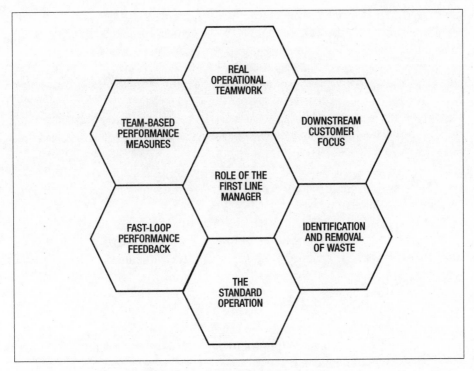

Figure 6.1 The elements of *Genba Kanri*

10. All barriers to the flexibility, commitment and profitable motivation of the workforce must be identified and removed.

The meaning and purpose of all these principles will be further explored in succeeding chapters, dealing particularly with the three cornerstones of *Genba Kanri*: the role of the production First Line Manager, the importance of the Standard Operation and the weaving of the PDCA cycle into the daily operational fabric of the business.

NOTES

1. Imai, *Kaizen* (p. 42); see Select bibliography.
2. 'Eliminate slogans, exhortations and targets for the workforce.' Deming, *Out of the Crisis*; see Select bibliography.
3. *Genba keiei*, translated as 'workplace management'; see Select bibliography.
4. Some writers and consultants refer to *gemba* and *gemba kanri* in their literature. Both spellings are acceptable: they are after all romanised renditions of Sino-Japanese characters. Phonetic accuracy favours the *m* form since the *n* sound changes to *m* when followed by *b*. (Similarly: *kanban* or *kamban*.) Assuming the concept to be of greater interest than the pronunciation I opt for *genba* and *genbutsu* in order to maintain a common prefix for each of the 'three reals'.

7 The First Line Manager

Do you see a man skilled in his work?
He will serve before kings; he will not serve before obscure men.

Proverbs 22:29

Despite all the literature to have been published about the various manufacturing tools and techniques to have come out of Japan – TPM, cellular manufacturing, SMED, visual management and the rest – no writer feels particularly inclined to specify whose is the main responsibility for employing them. But let there be no ambiguity in the matter: it is the Japanese 'foreman' who drives the wheels of the world's great manufacturing juggernaut.

Therefore, of the seven essential elements of *Genba Kanri* introduced at the end of the previous chapter, the nucleus, around which the others are clustered, is the first level of production management.

OF MANAGERS AND LEADERS

The term 'First Line Manager' is used here, and throughout this volume, only after much deliberation and an exhaustive search for a better alternative. The word 'supervisor' was a candidate but it has too many negative associations. This is especially true in the United States. Although, in Europe, the word 'supervision' is often used simply as a collective noun for the first layer of management, in the United States it almost invariably makes a statement about the *style* of management, equating it to the base, primitive and seldom justifiable practice of *overseeing*. This style has no place in GK companies even though the job title is still commonly found in them.[1] The term 'team leader' would be especially confusing since most GK companies have Team Leaders *as well as* First Line Managers (the upper case is used deliberately to apply specifically to GK organisations and within the context of the GK FLM role).

Of course, semantics are of no great significance to companies seeking to adopt GK principles. Supervisor, cell manager, foreman, *Meister*, product manager, superintendent: we can call these people whatever we like. It is the *role* and *remit* to which the titles are attached that is important.

I therefore adopt the simple expedient of First Line Manager, dry, sterile and unwieldy as it is, without, at this stage, wishing to imply any view as to the relative merits of management or leadership. For convenience and brevity this becomes FLM in the remaining pages. 'GK FLM' is specifically applied to those who possess the roles and responsibilities that apply in a GK company.[2]

It has already been asserted that the underlying reason for the failure of Western industry to compete with Japan and the other emerging 'dragon economies' of Asia is the development of 'remote control management', and the emasculation of the FLM role. This legacy has proven to be a seriously diminished capacity for deploying effective manufacturing disciplines, for managing the detail of productive work, for eliminating waste and variability from processes and for implementing a high volume of incremental process improvements quickly and easily.

We know well enough how this came to pass. Scientific management made the first incursions by insisting on the separation of the planning and execution of the task and introduction of piecework. This not only ostensibly eliminated the need for the foreman or supervisor to provide motivation and encouragement, but also put far greater onus on the newly emerging profession of industrial engineering ('time and motion study', as it was called then) for the detailed analysis of work and for specifying how it should be carried out. The industrial strife which characterised the middle part of the century accompanied the growth of the industrial relations or personnel function, which gradually eroded the FLM's traditional responsibilities for the management of people. Finally, the postwar boom and the desire to respond to what appeared to be almost unlimited demand for consumer products led to further specialisation, not only of labour but of management too. Every self-respecting factory now had to have a separate quality department, a process engineering department, growing numbers of schedulers, planners, expediters and progress chasers. Management structures became increasingly multi-layered and complex.

As a result, the FLM's role became a mere shadow of what it had been in former generations. All that remained was the perceived need for supervision in the basest sense of the word: for people who would oversee and keep a vigil in the workplace; who would ensure that everybody was kept busy and nobody shirked or strayed from their place of work. The impoverishment of the FLM's role reached its climax in the mid-1970s when the oil crisis and worldwide recession were making the lack of Western competitiveness all too apparent. In the 1970s and early 1980s, therefore, reduction of the numbers of supervisors, foremen and chargehands was firmly on the agenda of virtually every manufacturing firm, in the name of reduced overhead costs and lower 'indirect headcount'. Of course this was perfectly rational. The fault lay not in thinning the ranks of supervisors. This was simply the logical consequence of an unsound premise that operational effectiveness could be achieved and sustained by remote control at middle-management level.

A few years ago I was preparing a seminar room at a venue used by a number of manufacturing companies in the North of England. I came across a supervisory training handout issued by the previous occupant, a well-known 'blue-chip' manufacturer of electrical goods. (It had clearly been abandoned by some discerning trainee.) The subject matter made it impossible for me to resist the temptation to skim through its content. This bellhop's charter reflected the three broad sections into which it was divided. The first was entitled 'Managing Downwards'. This stressed the importance of FLMs in communicating the decisions of higher management to their charges and ensuring that these decisions were effectively carried out. Second, 'Managing Upwards' emphasised the need for supervisors to ensure that management were constantly and promptly informed of events and occurrences on the shop floor to enable them to take swift and effective action. Finally, 'Managing Sideways' stressed the importance for FLMs of building a good relationship with the union shop steward and ensuring that they were always kept 'informed of all events and matters relating to the management of the section'.

The symptoms of this climate of inertia and powerlessness were most aptly and concisely described to me by Peter Dobbs, the manufacturing director of Parsons Turbine Generators Limited. He has done much to introduce the principles of simultaneous engineering and cellular manufacturing within the group, and was quick to realise that these new approaches would require a radically different style of first line management from that which he had previously experienced. He described a phenomenon which cannot fail to strike a familiar chord with many industrial managers. On visiting the shop floor, discovering the instance of a stoppage, breakdown or quality problem and enquiring of an operator as to the cause, he noticed that the response was almost invariably prefixed with the same four words: 'I am waiting for ...'. Thus: 'I am waiting for a fitter ... parts ... tools ... a crane ... an engineering drawing ... an inspector ... the next job.'

When asked the same question, FLMs would prefix their responses with three words: 'I have told ...'. Thus: 'I have told the fitter ... purchasing ... Fred Smith ... engineering ... the QA manager ...' and so on. It is as if, after identifying and notifying the appropriate problem holder, the obligations of the supervisor have been fulfilled.

Some progress has clearly been made by *some* companies, but not nearly enough and, though the decline in the FLM remit and authority seems to have been halted, there has been no great Western enthusiasm for making a full restitution. Why is this?

The reason probably stems from the fact that, whereas we tend to look to Japan, to GK organisations for tools and techniques, we understandably turn to Western literature for guidance on management and organisational issues. As ever, discourse on these issues tends to be dominated by fashion; during the

1980s and 1990s, the subject of supervisory management has been especially unfashionable. Few commentators felt inclined to deal with the subject at all and most who did were disparaging. In the early to mid-1980s, Japanese transplants into Britain and into the US provided incontrovertible local evidence that these factories relied heavily on a very imperial remit of responsibility for their FLMs and on investing in low FLM–worker ratios. But the climate of fashionable convention conspired to ignore this.

'Remove supervision!' was the battle-cry of the 1980s. 'Substitute real leadership in the workplace.' Noble sentiments, but how? Leadership by whom? The only commodity on offer was something called MBWA, variously rendered as 'Managing By Walking About' or 'Managing By Wandering Around'. Despite the undoubted merits of having top managers re-acquaint themselves with the workplace and with the people who spend so much of their time there, it can scarcely be expected to fill the vacuum. Coupled with another of the maxims of popular passion of the 1980s, that of reducing layers of management, many senior executives were given what seemed to be legitimate cause for turning a blind eye to the lessons of the transplants and for resuming their onslaught on the ranks of FLMs with renewed vigour in order to secure the short-term *prima facie* benefits of lower 'indirect labour costs'. Small wonder that, in their well-intentioned efforts to flatten organisation structures, so many firms pruned the wrong parts. Thus, burgeoned ranks of middle managers and specialists, spawned by remote control management, remained largely untouched while the capacity for *real management* in the workplace was weakened still further.

The 1980s and 1990s witnessed much academic discourse about 'leadership' and 'management', generally extolling the virtues and value of the former over the latter.[3] Much of what has been written has been chiefly concerned with studies of powerful corporate figures. We in the West seem to have an insatiable interest in the great and the infamous; we never tire of trying to extrapolate universal truths from the actions and behaviours of Harold Geneen, Lee Iacocca, Sir Michael Edwardes or Giovanni Agnelli, not to mention innumerable statesmen and generals since the dawn of history. An interesting observation made as early as 1911 by Harrington Emerson, one of the leading apostles of scientific management, follows:

> It is not the flesh and blood and brains of the Japanese that make them industrially dangerous; it is not their money, for they are poor, not their equipment, for they have but little, not their material resources, because they are meagre. They are dangerous as industrial competitors ... because we have not even awakened – and they have – to the fact that principles applied by mediocre men are more powerful for good than the spasmodic floundering of unusually great men.[4]

GK is concerned with the practical disciplines of the everyday struggle for supremacy which takes place where the product is made. For our purposes the leadership versus management debate is as sterile as it is abstract. Out in our factories we require both leadership *and* management. Competence in each greatly enhances capacity for the other. We have teams to lead; processes and resources to manage.[5] We need both maintenance and improvement. We need both effective control and true empowerment. True empowerment cannot be simply trained or exhorted; only a challenge will do it. The kind of leadership we need in our factories involves pointing to a clear horizon and making people want to go there, but it also requires that we advance from the secure position of stable processes, a robust standard of job skills and knowledge and a full and detailed comprehension of the current situation in the *genba*.

THE ILLUSION OF THE 'SELF-DIRECTED WORK TEAM'

The fad of the hour is something called 'self-directed' or 'self-managed team working': the latest development of the theme 'manage equals bad; team equals good'. I have no problem with the concept; I can well imagine such a thing. After all, my little girl, familiar with Irving's 'Legend of Sleepy Hollow', imagines the Headless Horseman and I have sometimes had to dissolve that image before she goes to sleep. But she has never seen the Headless Horseman and I have never come across a leaderless team. The fact is that, in sport, in combat, in competitive business of any kind, teamwork and leadership are inseparable.

Even the proponents of this approach have been forced to make concessions in this direction. 'Team leaders' emerge as a common feature, though the role ascribed to them is rather limited and nebulous, to say the least. And, of course, it wouldn't do to appoint the best person for the job or to put somebody 'in charge'. Somebody might feel slighted. One option is for the team to elect the leader.[6] Another is to rotate the leadership so that everyone gets their turn. Some day, we might finally stop treating production workers like children.

Where does this approach come from? What is its appeal? What can be said for it? How does it measure up against GK?

Suppose we were to send a group of business psychologists and organisational development specialists – astute and perceptive within their specialities but lacking practical experience of manufacturing – on a study of GK companies. Something not unlike the packages currently labelled SDWT or SMWT would probably be the outcome, and I suspect that this has already happened.

That SDWTs and the like appear to be claiming a degree of success in some manufacturing organisations should not be surprising, since the approach relies heavily on some key GK elements, especially those discussed in the next two chapters. They also necessitate the removal of methods of payment, measures of performance and working practices which are inconsistent with any practical kind of teamworking. (See Chapters 12 and 13.)

The missing items, however, are *fundamental*, and this is where SDWTs and SMWTs are at 180 degrees variance with GK principles. Companies who adopt this 'technique' are in fact making progress along the course of a boxed canyon.

The problem remains that conventional Western production functions are *too weak*. GK is about creating a *strong shop floor*, a strong production department to complement existing strengths in engineering and commercial disciplines. This cannot be achieved by denying it strong leadership and management, especially at the front line. We would not seek to eliminate strong leadership from the senior management level or in other departments. This is *more* important, not less, on the shop floor, in the *genba*, where the *real work* is done. Given the lack of emphasis on shop floor leadership it is inevitable that the methodology of SDWT introduction involves the fully panoply of steering committees, facilitators, moderators, coaches and mentors described in Chapter 4 as having characterised previous initiatives.[7]

The approach cannot resolve our central problem. It does not address the issue of process ownership. It does not confront the apparent conflict between process control and rapid and frequent improvement. It ignores and widens rather than fills the gap which has evolved between management and the actual work. Those who argue the case for SDWTs cannot be altogether blamed for the oversight. They are not manufacturing people. I doubt if they are even aware of the problem.

The best way of fully empowering a work team is to give them a leader: a man or a woman of real stature and authority and a full portfolio of complementary leadership and management responsibilities which enables them to deliver the goods for the team, for *their* team, and who can put a permanent end to 'I have told ... ' and 'I am waiting for ... '.

THE ROLE OF THE GK FIRST LINE MANAGER

Figure 7.1 shows a model of the main components of the FLM role in GK companies. Allowing for only slight variations in format, it would be instantly recognisable to them all, including the major manufacturing corporations of Japan.

There are two overriding requirements, of which everything else is part. These are to achieve production goals and to educate and develop team members. GK principles admit no separation or contention between these demands. Only in

ACHIEVING PRODUCTION TARGETS				
1	2	3	4	5
ESTABLISHING STANDARD OPERATIONS	ENSURING STANDARD OPERATIONS ARE CARRIED OUT	IMPROVING STANDARD OPERATIONS	IDENTIFYING AND ELIMINATING PROBLEMS	CULTIVATING A GOOD PRODUCTION ENVIRONMENT
EDUCATING AND DEVELOPING STAFF				

Figure 7.1   The role of the GK First Line Manager

underperforming and ineffective organisations is the latter activity treated as some holy icon to be worshipped periodically, when operational conditions permit a breathing space, and the former regarded as the normal eight-'til-five activity. Each and every one of the five divisions of the FLM role are concerned with fulfilling *both* requirements.

Three of the FLM role divisions are concerned with process management: defining, teaching, observing and improving the best current methods for carrying out the work. The importance of the FLM ownership of the manufacturing process, the Standard Operation, the chief distinguishing characteristic of GK, was described in the previous chapter; its practicalities and benefits are described in Chapters 14 and 15. For now, it is perhaps enough to note that this aspect of the role accounts not only for 60 per cent of the whole, but should also consume 60 per cent of the GK FLM's time and efforts: such is the importance placed on the maintenance and improvement of production methods by such companies.

The fourth division is mainly concerned with maintenance. It requires the FLM to establish, monitor and uphold a range of standards pertaining to the effective running and order of the workplace and its resources. Such standards are highly visual and easy to use, giving a clear and prompt signal of all inconsistencies and irregularities which need to be addressed before they result in operating problems. The final division comprises all the leadership aspects of the role.

The precise nature of this activity of course varies among companies and among the various functions of those companies according to processes and the manufacturing technology. But what is common to all of them is a fully comprehensive and complementary set of responsibilities for *all four* phases of the Deming/Shewhart cycle – Plan, Do, Check and Action – and for *all seven* of the components of our model of manufacturing capability (Figure 1.1) – man, machine, materials, quality, cost, delivery and the process by which they are joined.

In this way GK FLMs become the CEOs of small businesses. In a high-volume, shallow process this will probably mean that they and their teams are responsible (for a given range of products or for supplying one or more stipulated customers) for *all* operations, from receipt of raw materials and bought-in parts through to final dispatch. Team size permitting (see next chapter), this is the ideal configuration, since it completely eliminates in-process 'hand-offs'. In longer, more complex processes (such as an assembly line or where there are very large fixed facilities) it will usually be necessary to segment the process to create these small businesses. All that is required is that there is a clearly defined *end point* by which the product can be regarded as, in a sense, completed and shipped, to the satisfaction of the next zone – the downstream process or *downstream customer*. The prerequisites of this approach are clear and unambiguous standards for quality and delivery at the end of each segment. Once these are in place we have an interlocking chain of customers and suppliers where each link can apply itself to the daily task of improving its performance in terms of quality and delivery and

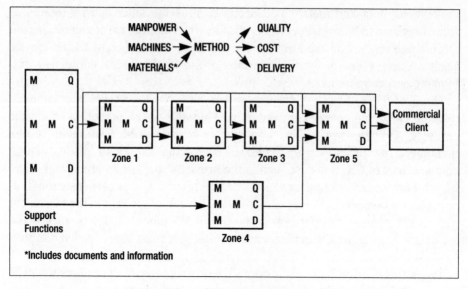

Figure 7.2 Creating small businesses for FLMs

reducing the consumption and costs of its own resources: man, machine, materials. This approach (illustrated in Figure 7.2) applies not only to direct production FLMs, but to those in charge of maintenance, quality assurance and material handling teams and also to the departmental and sectional heads of all engineering and commercial support functions.

The downstream-customer discipline, having clearly established the performance requirement of the small business, has also effectively defined the scope of the FLM's role, since, on a daily basis, what happens *within* the business, and how they manage their resources to achieve what is required, is primarily their own concern. Yes, there are specialists from outside who can be called on to give valuable support, just as in any other business. But it is the FLM who remains in the driving seat, who assumes ownership of problems, and who is accountable for the performance and wellbeing of the business.

The following may give some idea of the extent of this remit as it applies to our three factors of production.

MANPOWER

GK FLMs are responsible for their own manpower budgeting and forecasting. They hire their own staff, determine the start date and personally give the offer of employment. They are responsible for the training and development of all their team members. They are responsible for all disciplinary matters relating to their team; GK companies ensure that their policies and procedures recognise and support this responsibility.[8] They, and not industrial engineers, design and constantly revise and improve the distribution and content of work assignments. Where there is provisional overtime they hold the budget for it and determine whether, when, and for what purpose it shall be used. As will be made clear in subsequent chapters, they communicate daily with their team members, giving feedback on team performance, explaining and listening to problems and informing of improvements and corrective actions to be undertaken. Above all, they are responsible for the safety and wellbeing of their team members. This does not just mean ensuring that people adhere to company regulations or state legislation. (That requirement is fairly standard for the supervisors of all self-respecting companies.) It means paying particular attention to the design of working methods, making sure that Standard Operations are inherently safe and do not involve awkward movements which lead to stresses and strains on joints and muscles, causing fatigue and injury (as well as being wasteful and inefficient). It means carrying out regular audits of the workplace, not just to ensure conformity to the rules, but to make sure that it is clean, uncluttered and in good order.

MACHINES

GK FLMs are involved and consulted at the earliest opportunity before the selection, purchase and installation of new equipment. They have an important role in deciding where it will be situated. They will often accompany plant engineers to contractors' factories to assess progress and demand modifications. They work with their fellow FLMs in maintenance to identify and establish procedures (Standard Operations) for planned preventive maintenance (PPM) and devise and monitor visual formats for ensuring that it is effectively carried out. (In GK companies, most basic, cyclic maintenance activity is undertaken by production team members.) They establish their requirements for machine spares and replacement parts and produce and maintain a budget for this as well as for their own supply of hand tools.

MATERIALS

GK FLMs determine the delivery point and layout of all direct materials, whether bought-in parts or part-processed materials from upstream production teams. Where there is a separate team for material supply or linefeed, they will, with the FLM of that team, establish appropriate linefeed quantities and frequencies. They determine the method of presentation of parts to the line in a way which optimises working conditions and eliminates waste. They have a major say in determining the design and application of commercially produced stillages. They frequently devise racking, workbenches and gravity-feed systems and involve the team in making them. They establish their own budget for indirect (consumable) materials such as protective clothing, paints, adhesives, lubricants, detergents and cleaning materials.

For each of the '3 Ms' they agree appropriate (challenging but achievable) targets for cost reduction with the second line production manager. They also agree targets for the same (marginally more challenging) with members of their team. They measure, display and monitor progress towards these targets.

This degree of authority and broad scope of operational remit and accountability is a double-edged sword for GK FLMs. There is no hiding-place from the failure to perform, no easy refuge in the real or alleged failings of others. They cannot blame the capabilities or attitudes of their people; they themselves selected and trained them. They cannot blame the tools and equipment; they themselves were fully involved in determining what was required and where it should be placed. They cannot blame the work assignments, for it is they – not industrial engineering – who determine these. They cannot blame the manufacturing process, for it was written by themselves and not by a process engineer. They can no more attribute their failings to their suppliers than can the company blame its own failings on the performance of its commercial vendors. In this way GK FLMs and their teams take fierce pride in the ownership of their problems and in their ability to take swift unilateral action in 90 per cent of cases. Where specialist support *is* called for, FLMs still regard themselves as the owners of the problem and vigorously pursue the required standard of service from their suppliers. There can be no 'I am waiting for ... ', 'I have told ... '. Combined, complementary and mutually reinforcing responsibilities for all aspects of production bring about true empowerment and total operational accountability.

NOTES

1. A requirement to *oversee* would in any case be impractical since, to fulfil the requirements of the role, they must frequently be absent from their section, visiting downstream customers and upstream suppliers. On specific occasions they may even need to be absent for a whole shift or a number of shifts. The production team is expected to perform and achieve its daily tasks as usual, without anyone looking over their shoulder.
2. However, it is not my intention to start a fashion, and I would certainly urge companies to abandon this dull acronym and find something both more applicable and uplifting for their own use. It is, in any case, no bad thing for companies undertaking a thorough-going enhancement of the role to find a new job title. This helps to underline the fact that the role has changed.
3. Prominent among the writers who have done much to popularise *leadership* at the expense of *management* have been Warren Bennis and Burt Nanus. Bennis's ideas, in particular, were a significant influence on Tom Peters. Bennis: 'I tend to think of the differences between leaders and managers as the differences between those who master the context and those who surrender to it.' See W.G. Bennis (1989), *On Becoming a Leader*, New York: Addison Wesley.
4. H. Emerson (1911), *Twelve Principles of Efficiency*, New York: The Engineering Magazine Co.
5. Two prominent writers on leadership also question the alleged contrast and contradiction between leadership and management. First, John Adair: 'Leadership is about a sense of direction. The word "lead" comes from an Anglo Saxon word ... which means a road, a way, the path of a ship at sea. It's knowing what the next step is ... managing is ... from the Latin "manus", a hand. It's handling a sword, a ship, a horse. It tends to be closely linked with the idea of machines.' See J. Adair (1988), article in *The Director*, November. Second, John P. Kotter: 'Nor is leadership

necessarily better than management or a replacement for it. Rather, leadership and management are two distinctive and complementary systems of action. Each has its own function and characteristic activities. Both are necessary for success in an increasingly complex and volatile business environment.' See J.P. Kotter (1990), 'What Leaders Really Do', *Harvard Business Review*, May/June.

6. One international company which opted to allow its production 'teams' to appoint their own leaders found that there was some considerable variation in the capabilities of those chosen. It emerged that the common denominator was that the person was usually the oldest in the team. Team members later confided that, though they had an imprecise understanding of the duties and responsibilities required of this person, they knew that the position attracted an incremental pay award and they saw an opportunity to increase the pensionable salary of the team member closest to retirement. A company which takes its responsibilities for people development seriously would be unlikely to countenance such an approach. It certainly does not characterise an organisation which seeks to identify, recognise and promote talent and ability from the shop floor. (See Chapter 16.)

7. The establishment of these structures and the training of those people who will participate in them is itself a considerable undertaking. As a five- to six-phase exercise, taking between three and five years to implement, SDWTs must be a goldmine for those consultancies who market the approach.

8. It is invariably the unempowered supervisor who is forced to display the most negative and unpleasant of management styles. These are the ones who engage in sarcasm, intimidation or ridicule, for they are the only sanctions at their disposal. Though GK FLMs usually have the authority to fire as well as hire, dismissals and, indeed, resort to formal reprimands of any kind are extremely rare in GK companies. GK FLMs have a vested interest in making their people winners – not just to weld together an effective team which regularly achieves and surpasses production goals. How does it look if FLMs have to go to their boss or to personnel to start dismissal or formal disciplinary procedures? Who has failed to hire the right person? Who has failed to bring out the best in him or her by training, coaching, encouraging? Staff turnover and absence are also exceptionally low relative to conventional organisations.

8 The Requirements of Leadership

Pity, oh pity the poor baritone ...
'Cause he can't quite sing high and he can't quite sing low.

Mike Elliot, *The Poor Baritone*

For many managers in conventional companies, the broad remit of responsibility expected of the GK FLM is extremely daunting. They presuppose that few among either their existing supervisors or their existing middle managers could match this requirement.[1] Usually they are mistaken. Partly, this can be attributed to the extent to which Western organisations tend to undervalue their own people and to the lack of appreciation of what can be achieved by a modest amount of training. *Mostly*, it is a lack of understanding of the synergistic benefits of combining responsibilities: real authority gained in one aspect of the role increases the capacity to fulfil the demands of the others.

Sometimes people ask me how I believe that 'the average Ford or GM foreman' would cope with a supervisor's job at Nissan or Toyota. Having met and spoken at length with a fair number of them, invariably my response is that, far from buckling under the weight of their responsibilities, most would feel both that a considerable burden had been lifted from them and that, all of a sudden, they would find that they could *make things happen*.

Four factors allow GK FLMs to fulfil the demands of their role and to take full responsibility for their teams and their businesses. They can be represented by the word TAKE and are: Time, Authority, Knowledge and Encouragement.[2]

TIME

The GK FLM's role is principally *proactive*. It is at least as concerned with improvement as with maintenance. GK FLMs need to be spending time with their customers, to ensure that the outputs of their business are meeting requirements; with suppliers, to ensure that their business is getting the standard of product, service and support it needs to do this. There must be time for data collection and analysis, for training and coaching, for *real* communication with team members and, especially, for observing and improving working methods.

Two contributory features go a long way to providing this time. The first is team size. Given the demands of the role, there must be a strict limit on this. Production teams of 40, 50, 70 people are simply not compatible with GK practices. Precise maximum numbers will vary in accordance with the base manufacturing process and the level of technology but, as a general rule, no FLM team should have more than 25 people. Capital-intensive businesses or those requiring a particularly high level of technical skill and knowledge might require team sizes which are even smaller.

Isn't this a considerable investment? Yes: but it pays back a hundredfold in terms of the *manufacturing capability* that it brings. Companies who spurn this investment, who have FLM team sizes of 30 or more, pay the price not only in poorer standards of production discipline and lost opportunities for improvement, but in *more* production planners, *more* HRD staff, *more* IEs, *more* quality assurance people, *more* middle managers and a poorly utilised engineering resource. More FLMs of the right calibre and with appropriate responsibilities actually *reduce* the overall indirect headcount and lead to *lower* overhead costs.

Doesn't this detract from our aim to have a flatter organisation structure? No: GK companies *invented* the flat organisation structure. It means, rather, putting the management emphasis where it *should* be, where it is of most use, at the front line, in the *genba*. The key to creating an effective, responsive and truly flat organisation is to do it from the bottom up. We begin by establishing our operational teams and the roles and responsibilities we wish to give them. We make these as broad and flexible as we can. We then determine those of our first layer of management, making the remit as comprehensive as possible. The rest of the structure must fit around these basic building blocks. If a production worker at Nissan's British plant is promoted just six times, then he or she is running the whole show: but it will take half of those promotions to reach 'senior supervisor' rank.

But hasn't it now been established that 'span of subordinate control' is unimportant? Must we kowtow to the hierarchies invented by the medieval Chinese? Are we, though? What about the Judges of Israel and their 'captains of tens' and 'captains of hundreds'? What about the military organisation of the Greeks, the Romans, the Zulus and every modern army since Gustavus Adolphus? *But these are not administrative structures; they are killing machines.* Indeed they are. But then, what is production in the modern competitive world? The Japanese know the answer only too well: it is *war*.

There does seem to be a strangely ironic paradox at work in that those writers who have done most to debunk the notion of 'span of control' tend also to be those who have most consistently called for the removal of supervision. Yet, if we mean supervision in the crude and primitive sense of the word that such commentators rightly criticise, we can indeed supervise as many people as we like. A tennis umpire's chair, a pair of binoculars and a loudhailer are the only devices we need. Leadership and management make different demands. But 'subordinate span of control' is not really the issue. In a modern competitive factory it is not subordinates, not people, but *processes* which need to be controlled. *Process responsibility*, requiring detailed job knowledge, is the real constraint on team size.

The second key contribution is made by the FLM's deputy, most commonly called the Team Leader. Some explanation is called for concerning team leaders. For example, where did they come from? Before the mid-1980s the job title hardly existed. Now it is everywhere, not only in manufacturing but in the commercial and retail sectors and in government service. This is no bad thing, perhaps, but, certainly as far as manufacturing is concerned, we should be aware of the history; the term itself has been very misleading and has sent a number of organisations down completely the wrong track.

The job title has proven to be the most popular and infectious label of GK companies. Not even JIT and *kaizen* are serious rivals. It spread in the wake of the Japanese transplants in the US and the UK. Of course the reason that visitors and observers latched onto 'team leaders' and not the roles and responsibilities of GK FLMs is perfectly clear. In the mid-1980s, when the transplants appeared, 'teams' and 'leaders' were *in*, 'managers' were *passé*, 'supervisors' and 'foremen' were definitely *out*. But what many people failed to realise was that the GK term 'Team Leader', though composed of English words, was a Japanese expression based on a mistranscription. It actually meant 'leading hand' or 'lead operator in the team'. Though the role of the Team Leader was and is a vital component of GK, in these companies the team is *the FLM's team; the leader of the team is the FLM.* So what? I am prepared to concede that 'team leader' is a much better-sounding job title than foreman, or cell manager or supervisor. But it is not just a question of semantics. By focusing on the Team Leader many Western organisations missed the point. Realising that in most GK companies they were part of the direct headcount, working members of the team, they hoped to compete with GK companies on the cheap – without reversing their previously declared strategies of reducing the number of supervisors and without increasing 'indirect headcount'. They opted for Robin without Batman and wondered why the result was so disappointing.

You cannot take the role and remit outlined in the previous chapter – a challenging and demanding role, a *manager's* role – and give it to workers paid a few pennies per hour more than the others, who do not feel themselves to be managers, who are not respected as such by other managers and who probably have to spend at least half of their time carrying out production work. You either believe in the benefits of investing in real management and leadership for fairly small teams or you do not. You cannot compensate just by giving an extra stripe to a greater number of direct production workers. Table 8.1 tells its own story.

GK Team Leaders deputise for the FLM, deal with the majority of reactive tasks

Plant	FLM job title	Typical size of FLM's team	FLM deputy's job title	Typical no. of deputies per FLM
Nissan	Supervisor	20	Team Leader	2
Toyota	Group Leader	25	Team Leader	5
Ford	Foreman	60	Group Leader	5

Table 8.1   Assembly teams at UK car plants

(providing a first response to breakdowns, material shortages and other running problems) and handle much of the on-the-job training within the team. They also carry out many of the maintenance aspects of GK (ensuring that basic production quality procedures are faithfully carried out, and collecting, recording and displaying production and performance data). This frees the FLM to concentrate on improvement and on the leadership aspects of the role, and to pursue vigorously the resources the team needs continuously to enhance its performance.

The position also provides a stepping stone, a development link between production team member and FLM. This is essential, given the demands of the latter role. The competence gap would otherwise be impossible to bridge. All Team Leaders are in effect FLMs in training, since this is the level from which most FLMs are appointed. Not all will make the transition. One thing on which most authorities *do* agree is that job knowledge and skill are not, of themselves, sufficient evidence of an ability to lead or to manage. Nevertheless, it is incumbent on FLMs to develop their Team Leaders as much as possible. In addition to receiving formal off-the-job training, they are progressively exposed to aspects of the FLM's role. Development activities may include sitting in on selection interviews, delivering the pre-shift briefing (see Chapter 10) or drafting Standard Operations (see Chapter 14).

AUTHORITY

No academic study of leadership would be complete without substantial discourse on the nature and derivation of authority. Fortunately, this is an empirical exploration and not an academic study. Brevity must be our aim. There is a grand old Anglo-Scottish word which furthers our practical ends. The word is 'clout' and it sums up in one syllable what FLMs need in order to fulfil the duties and responsibilities required of them by GK principles. Clout is what summarises the capacity to get things done, to be able to make things happen without calling on the support of your boss, to afford the luxury of being genial, polite and saying 'please', comfortable in the knowledge that the request may as well be treated as a command. Whereas leadership is the most important quality for dealing with the team, clout is frequently the most fecund commodity for dealing with others, particularly with peers in vital support groups. First among the ingredients of clout, whether we like the word or not is 'status'.

Of course, many companies make and have always made great claims for the importance and authority of their supervisors. They are often referred to as 'the key people in the organisation', 'the chief executive of their section' and so on. The truth of the matter, however, is frequently very different. The following checklist may serve as a guide to studying the real situation in a given company.

- In any formal description or informal understanding of the FLM's role, how much emphasis is placed on action and decision making and how much on 'keeping the management informed' and 'communicating policy and decisions to the workforce'?
- Is senior management truly free to concentrate on strategic improvements and future goals, or is it frequently engaged in managing or controlling the operational detail of daily activity?
- What are FLMs' chances of further promotion? Are they at the threshold of a long and promising career with the company, or can they only look forward to retirement? What was their boss's previous job? Was he or she an FLM? ... a production manager at another company? ... still at college?
- Would most of the workforce sell their very souls for an FLM's job or would they rather not touch it with a ten-foot pole?
- How does the salary and status of an FLM compare with that of an engineer? ... a personnel officer? ... a buyer? ... an accountant? ... a graduate trainee? ... or with that of their own team members?
- What would be the reaction of a holder of any of the above positions if it were suggested that they take an FLM vacancy? Would they get excited? Would they feel flattered? Would they ask what they had done wrong? Would they hand in their notice?
- What levels of support can FLMs command from other departments without the support of their own boss (particularly from vital semidirect areas such as maintenance, quality assurance, material control)? When FLMs call for help, who comes running?
- Are they told when visitors are coming through their section? Are they introduced?
- Do engineers and other support staff seek them out when they have business on the section? Or do they simply clamber over equipment and rummage through materials without paying them any regard?

Though 'status' is a Latin word, the ancient Roman republic had another, which conveys the second ingredient of clout. That word was *imperium* and it had less to do with mere prestige than with real discretionary power. *Imperium* was granted by the senate to specific magistrates, generals or officials. Those who possessed it could not and *would* not be overruled, provided they operated within the limits and regulations pertaining to it. Something akin to *imperium* must apply to FLMs if they are to be empowered to take effective action, to take full responsibility for their production zone and for the work team and if their authority is to be upheld. This means that Second Line Managers must do everything they can to avoid undermining their authority. Rather their goal must be to support their FLMs (*their* team members) whenever possible.

FLMs, of course, are not infallible. There must be standards for *their* behaviour as for everyone else's. They also need guidance, coaching, counsel. And the extent to which they are given free rein is largely conditional on results, on the outputs of their zone. At the most basic level, however, it is worth noting that, though GK Second Line Managers may occasionally give their FLMs a hard time, they *never* become involved in instructing or reprimanding production team members. They also make a point of defending the actions of their FLMs when communicating with other departments. The same principle is followed by FLMs themselves. They are fiercely loyal to their team members. They are big enough to take all the flak, all the responsibility for any real or perceived failing of their business. That is what they are paid for.

KNOWLEDGE

Job and process knowledge is a prerequisite for both leadership and management. Some people still run away from the proposition that FLMs must know and be able to perform the operations of their team members. They take refuge in the fallacious assertion that 'man management' or 'interpersonal skill', charisma, persuasion, charm or some other virtue will compensate. But every other profession demands both job knowledge *and* leadership skill. Imagine a finance manager who cannot read a balance sheet, or a technical director completely ignorant of engineering principles. Soldiers will not follow officers who do not know how to fire a rifle or who cannot climb a six-foot wall carrying 40 pounds of kit. They need not be the very fittest in their units nor the very best shot. But they need sufficient knowhow and ability to instruct others and give guidance. They need to be able to demonstrate performance of the task *personally* if required to do so.

Discipline in the *genba* has little to do with admonishments, still less with written warnings and suspensions; it is about *teaching*. Teaching requires knowledge. Of course job knowledge is not itself enough. Many are fond of citing the problems which arise from the promotion of someone with excellent job skills but limited management or leadership ability. But the reverse of this is just as bad. An example from Deming:

> *Production worker* (recorded): They give you no instruction. What they do is set you down at a machine and tell you to go to work.
> There is nobody to teach you?
> My colleagues help me, but they have their own work to do.

Don't you have a foreman?
He knows nothing.
Isn't it his job to help you learn yours?
If you need help, you don't go to somebody that looks dumber than you are do you?
He wears a neck tie, but he doesn't know anything.
But the neck tie helps doesn't it?
No.[3]

I often wonder how much of the failure, over time, of a highly skilled and knowledgeable worker satisfactorily to perform an FLM role can be attributed to a perceived lack of management or leadership skill, and how much to the lack of opportunity to exploit those very qualities which brought him or her to prominence in the first place – qualities which themselves are a vital ingredient of management and leadership ability. It should not be forgotten that, especially in the period from the 1960s until the early 1980s, such FLMs were neither required nor expected (and in many companies not even *permitted*) to be practically familiar with production operations. From the moment we conferred on them the legitimate authority to instruct others, we at once separated them from the activity which yielded knowledge of what should be done.

ENCOURAGEMENT

This final factor can take many different forms in any organisation. Naturally it should be expected that much of the encouragement given to FLMs comes from their boss. What then is the role of the Second Line Manager in a GK manufacturing organisation?

In some respects there are similarities with the role of FLMs, although the role relates to responsibilities for the larger business – the manufacturing operation as a whole or a major production unit in a bigger company. Second Line Managers also have systems and processes to manage and a team to lead; they are, too, concerned with both maintenance and improvement.

To begin with they have responsibility for strategy, budgets and costs for the plant or unit, and it is their task to convert key business goals into specific objectives and actions, including the identification of appropriate performance measures and targets for FLM teams.

Second, it is their task to manage the disciplines of *Genba Kanri*: to maintain and improve the practice of those disciplines; to audit and benchmark against best GK practice; to set the attitude and attune the focus of the plant or production unit; to establish the character and calibre of the *genba*; to build a strong shop floor, a strong production department.

Third, the FLMs are not only the leaders of teams but are themselves members of a team of production managers. The Second Line Manager is the leader of that team who must ensure that its members are mutually supportive in the collective endeavour to fulfil the daily and longer-term objectives of the unit. Just as FLMs must be responsible for their part of the chain of internal customers and suppliers, the Second Line Manager must preserve the links of that chain, and must ensure that the transactions and operating practices which enable it to function are properly maintained. The Second Line Manager must give coaching, guidance, training and development to FLMs and ensure that they receive the support they need from suppliers in other departments or functions.

In a GK company there are also inherent mechanisms which encourage action related to the resolution of problems and the prompt identification and seizure of improvement opportunities. These are the subject of the next three chapters.

NOTES

1. Some companies conclude that graduates are called for to meet this need. I share some of the sentiment, for I can conceive of few more propitious signals for the future wellbeing and prosperity of my own country than that graduates should be eager to enter the production function and that they be encouraged to do so. However, there are practical problems. First, I am convinced that very few of the newly graduated have sufficient maturity and credibility with the workforce to make a success of it – in *any*, much less a GK company. It is far better that they gain their experience in another function, such as engineering, and then move laterally into an FLM position. Second, we must remember that being academically or even technically qualified and being able to do the job are *not the same*. A graduate engineer as the FLM of a team which extrudes aluminium may seem like a very sound proposition but, even if he or she is a metallurgist whose specialised field is non-ferrous metals, this gives no assurance that the person will have the knowledge and experience of how to use and maintain the equipment effectively or of the multitude of factors affecting the yield of high-quality aluminium strip; nor does it say anything at all about their abilities as a leader or manager.

   The original 22 supervisors at Nissan's British plant were principally selected on their ability to grow quickly with the company into more senior positions. But, even so, only three of them had university degrees. Just over half of them had left school at the age of 16. Of these, five are now senior managers, five are operations managers, five are senior or middle managers at other companies and five are management consultants. Virtually all the 200 or so supervisors now at the company were promoted from the ranks of the factory floor; before that, they were coal miners, garage mechanics, shipyard welders, farmworkers, and some would have been unemployed. 'Graduate supervisors', therefore, are not the answer. In spite of, indeed, *because of* the demands of the role, most GK FLMs *can* and *ought* to come from the *genba*. (There is also an important issue concerning the morale and encouragement of the workforce: see Chapter 16.)

2. This particular construction was first used and developed by David Redpath and Tim Waddington of Forward Vision in 1996.

3. Deming, *Out of the Crisis* (pp. 52–3); see Select bibliography.

Part III
The Levers of Improvement

9 Teamwork and Customer Focus

A long pull, and a strong pull, and a pull all together.

Charles Dickens

Chapter 7 described how the role and responsibilities of the GK FLM are crucial for the application of direct management and real leadership in the workplace. There is another, which will be dealt with in later chapters. First, however, we turn to the four elements in our model: those which, collectively, provide *Genba Kanri* with its motive power and drive the engine of improvement.

It would be possible to devote a whole book to each of these subjects but, since some people have already done so, I hope that those readers who feel the need to explore them in greater detail will make use of the select bibliography. The main purpose of these chapters is to record sufficient observations to demonstrate how they work together and are interdependent.

REAL OPERATIONAL TEAMWORK

It often seems strange to me that Japan, a nation so renowned for its teamwork in business, should have, as its national sports, activities which consist of two very big men each trying their hardest to throw the other to the ground, or of two people hitting each other with sticks. In terms of international sports, the Japanese have a tradition of producing fine gymnasts and, latterly, some very competent long-distance runners and tennis players. They also have an abiding passion for golf.

By contrast, Western nations generally revere and excel at team sports: football, cricket, baseball, basketball, hockey and so on, and yet it seems that we ignore everything that our sporting tradition has to teach us when we seek to create teamwork in our factories, where it is often little more than a much espoused corporate value, something which merits a line or two on our company mission statements.

A few years ago I was visited by the HRD manager of the freight division of a leading European airline. His purpose was to learn about teamwork and to find out about training given to supervisors concerning teamworking and teambuilding. After some discussion, it was clear that my visitor was very knowledgeable about the subject, and also that his company had already made a large commitment in terms of time and money spent on training and education. I was beginning to wonder about the need for his visit at all; then, as he started describing the organisational and working practices at his company, his difficulties became all too apparent. It emerged that supervisors and freight handlers worked completely different shift patterns. Arriving at work, at the start of any given shift, a supervisor would only then discover who would be working for him on that shift. He may not have seen several of the freight handlers for a number of weeks. Similarly, a freight handler might find himself working for a different supervisor, as part of a different managerial regime, on each successive shift.

Here was a manager charged with the task of introducing teamworking into his organisation, and yet it was clearly not organised in teams in any realistic or practical sense. This is the first and most basic requirement for teamwork. If people are not organised in teams, then there is no point or benefit in pursuing strategies to develop some notion of 'teamwork'. Nor is there any advantage to be derived from educating personnel in either the benefits or techniques of teamwork; it is simply a waste of time and resources. It is rather like paying for some very expensive piano lessons without any intention of giving the intended pupil a piano.

The basis of a team is that it *works together* and *shares common goals*. If it does not do these things, it is not a team. Some people will, no doubt, argue that it is possible to have 'teamwork' in an organisation, irrespective of working arrangements and formal organisational structures and systems, in so far as members of an organisation can demonstrate that they are capable of positive interactions, are well disposed to one another, identify positively with the company, maintain a high level of morale or communicate effectively. This is thought to be teamwork 'in a sense'. But either there is teamwork or there is not. Teamwork is not merely a catchphrase for every virtuous aspect of the human condition. It is a real and practical thing. There can be no teamwork unless people are practically and realistically organised in teams.

I recall a glossy poster displayed in a factory. On it was a picture of some rock climbers, a rowing eight or a pyramid of trick motor cycle riders or something of the sort. I think there was a glowing sunrise in the background. I do remember the acronym beneath. It said:

Together
Everyone
Achieves
More

Now, with deepest respect to anyone who has parted with hard cash to put this kind of thing on their factory walls, I want to ask a question. Just how many times do people in our organisations have to look at this stuff before they feel themselves to be part of a team?

Real operational teamwork is not a bland abstraction. To secure the fruits of continuous improvement, teams must comprise members who work together, have the same leader and the same shift pattern. They must be assembled rationally and logically, reflecting the needs of the business and the product flow of the base technology – all else is mere metaphor.

They need to be able to assess their progress towards stated objectives and to obtain regular feedback on their results in order to learn from disappointments and to celebrate their successes. The concept of the downstream process as the customer is not only a vital feature of quality control but also an essential part of real operational teamwork. Many are familiar with the three circles model of John Adair,[1] showing the link between the task, team and individual. The task does not merely justify itself. It is also the cement which holds the team together. In daily commercial activity that task will be to serve the needs of the customer.

TURNING THE ORGANISATION ON ITS SIDE

The common focus of teams and their leaders in GK companies is the needs of customers, both commercial customers and *internal* customers who comprise all downstream processes. Of course there is almost as much lip-service paid to the maxim of the downstream process being the customer as there is to the desirability of teamwork. Most companies do not appear to understand the necessary link between the two and, consequently, neither usually features in the practical realities of conducting their daily business.

I recall carrying out an extensive training programme in teambuilding and leadership for production managers and foremen in a big heavy engineering company. The company is well established and most of its 2000 or so employees have long service histories. Two recipients of the training had almost 80 years of service between them. Each had been a foreman for between 15 and 20 years: one in the foundry and one in the heavy machine shop; one the supplier, the other the customer. They met each other for the first time as a result of attending the training programme.

GK principles require all manufacturing and support teams to treat themselves as businesses serving the needs of downstream customers and being responsible for their own supplies, resources and processes. For this reason GK organisations put far more emphasis than their conventional counterparts on horizontal rather than vertical demands (Figure 9.1), especially where daily operational activity is concerned.

This concept is as important for indirect, 'support' functions as it is for direct

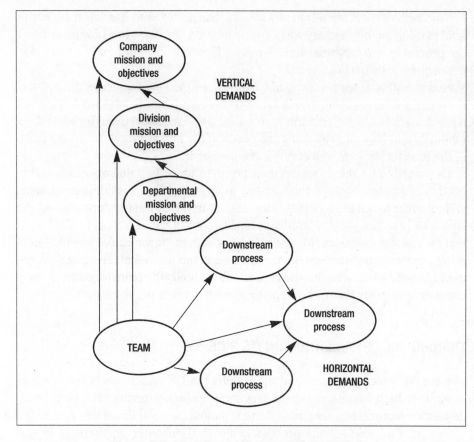

Figure 9.1   Team focus: vertical and horizontal demands

production teams. Departments such as engineering, production control and purchasing must focus on the needs of customers; all too often companies fail in this. In many respects what we are doing in introducing these ideas is tantamount to turning the organisation on its side. Whom we work for is our customer rather than our boss; and yet the latter will be gratified by our customer-driven endeavours because by them he or she will also be judged in the organisation.

The ethos that we need is very similar to the sentiments attributed to Company Sergeant-Major Moran of the Royal Regiment of Fusiliers. When dealing with 'support personnel' who expressed difficulty in giving his unit the *matériel* or service it required, he would reply: "'Can't" means "won't". "Won't" means "jail"!' This is only a slight overstatement of the kind of spirit that we need when impressing on suppliers the requirements of downstream customers.

To achieve this there must be swift and unhindered channels of horizontal communication between teams of internal customers and vendors. Middle and senior managers must be educated not only to tolerate but actively encourage such transactions.

Alpha Corp. and Omega Inc. are two fictional companies, each of a similar size and each employing approximately 3500 employees. They make diesel engines for commercial vehicles and for the marine sector. Three main processes are carried out on their respective sites: aluminium and ferrous casting; machining; and engine assembly and test.

The two companies are also of a very similar organisational structure. Following through the rungs of their manufacturing division we have: production worker; team leader; supervisor; shift manager; unit manager (one for each of the three main manufacturing operations); manufacturing director; chief executive.

One morning, an assembly worker at Alpha finds that a proportion of his supply of a particular machined component is contaminated by swarf and other debris which he is having to remove before assembly. This is making it very difficult for him to complete his assigned job of work. He brings this matter to the attention of his team leader. The team leader tells the supervisor, the supervisor informs the shift manager, the shift manager informs the unit manager. The unit manager, at this point, may take the matter up immediately with the unit manager of the machine shop, depending on the volume or nature of other problems which may be besetting him at this particular time. Assuming he does so, the unit manager in the machine shop is now, perhaps, a little embarrassed and irritated at being 'caught out' by his downstream peer and colleague. He calls in his own shift manager. He tells him of the problem and demands that it be dealt with. The disgruntled shift manager visits the supervisor from whose section the contaminated parts originated, and the supervisor admonishes the team leader, who then remonstrates with the machine operator deemed responsible for the problem.

There are obvious difficulties with this performance. The first is that this form of communication inevitably makes Alpha a particularly unpleasant place to work. Second, it oftens means that problems detected downstream and fed back by this very tortuous system of Chinese whispers are often totally misunderstood by the time they reach their eventual destination, rather like the old example, 'send three and fourpence we're going to a dance'. Third, and most important of all, this process takes *far too long*. In reality it may have proven very difficult to feed the problem back to its supposed originator while it was still 'live'. The time required for this particular chain of command to run its course probably means that there were two or three changes of shift in the intervening period. The person thought to be responsible may well be in bed, asleep, by the time word of the problem reaches the machine shop. When they return to work the problem is history, yesterday's news – until the next time.

Of course, not all companies behave quite like Alpha. Some, instead, would have expected the assembly supervisor to bring the problem to the attention of quality assurance personnel, who would themselves either report the problem directly upstream or log the problem as a 'concern'. Another approach might be for the supervisor to raise the item at the next weekly meeting of the 'Quality and

Productivity Improvement Forum', a mechanism to promote 'cross-functional teamwork' and 'continuous improvement'. In fact, in this latter case, the supervisor may well be grateful for the contaminated components incident. It gives him something to contribute to the agenda and thus prevents him from feeling uncomfortable and inadequate at the meeting.

At Omega, they do things very differently. On learning of a similar problem, the team leader walks straight to the nearest telephone and calls his opposite number in the machine shop. This is no great trouble for him; he makes such calls maybe two or three times on every shift and is often in receipt of the same from his peers working in engine test and other downstream assembly teams. This frequency of dialogue means that he is on easy terms with the team leaders in the part of the machine shop whence the parts originated. He knows that they generally give good service and is accustomed to receiving clean, good-quality parts on time and delivered just where he wants them. Clearly, there must be some reason for this shortcoming, and he describes the problem to his colleague without animosity or recrimination. Within five minutes the machining team leader is in the assembly shop examining the contaminated components. On this occasion, he has been able to bring with him the operator of the machine whence the products originated. Both are at a loss as to how the contamination might have occurred. Clearly they will need to investigate the cause and ensure that it does not happen again. But their first obligation is to make certain that the existing components lineside are uncontaminated, and they quickly set about the task with clean rags. Before they return to their own section, the machining team leader pledges his assurance to purge the system of all contaminated components so that, pending a final resolution of the problem, there will be no more defective products reaching assembly.

Fifteen minutes later, the supervisor of this particular section in assembly asks his team leader how things are going.

'OK,' is the response. 'Harry had some problems with dirty components but I've spoken to Dan in Machining and it's been sorted.'

Incidents like this occur at Omega quite frequently. After all, the *genba*, as we know, is, by its very nature, an imperfect place and Omega is forever looking for improved performance, making ever more stringent demands for better-quality products and services from internal and external suppliers. But, at Omega, such problems are dealt with swiftly and efficiently and without acrimony. In this way most are identified and resolved without anyone in middle or senior management being involved or even knowing of the problem in the first place. Instead, the latter are free to carry out the duties for which their salaries make them responsible rather than have to engage in the minutiae of everyday maintenance activity.

This approach requires a very different sense of managerial responsibilities and a very different management style from that which predominates at Alpha Corp. There, shift and unit managers feel decidedly uncomfortable when they see any of their people talking to those who report to their peers in other departments. To their way of thinking there are only two possibilities for such dialogue: either the subject matter is trivial and inconsequential – in which case the communicants are wasting company time and deserting their place of work; or the subject matter is of operational relevance – in which case they feel the need to be in full possession of every detail of every activity carried out within their empires. Anything less than this makes them feel extremely vulnerable.

A 'quality garment manufacturer' in the English Midlands was endeavouring to introduce 'cellular manufacturing' into its factory. As part of this change, it was acknowledged that the company's production managers and supervisors would need to develop a far better understanding of internal customer relationships. I was told that, only three years before, workers in the plant had been issued with different coloured overalls, depending on the part of the process in which they worked. Workers in the knitting section were issued with blue overalls. Stitch-room workers were issued with yellow overalls. The purpose of this was not to generate some form of departmental pride or team identity; rather, as one production manager admitted, such a policy made it very simple to detect and apprehend wayward operators who had strayed from their place of work. A yellow-clad figure amidst a sea of blue-clad figures was easily spotted and immediately assumed to be an errant individual clearly 'up to no good', and certainly up to nothing productive. Strays were invariably admonished and shepherded back to their 'own work area'.

BROKERS AND MIDDLEMEN

A characteristic often, though not exclusively, found in many heavy engineering firms frequently conspires not only to impair manufacturing performance and inflate overhead costs but also to prevent the development of effective internal supplier–customer relationships and rule out the possibility of real operational teamwork. This is the excessive reliance on large central planning and scheduling departments which have evolved to become the sole interface of every individual manufacturing section or functional group in the organisation. They are at once the only real supplier and the only real customer, the medium for and sometimes the jealous guardian of all transactions.[2]

When observing such companies, I cannot escape the mental image of a car with a highly sophisticated engine management system for optimised running and fuel economy. The hardware for this is so big and heavy that the car has to pull it on a trailer. Rarely do such companies ever seem to be particularly successful when it comes to delivery performance. Unfortunately the conclusion too often reached in such a case is: *we must have more planners*. It sometimes appears that the amount of real planning which takes place in a company is inversely proportional to the size of its central planning department. Usually what passes for planning in these companies is actually *repromising*. Every day 'planners' sit down to a repromising meeting. Having failed to meet the schedule, they simply issue another. This makes it very difficult to create real teamwork in the production department, for not only are production 'teams' either absolved or even prohibited from regular communication with downstream processes; they have no clear indication of schedule achievement, no concept of success or failure, no spur to resolve problems or make improvements.

EFFECTIVE TEAMS ARE COMPOUNDS, NOT MIXTURES

Nor is true teamwork fostered by taking people with different kinds of expertise, professional discipline, responsibilities, levels of seniority and salary and simply bundling them into the same corner of the organisation chart. This often serves to weaken the effectiveness of functions and of itself does nothing to further the ends of either real teamwork or better customer service. Suppose we all had a firefighter and a paramedic stationed in every neighbourhood. Would this actually improve the level of service we could expect in an emergency? I often reflect that 'multifunctional teams' have proven most attractive to companies who have simply failed to make the maxim of internal customer satisfaction, especially with respect to indirect support groups, a reality in their organisation.

Consider the team trainer, the man with the first-aid kit, the ice pack and the magic sponge, who crouches by the touchline during a football game. Does he care about the wellbeing of the players on the field? Yes, he does. It is his whole purpose for the duration of the game. When a player is hurt he *runs* on to the field to give treatment or assistance. So, is he actually a member of the team? No, he is not. There are and can only be 11 members of a football team.

If the issue is to get our support functions to give good service to their customers, then simply shoving them geographically or organisationally together is neither a necessary nor sufficient condition for achieving this. To draw a chemical analogy, an effective team must be a compound, as opposed to a mixture.The following case study provides a cautionary example.

An international manufacturing company employs direct, so-called 'semi-skilled' operators to perform production operations, and fitters and electricians to be responsible for the maintenance of plant and equipment. In keeping with common practice among most manufacturing organisations worldwide, it remunerates the latter group more highly in recognition of the marketability of their skills and the time taken to acquire them.

A senior executive of the company, while reflecting on the growing perception that the competitive edge of its rivals is frequently attributed to 'teamwork' and the removal of traditional job demarcations, walks past a maintenance workshop and observes that, because production is experiencing a day relatively untroubled by equipment failures, several fitters and electricians are reading newspapers and appear to have nothing to do.

An idea begins to germinate. What if these people could be required to carry out production operations on such occasions? The idea gathers momentum and captivates the imagination of the senior management team, who perceive an opportunity to galvanise their factories towards a more effective deployment of labour, under the banner of teamwork and flexibility.

'What? You mean put production workers and maintenance together in the same team? Wow! Not even the Japanese have gone that far. Let's do it! We'll teach them a thing or two about teamwork and flexibility!' Negotiations are undertaken with the elected union representatives of both groups of workers. The management of the company sells the vision of 'assimilated production units' (APUs), which will be 'teams' comprising both 'semi-skilled' and 'skilled' members led by a supervisor from either a 'semi-skilled' or 'skilled' background.

In APUs, direct operators will now be encouraged to perform some of the maintenance tasks historically undertaken by the 'skilled' group. There is, of course, a price for this flexibility: those who accept it will achieve an incremental grade and be paid accordingly. Of course, the company feels it has to make sure that the increment is seem to be *earned* and not 'given away for nothing'; so, as a prerequisite for the wage upgrade, it insists that the operators undertake a training programme. The company demonstrates its own commitment in that the programme is lengthy, expensive (four weeks off-the-job training) and, in keeping with the current fashion, to a 'nationally recognised and approved' occupational standard.

In APUs, indirect operators must declare a willingness to carry out production operations. Again, this willingness has to be bought: fitters and electricians in APUs are now paid a higher wage than their peers who are not yet in APUs, in recognition of their 'flexibility'.

At first, the introduction of APUs appears to be a success. There seems to be a marked improvement in morale and enthusiasm on the part of the workforce where they are introduced. This should not surprise us. Elton Mayo's famous Hawthorne experiments, carried out over 70 years ago, should have led us to expect as much. Furthermore, 'teamwork' and 'flexibility' are both universally lauded as 'good things' by everyone. Changes wrought in their name invariably invite interest and attract a positive disposition from all concerned. Eventually, however, the initial euphoria subsides.

It is observed that, even in the APUs, the fitters and the electricians, though happy with their pay increase, have no particular enthusiasm for performing what they still perceive as 'lower-skilled' work.

The company finds it difficult to fund the training programme which would legitimately 'qualify' production workers to carry out basic maintenance work, both in terms of the costs of the training and in releasing them in significant numbers from production activities. Production workers, eager to increase their pay but also to learn and practise new skills, become frustrated and cynical at what they see as a 'lack of flexibility and commitment' on the part of management.

In addition, the training which is provided proves to be of a very general nature and cannot hope to provide the few 'directs' who have partaken of it with the knowledge and skills which would equip them to undertake specific maintenance tasks on the company's machines (although it has, of course, qualified them for a wage increase).

Unlike its rivals, the company has no strong tradition of thorough and detailed on-the-job training which would provide this knowledge. Even if it had, this approach would not be acceptable in terms of the APU agreement to justify the wage upgrade and, of course, no upgrade – no maintenance activity.

It becomes clear that APUs have in fact changed things very little. Within the APUs themselves hardly any fitters or electricians engage in production work; even fewer production workers carry out maintenance activities.

It further emerges that, whenever there is a large maintenance project to be undertaken or a need to respond quickly to a breakdown affecting a complex and critical item of equipment, it is very difficult to deploy swiftly a team of technicians with the right combination of skills and knowledge, for they are now flung to the four winds and nominally work for different supervisors. The company finds itself increasingly dependent on outside contractors for such services and starts to lose valuable knowledge of its own processes and equipment.[3]

Some former 'production-only' supervisors confess to a lack of confidence in managing their 'skilled' team members, conscious of their limited technical knowledge. 'If he says it takes him half a shift to replace a drive motor, then who am I to argue?' says one.

One or two supervisors and middle managers start to question whether or not there has been a meaningful change in working habits and whether there have been significant operational benefits, either in terms of more effective or efficient labour deployment or in terms of better standards of maintenance and machine performance.

Retrospectively, there is a suggestion that there is something perverse and absurd about paying someone more money for 'higher-skilled' work and then paying them still more money for spending some of their time carrying out 'lower-skilled' work.

Meanwhile, in the rival company, teamwork and flexibility are not shibboleths but *real and practical* contributors to improved company performance. Most simple and cyclic maintenance functions are indeed carried out by production workers. The practice of planned preventive maintenance, by both skilled technician teams and production teams alike, has achieved a record of machine performance and productivity that continues to turn our company green with envy. At this rival company the very notion that, in a modern complex factory, a skilled maintenance technician could ever be in a situation of *not having enough maintenance work to do* would be greeted with total and dumbfounded incredulity.

We may be tempted to conclude that what this episode demonstrates is a costly, disruptive, time-consuming and ultimately futile response to a wrongly diagnosed problem – and all in the name of 'teamwork' and 'flexibility'.

Another company, perceiving that its engineering functions do not identify sufficiently with the needs of its customers in the production department, decides to take positive action to address the matter. It uproots a number of its more junior engineers and allocates them to production teams of which they are now deemed to be 'members'. (Actually there proves to be only sufficient of these engineers to allocate them to every *other* team as a shared 'resource'.) Some of these young engineers are far from happy with their new circumstances and they yearn for a time when, their exile completed, they will be able to rejoin their colleagues and resume the mantle of proper engineers. Others accept the situation and try to do their best for their new 'team mates'. Unfortunately, they now find themselves in a similar situation to that of the production FLMs. There is a limit to what they can achieve without the support of the central engineering functions, whose values, of course, remain unchanged. The vast chasm between supplier and customer has not been bridged. It has simply been resited around and behind these redeployed engineers.

In another case, a company tries something even more radical. Engineering, it concludes, is not the only 'errant supplier'. There are similar problems with quality assurance, purchasing and scheduling departments. The company assigns individuals, now labelled 'manufacturing and planning engineers' (MPEs), who nominally take on the responsibility of providing the services of all these disciplines. The great number of individuals thus spared from the support functions enables the company to appoint one of these multi-functional superbeings to each and every production team. But this strategy has all the failings of the previous approach, with the addition that there is an even greater reliance on the centre for specialist knowledge and support (a resource which is now somewhat depleted). As the new roles evolve, the new 'team member' simply takes on part of what should in any case be the FLM's responsibilities. FLMs are happy to be able to wash their hands of these obligations. What emerge are leaderless teams. The FLM tries to manage the people while the MPE tries to manage the task. Real leadership in the workplace cannot subsist whilst these two roles are separated.

The need unequivocally to re-focus *all* departments on downstream requirements cannot be avoided. This demands clear leadership and command at the highest level of management. Department heads must be expected to make these requirements their first priority, and workable *customer-focused* objectives must be cascaded down to all functional groups of technical and commercial specialists at an operational level. There can be no substitute for this. Tinkering with the organisation structure will not suffice.

NOTES

1. J. Adair (1979), *Action-Centred Leadership*, Aldershot, Hants: Gower.
2. Complexity of products, long lead times and the manufacture of 'one-offs' are frequently cited justifications for such an approach. But all these requirements simply reinforce the need for unobstructed communication and collaboration between production teams. It is perhaps nearer the truth to say that many companies with these characteristics have been accustomed to supplying governments and state utilities. Affinity and affection for the big and complex, fashionable in the 1960s and 1970s, has simply survived a little longer in these companies as compared with those who have long since determined that they can no longer afford to carry such baggage.
3. Toyota is a prime example of the reluctance of many GK organisations to contract out significant aspects of equipment maintenance and lose the knowledge that goes with it. To quote Taiichi Ohno: 'You must have the ability to tinker with and improve the machines you already have. If you only know how to use machines the way the manufacturer showed you, then you will end up with what you deserve'. See T. Ohno, *Workplace Management* (p. 124); see Select bibliography.

10 The Hunger for Improvement

I sometimes take calls from managers who are pursuing problem-solving training for their supervisors. I ask if they have already had any training on the subject and they quote from a formidable array of tools and techniques such as Kepner Tregoe, Taguchi, fishbone diagrams, situation analysis, process FMEA and CEDAC. I then ask why it is felt that any further training is needed.

'They're still not solving problems', is the usual response. In fact problem-solving skills and tools are rarely in short supply among FLMs and their workteams. Usually it is the *desire* and *appetite* for problem solving, or for improvement, which is lacking.

Other managers, aware that neither bonus payments nor financially rewarded suggestion schemes are a feature of GK companies, seem baffled as to why workers in such companies should *want* to improve their team performance. I sometimes point out that, every Saturday and Sunday in the winter months, my brother runs about in a field for three hours in all weathers and returns covered in mud and bruises. All he has ever received for his trouble is a torn cartilage and a broken cheekbone. He is not a complete eccentric. Twenty-one other men share his discomfort and another six stand in line for the chance to do likewise. Many thousands more are also doing the same in the British Isles alone, and many are the same people of whom it is claimed that they will do nothing without financial incentives.

'Ah, but that's *football!*', is the response. 'You can't compare sport with work!' No, sadly, in most companies you cannot. Suppose, after 90 minutes, we asked a player walking from the field what his team's result was. We would be astonished if he could not tell us the score and would reasonably expect that he could also tell us the team's position in the league, how many points it still needed to win the championship or avoid relegation, and possibly a whole host of other information relating to his team and its performance, both during the game and during the season. Now, suppose we stop somebody coming through the factory gates and ask them how *their* team performed in its last shift. Did it achieve schedule? How was its finished quality? How much machine downtime was there? Will they be able to tell us and will they be able to tell us *with numbers*?

VISUAL MEASURES OF TEAM PERFORMANCE

Very few companies, including those who claim to have introduced 'teamworking' to their operations, actually analyse their performance measurement in relation to team level – in marked contrast with GK organisations.

Visual measures of team performance are the key to providing the *essence* of teamwork, focusing clearly on customer requirements and creating the hunger for improvement. That hunger cannot be trained or exhorted; only a challenge will do it. But visual measures of team performance are not a device for impressing visitors, a senior manager's prompting aid for 'Managing By Walking About', nor a cudgel to intimidate FLMs or their workteams.

To understand the concept fully we need to distinguish between *actual* and *visual* quality. Actual quality is quality in the normally understood sense of the word: the combination of factors that combine to please a customer, fitness for purpose, the things for which customers actually pay. In a restaurant it is the taste of the food, the standard of waiting service, the atmosphere of the dining area, the presentation of the menu. Visual quality is the impression given by a tour of the kitchen, before the customer has actually eaten anything. Visual quality conveys a message, demonstrates competence and also expresses individuality. Visual quality says: 'This is who we are, this is what makes us unique, this is how good we are at doing what we do.'

Visual management is the catalyst for promoting improvement and problem-solving activities within an operational team as a normal part of the business. Each and every member of the team becomes conversant with its targets and goals and can direct energy towards them. The motivation to improve requires the team to be aware of progress towards objectives and to recognise that these objectives and goals are the *team's*, not the plant manager's or the FLM's alone. Only when a team has these objectives can real operational teamwork be practised.

Visual management aids the translation of strategic goals and objectives into operational teams. In large companies it can be difficult for employees to grasp the significance of strategic activity in a tangible way. Visual management provides a way of cascading meaningful objectives. If I take a leak in Lake

Superior then logic would tell me that I am making some contribution to the water level, but I would not expect to be able to see any tangible result of my efforts, which would literally pass unnoticed. Similarly, as the employee of a large company, there is very little I can do that will positively influence the gradient of a graph of, say, company energy costs. My conscious efforts to switch off lights or machines when not in use must help in some way, but are unlikely to make a noticeable difference. If it is possible to break those costs down to small teams of less than 25 people, or if my team is a maintenance squad or a group of site engineers who can take improvement actions to influence events significantly (such as installing infra-red sensors to switch off lights automatically when nobody is in an office), then that is a different matter entirely. In this way, team performance displays enable us to relate the contribution of our individual endeavours to the achievements of the team and the achievements of the team to those of the department or company as a whole.

Visual management reinforces an image of corporate professionalism. Work teams are seen to care about the quality of service they provide and the way in which it is provided. This image is portrayed to customers, clients, visitors and the workteam members themselves. As a pure tool for measurement, visual management enables trends and the results of improvement efforts to be identified. It can provide a focus when day-to-day progress towards longer-term objectives cannot be immediately ascertained. The data collected and charted are also valuable in solving problems.

There are two main aspects of visual quality and visual management in GK companies. The first concerns the organisation and maintenance of the workplace – not simply the disciplines involved in keeping it clean, neat and tidy (usually called 'housekeeping'), but establishing visual techniques for assessing its orderliness and capability. These enable us to see, at a glance, if something is in the wrong place, if a tool is missing, if there is too little or too much material, if a machine is not being properly maintained and so forth.[1] The other aspect concerns how the workteam, either a direct production team or an indirect support function, displays its performance in terms of achieving quality and delivery to its customers, its control and improvement of its production or business process and its ability continually to reduce the costs of its resources: manpower, machinery and materials.

The best and most familiar example of this comes not from any GK company in Japan but from the fuselages of Allied combat aircraft during World War II. I was once privileged to meet Otto Meikus, a distinguished American service veteran now living in Cambridgeshire. Mr Meikus served with the 91st Group of the Eighth Air Force, home of the legendary *Memphis Belle*, and was Crew Chief of two record-breaking B-17s: *The Ripper* and *Nine-O-Nine*. He and his team were responsible for the repair, upkeep and performance of the aircraft, employing maintenance techniques which would be easily recognised in the best GK companies, decades before anyone had a name for planned preventive or total productive maintenance. *Nine-O-Nine* eventually completed an unparalleled 125 successful missions. Each completed mission was signified by a bomb symbol. On *Nine-O-Nine*, eight of these symbols carried the letter B, signifying a successful mission to Berlin.[2] Of course each B-17 had its own expression of individuality in the form of the names and illustrations which proclaimed, on the part of combat and ground crews alike, 'This is us. This is our team. This is our plane. Look at what it has achieved.'

WALLPAPER

By contrast, let us compare this simple and effective example with some of the sophisticated performance graphs that can be seen in so many organisations. The example in Figure 10.1 is taken from the wall of the production scheduling department of a large manufacturing company. I cannot do full justice to the original, which was produced monthly by the IT department, on A3 size paper and in glorious technicolour.

The senior manager who was showing me around the plant was particularly proud of this item. It was only one of a number of graphs, displayed at several locations throughout the site, produced after a top management 'workshop' to establish what cost items the company could measure and display. (Never a good

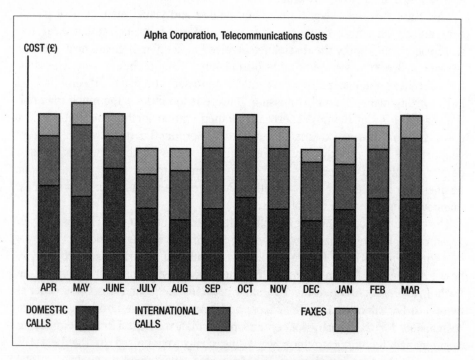

Figure 10.1 Display of telecommunications costs

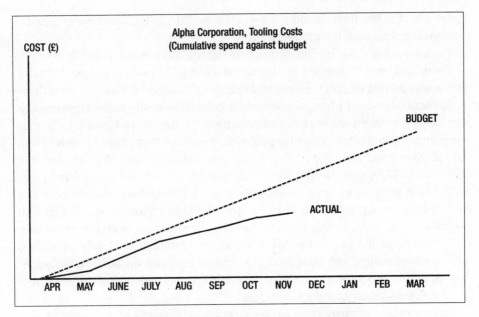

Figure 10.2 Display of performance against budget

way to begin.) A little while later I had the opportunity of asking one of the administrative assistants working in the department to spell out the significance of this item to me.

'It's a graph of our monthly telephone and fax costs', she said, with the patient air of one explaining the obvious to a child.

'Yes, but does it actually tell you anything?'

She thought for a moment and then smiled broadly.

'It tells us that our summer vacation is the last week in July and first week in August and that Christmas always happens in December.'

I was hardly surprised to discover later that these displays, of which the management team were so proud, were known throughout the company as 'bullshit boards'.

Expenditure against budget is often a favourite. Figure 10.2 provides an example. What are people supposed to infer from this? That we have achieved some magnificent cost savings through continuous improvement? That we have under-invested in new tooling and had better rush out and spend before the end of the year? Or that somebody really screwed up when they set the budget?

I recall an episode from a plant which used an 'off-standard' calculation as one of its main operational performance measures. This gives a percentage ratio of unrealised production capacity and as such is a witches' cauldron of all things which adversely affect production performance. A large graph of the average weekly 'off-standard' was prominently displayed near the coffee vending machine in one of the manufacturing units. The gradient showed a steady increase in the figure over the last three months. One of the workers in the factory was asked if he could explain what the graph meant.

'I'm not too sure', he replied. 'But it's on the up, so we must be doing well.'

There are visual displays of performance which inspire people to solve problems and make improvements and therefore have profitable ends – and there is *wallpaper*. Much of what gets pinned up in factories is the latter. Occasionally, the wallpaper might impress top management or undiscerning clients. It may even impress some agencies charged with giving out 'best practice' awards on 'world-class manufacturing', who rarely see beneath the obvious and the superficial. Wallpaper is the stuff that absolutely nobody in the company, including management, truly gives a damn about. Rarely does anybody look at it and nobody really cares whether or not the information is up to date. (If somebody *did* care, it would be.) The only time we do anything about our wallpaper is on the eve of the VIP visit, when we find some newly graduated management trainee and have them run around the plant updating it. Wallpaper has no influence whatever on how people in the organisation work, think or feel – except occasionally to induce cynicism.

To make the vital distinction between profitable displays of performance and wallpaper, we simply select any display, anywhere in our factory, and apply this simple test. (A randomly selected worker from the vicinity might help with some of the questions.)

- Does everyone understand it?
- Does everyone appreciate the factors which influence it? (If not, how can they do anything about it?)
- Does everyone understand the difference between a good result and a bad one, and why?
- Can everyone, alone or with others, do something about it?
- Are the results statistically valid?
- Is there a clearly indicated, challenging yet attainable *target* which can be achieved by the team, section or department?
- Is there still room for improvement? (Visual management should be *live* and deal with real and current problems or improvement opportunities: when an item ceases to be significant it should be taken down and replaced with something else.)

If the answer is *no* to two or more of the above, then the item is wallpaper.

WHAT GK TEAMS MEASURE

For the purposes of establishing GK disciplines, satisfying the needs of customers, implementing real operational teamwork and creating the hunger for improvement, we are mostly concerned with performance measures and displays

Primary: customer satisfaction	Secondary: main influencing factors and key cost items	Others (non-exhaustive)

• Off-line product or service quality
• Achievement of schedule
	• Downtime: lost time due to machine
	  breakdowns
	• Lost time due to non-receipt of
	  materials
	• Scrap/repair
	• In-line product quality
	• Attendance
		• Labour efficiency
		• Skill matrices
		• WIP levels
		• SPC charts
		• 'Housekeeping' audits
		• TPM (total productive
		  maintenance) monitors

Table 10.1 **Three tiers of team performance measurement**

which relate to teams. Here are some examples of the kinds of item that we might expect to see recorded and displayed by production teams in a GK company. The items have been categorised into three levels of precedence and importance. (Table 10.1).

PRIMARY MEASURES

There are only two primary measures: the quality of the goods or service delivered to the customer (either the commercial client or the downstream process) and the prompt delivery of the goods or service. These items override everything else. They constitute the *raison d'être* of the team itself. They are the outputs of our model in Chapter 1 (Figure 1.1). Team performance against these two items, quality and delivery, should be measured, recorded, displayed and communicated to the team, each and every production shift.

SECONDARY MEASURES

Secondary measures comprise the factors which either have a direct bearing on the team's ability to achieve the primary measures or else relate to key cost items. ('In-line product quality' refers to defectives produced within the team's area but which were discovered by the team and prevented from reaching its customers. These naturally constitute problems which must be resolved by the team, since they carry the risk of eventually reaching the downstream, disrupt the team's operation and obviously increase its real operating costs.) Frequency of feedback on secondary measures depends largely on the contributory effect of each item and the ease and frequency of data collection.

A company seeking to introduce team performance measures should always start with one or both of the primary measures. In so doing it makes a clear and meaningful commitment to profitable outputs and to the maxim of treating the downstream as the customer. To begin elsewhere – for example with attendance or with labour efficiency – would send out completely the wrong messages to workteams, who would immediately be suspicious of corporate intentions and consider themselves 'got at'. On the other hand, once teams and their FLMs set about understanding and improving their performance to customers, their attention will inevitably be drawn towards any secondary items which inhibit their achievements.

Once the primary and secondary measures are in place, there may be other items of interest either to the team or to the organisation, depending on its specific aims and circumstances. Some will no doubt be surprised at the low priority accorded to labour efficiency, machine utilisation and production volume. The reason for their relatively humble status is that they are not *outputs*. Though we are accustomed to referring to production volume as 'output', this is a misnomer. Quality, cost and delivery are our only process outputs. Production volume *per se* is only relevant in so far as it relates to the efficient use of our resources, our inputs: manpower, machinery and materials. Where an inability to marshal these resources effectively may threaten the fulfilment of the production schedule, this will be revealed in our more direct and specific secondary measures.

PERFORMANCE MEASURES AND SUPPORT GROUPS

Performance measures, and not some nebulous notion of organisational 'culture', are the biggest influence on what happens in companies and on what groups and individuals actually do at work. This influence can be either beneficial or maleficent, depending on what is actually measured and especially on its relevance to customer needs.

A purchasing department whose only significant performance measure is the extent to which it can hold down vendor prices will not be greatly concerned with the effects that poor vendor performance on delivery or quality have on production. The accounts payable section of a finance department, whose sole measured purpose is to optimise cash flow, will never feel discomforted by the effects of missed deliveries arising from dishonoured payment obligations to vendors.

This is not to say that holding down vendor process and prudent cash flow management are unimportant.[3] Rather, it means that their importance is as a measure of the costs of providing a service. We must not lose sight of the service itself. It is a matter of ensuring an appropriate balance. As we have seen, with our model of inputs and outputs in Chapter 1, real improvement does not constitute reducing costs at the expense of the customer, nor improving customer service at a commensurate increase in costs. If the key to real operational teamwork is that both direct manufacturing and support function teams are to treat themselves as true businesses, they must have all the dials and gauges in front of them. They cannot always be given easy options. Business is not supposed to be that easy.

The production department of a small company in the North-East of England making air conditioning equipment found that the biggest inhibitor to achieving the production schedule was the poor supply of parts and materials. One of the production managers erected a two-by-one-metre board in the middle of the factory, on which he displayed a simple Pareto analysis of causes of lost production. Materials shortages clearly accounted for more disruption than all the other factors added together. The materials manager was incensed when he first saw it. He demanded that the display be taken down. The production manager refused and the production director backed him up. Within two weeks the amount of lost production time had halved and 'lack of parts' moved three places to the right on the Pareto board. The materials manager and his team were pleased by their achievements and resolved to do more. The biggest problem was now the late release of engineering documentation, and it was the turn of technical director to feel embarrassed. Hitherto he had observed the board with amused detachment.[4]

GUIDING PRINCIPLES FOR VISUAL PERFORMANCE DISPLAYS

VISIBILITY

Displays must be seen by all team members and make an impact. The most important items (outputs) should be simple and colourful and should not need to be read close up. Very few visible live and relevant charts are better than a display board which resembles the instrument panel on the space shuttle. Six or seven items per team are more than adequate. A dozen is too many. Following the 80–20 principle,[5] one or two items which concern outputs to customers will reap most of the dividends.

Displays should be in the team's workplace, a team meeting room, engineering office, maintenance workshop – a focal point for the team. Scarcely better than the remotest corridor is the company dining area or just outside the washrooms. It is an oft-stated but erroneous assertion that people look at visual displays in these places.

THE TEAM AS THE FOCUS

The importance of team measurement is not only as an indispensable ingredient of real operational teamwork but also in providing a medium whereby, on a daily basis, individuals in the organisation can relate their endeavours to company achievements. It is natural, therefore, that many consider extending this logic down to displaying *individual* operational performance, such as individual attendance records or individual quality performance. But this is never as effective, has an adverse effect on morale and is usually a symptom of remote control management.

One company of about 300 employees would, as part of its approach to BS 5750, place most of the burden for observing and auditing processes on its quality assurance department (a practice inconsistent with GK principles in any case). The quality manager would compile a monthly report of statistics to include a breakdown of instances of process errors and of non-compliance with quality systems which could be attributed to individuals. The report would be discussed monthly at a special meeting of the senior management team. No profitable purpose was served by this. No practical action could be taken by such a body, especially after considerable time had elapsed since the incidents. For real operational teamwork and effective leadership the measurable successes and disappointments must be collectively those of the team. The *accountability* must be that of its leader and manager, the FLM. In this way the FLM will be impelled to take appropriate action regarding individual contributions to the outcomes in accordance with his or her own judgement. That action is the legitimate concern of the team member and the FLM – nobody else.

TEAM INVOLVEMENT

It is unfortunate that these days we seem to have so much contempt for anything not produced by a laser printer. A single, meaningful, hand-drawn chart of customer-related performance, for which team members themselves have collected, displayed and updated the data, is far more valuable and effective than half a dozen centrally produced, mundane and uniform little computer printouts stuck in neat little rows of plastic envelopes. The task of compilation promotes greater ownership of the process, greater awareness of customer requirements and a better understanding of problems.

Data should be easy to collect and readily available. The costs and efforts of this exercise must not be allowed to exceed its value. Moreover, much depends on creating a climate for action, especially the swift resolution of problems which cause difficulties downstream. Therefore output data in particular should be collected and digested while they are still 'warm'.

This criterion is rarely difficult to fulfil providing that the real and relevant factors are being measured. Output data which specifically address the real issues for customers and the downstream will easily and most willingly be quantified by the customer. Virtually all the other items are within the control of the team and of the GK FLM. No one will have to look elsewhere for the information.

PRESERVING THE PURITY OF PERFORMANCE MEASUREMENT

In creating a climate which promotes continuous improvement, the resolution of problems and continual, direct and horizontal dialogue between suppliers and customers within organisations, there must be no doctoring of data to accommodate the failure of upstream processes. All teams must take full responsibility for their outputs and thereby behave as *true businesses*. Only unadulterated performance figures will drive home the resolution of upstream problems.

We are all too aware that if a company fails to meet its delivery requirements to a commercial client, it cannot expect to be exonerated because its own commercial vendors failed to perform adequately. That may not always be fair, but it is business. Companies are expected by their clients to manage their own suppliers as part of the deal. So must it be with our internal transactions between teams of suppliers and customers.

If a team required to pack and ship 2000 doughnuts every shift only ships 1000 doughnuts, then it has failed its customer obligations by 1000 doughnuts. That there were no doughnuts to pack until lunchtime does not alter the fact. The doughnut-frying team has also failed to supply doughnuts according to schedule, a fact not altered by the breakdown of the doughnut fryer for four hours or by the maintenance team's difficulties in fixing it because of the purchasing team's inability to procure spare parts on time. But if, in furtherance of a false concept of 'fairness', the packing and despatch team is allowed to be credited with shipping the 1000 doughnuts that it feels it certainly would have shipped had they arrived on time, then all the pressure for better service from suppliers, and all the hunger for problem solving and improvement evaporate.

This only appears 'harsh' or 'unfair' if the purposes of team performance measures are misunderstood or misapplied. The importance of notional fairness and the habit of building in fudge factors and allowances derives either from a climate of condemnation and reproof or is rooted in current or historic systems of monetary reward for operational performance. Neither applies to GK organisations. The daily task is not to calculate just reward nor to apportion blame, but to resolve problems at source.

RAPID PERFORMANCE FEEDBACK: PDCA IN ACTION

Chapter 2 described the need to weave the improvement cycle or 'Deming's wheel' into the fabric of how companies actually carry out their business. Fulfilling this need is the fourth element which sustains the drive for improvement by adding bite to the visual measures of team performance, providing an assurance of communication between upstream and downstream processes and service groups, giving a framework for effective leadership in the workplace and creating a climate which assumes prompt action to resolve problems and the swift exploitation of improvement opportunities.

The heralding of each production shift by meetings, conducted by each

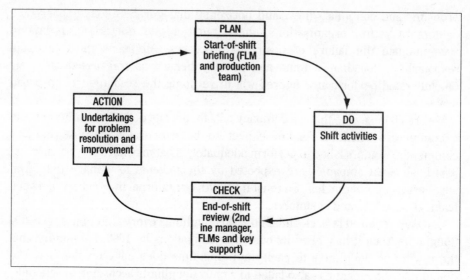

Figure 10.3   Performance evaluation, feedback and PDCA

production supervisor and attended by all of his production team, is a well-known practice of GK companies. Far less is known, however, about the content and *true purpose* of these meetings and still less about the post-shift reviews attended by those self-same FLMs and conducted by Second Line Managers. Both these sessions need to be fully understood as a prime example of how the PDCA cycle of continuous improvement is structurally integrated into the operational life of a GK company (Figure 10.3).

There can be few things more distasteful to managers in most organisations than any proposal involving the introduction of meetings. Initial feelings of revulsion may perhaps be quelled by two important features of this approach. The first is that these meetings are *substitutional*, not *additional* to many of those that already take place in companies. In fact most companies discover that, because these meetings consciously follow the discipline of the PDCA cycle, the net amount of time spent in meetings generally is dramatically reduced. It could almost be said that these are 'meetings to end meetings'. Second, unlike the more familiar regular and *ad hoc* discussions which take place in most conventional organisations, their significance lies not so much in what is discussed *at* them as in what they cause to happen *between* them.

THE POST-SHIFT REVIEW

As soon as possible after production has finished and most production team members are making their way home, the post-shift review takes place, religiously and without fail. There are no exceptions.

This meeting is the occasion for the production unit to make its assessment of its business performance in terms of quality, cost and delivery, the manufacturing process and manpower, and machinery and materials during the newly completed production shift. It makes this assessment while the issues are still fresh and the problems are still at the forefront of the minds of the attendees. Across the production unit this is the formal management exercise of conducting the CHECK phase of the PDCA cycle and laying the foundations for the ACTION phase. Its purpose is to establish what happened and why and, in respect of any problems, what is to be done, when and by whom. It also reinforces the customer focus of support departments and promotes teamwork among the FLMs themselves.

The session is conducted by the Second Line Manager and lasts between 15 and 40 minutes in most GK organisations, depending on the quantity and complexity of problems encountered during the shift. In attendance is the Second Line Manager's own team of production FLMs plus representatives of the main functions which support production activity – whether they formally report to the Second Line Manager or not. Representatives of some functions will be summoned to attend as and when required, such as purchasing or personnel. Others, such as maintenance, material control, quality assurance and engineering, will be represented at every post-shift review as a matter of course. Attendance at this meeting by support staff is *not optional*. After all, they represent *supplier departments*. Failure to attend would be regarded as a very serious breach of customer obligations. Out of consideration to them, however, the Second Line Manager will usually place items concerning support groups near the top of the agenda and they are free to depart once the relevant items of business have been resolved. Some will then attend post-shift reviews of their own functions. All will be communicating any undertakings and commitments made at their various pre-shift briefings.

The precise agenda and the time spent on each item will of course vary between GK companies and between production units with differing base technologies and characteristics. Assembly plants may tend to have a more varied range of quality problems. Machining, casting, moulding and similar processes may be more concerned with scheduling and maintenance issues. But, broadly speaking, the pattern of discussion is as follows:

1. Quality performance
2. Schedule achievement (including any imminent schedule changes)
3. Breakdowns, tooling problems and process concerns
4. Workflow problems, parts and material shortages (including any anticipated problems on the next shift)
5. Safety incidents
6. Updates on trials, countermeasures and improvement activities
7. Other items.

Items 1–5 have numerical ratings and will usually correspond to displayed measures of performance for the production unit as a whole. For each agenda item, main contributory problems are listed. Each problem requires an *action*. This action may be undertaken by the appropriate production FLM, by one of the indirect representatives in attendance or by a combination of both, depending on the nature of the problem. It may involve agreeing to implement an immediately apparent practical countermeasure. It may consist of the 'owner' of the concern giving a firm promise to resolve or, as a temporary measure, to 'cut off' the problem by inspection or repair by a particular time, date, unit or batch number. It may involve assigning responsibilities for undertaking further investigations and reporting back by a particular time.

The Second Line Manager ensures that no problem item slips through the net, that *someone* takes ownership of each and that all promises of action are assiduously recorded.

Rarely are FLMs or support representatives caught off guard by the items, since they are related to the processes and services for which they are responsible. During the course of the production shift, they will have made frequent visits to downstream customers and final testing and inspection areas to evaluate their performance and that of their teams. In many cases, they will not only be aware of the problems, but will have already taken appropriate action to resolve them fully. Production FLMs and their Team Leaders will have faithfully recorded any disruptions to the smooth running of key items of equipment. They will detail the nature of the problem, the precise time and duration of any breakdown, the current status of the equipment and all actions taken or to be taken – by the production teams themselves, by maintenance technicians, or by a collaboration of both. Of course, during production, maintenance technicians will have recorded the same information, thus ensuring that the maintenance FLM is well prepared to discuss items which are unresolved or still causing concern. So it is also in respect of the supply of materials and other factors.

The consequence of this is that, with the occasional exception of problems that first occur near the very end of the production shift, attendees of the post-shift review are bringing data, solutions and firm undertakings to the meeting, not problems. That is how this session can be so concise and yet so productive. The post-shift review is not a problem-solving session. Problems should be solved in the workplace, in the *genba*, during the shift; ideally in the shift in which they were first recognised. The post-shift review can best be described as a 'reckoning', in both commonly used senses of the word. It is the definitive tally of what the unit has achieved during the shift against its main performance criteria, and an exposition of all main contributing factors so that all attendees can obtain a common understanding of that performance. But it is also an occasion when all present are called to account for their activities.

This is how internal customer service becomes a reality in GK factories. FLMs make regular visits to their customers during the shift, not simply because, either by nature or by dint of training or education, they are considerate of customer needs, nor because of a line or two on the company mission statement. They have two vested interests in learning promptly about problems found by the customer and for taking swift and appropriate action. The first is their customer-focused measurements of team performance. To learn sufficiently early about downstream problems enables them to act quickly and limit the damage to team achievements. That is why they are usually genuinely appreciative of any feedback from their customers about problems with quality and delivery. Second, they do not want the embarrassment of learning about the problem at the post-shift review. There are always problems in a company which recognises the natural imperfections of the real workplace and yet on a daily basis is straining every sinew to achieve ever more stringent standards of product and service and, at the same time, reduce operating costs. To have problems is therefore forgivable. But to be in ignorance of them and of the discomfort they cause to the downstream is not. The post-shift review is the practical and operational manifestation of this maxim.

Following the gradual departure of the various support function representatives, the unit's production management team – Second Line Manager and FLMs – discuss those matters which principally concern themselves. These may relate to unit and team targets and budgets, the training and development of staff, issues connected with cost reduction or improved manufacturing performance, items about sporting or social events and also, of course, any disclosures related to company-wide performance and activity, some of which the Second Line Manager may wish to disseminate throughout the manufacturing unit.

THE PRE-SHIFT BRIEFING

FLMs are thus armed with the information concerning all the quality, cost and delivery achievements of the previous shift, plantwide, for the production unit but, most important, *for the work team itself.* They are able to tell of specific quality and process problems fed back to the team, of the actions being taken by support departments, and of the specific commitments to action on the team's behalf; they can forewarn the team about anticipated problems involving the schedule or the supply of materials and, finally, they can add any other items of general information or interest which they wish to make known.

In a nutshell, the FLMs are reporting on the CHECK and ACTION phases from the previous shift and giving their outline PLAN for the team on the forthcoming shift. All this occurs at the pre-shift briefing – a short, sharp activity which takes place immediately before production begins. Present are all members of the production team and the event is conducted by its leader and manager, the production FLM.

The briefing takes place at or adjacent to the team's work area, on the factory floor or, in the case of an indirect support team, in the office where they normally work. The visual measures of team performance are close at hand so that the production FLM, senior engineer, purchase manager or whoever can illustrate the performance of the team by referring to them.

In most GK organisations, the session lasts only five minutes and the guillotine of the start of production imposes a strict discipline. Nevertheless much information can be disseminated, even allowing for some discussion and clarification between participants. A typical pattern of the content of such briefings for production teams is as follows:

1. Previous shift's quality performance for the production unit and especially for the team
2. Internal quality concerns (problems of which the team is aware but which have not affected the downstream)
3. Actions to be taken in respect of 1 and 2 – by support services or by the team
4. Delivery performance for the unit and for the team, the schedule for this shift
5. Any concerns regarding safety, orderliness of the workplace from the previous shift
6. Previous shift's machine performance – actions to be taken
7. Update on materials position, parts shortages
8. Process changes, trials, improvement activities to be undertaken
9. Manning and training deployment of the team on this shift
10. General company and team news
11. Final statement of priorities, targets and objectives for this shift.

In this way, every single team member, every single employee throughout the company, is fully aware of how their team has performed against targets of quality, cost and delivery time in quantiative terms, on the previous shift. They are also aware of outstanding problems and the actions which need to be taken to address them if they are to improve on that performance.

Pre-shift briefings are a vital feature of the business in a GK organisation, not a voluntary activity or an occupational hobby. They are regarded as a normal part of the working day. Attendance is *fully remunerated* and *compulsory*. Team members are expected to be at their place of work at the time stipulated in their employment contract. This means, to all intents and purposes, that they should be in attendance at the pre-shift briefing before it begins. A valuable by-product of the team briefing is that it enables FLMs themselves to confirm attendance. This is what enables GK organisations to eschew time-recording devices.[6]

It should be made clear that these pre-shift briefings, as practised in GK companies, are fundamentally different from the 'team-briefing' initiatives attempted in many organisations, ostensibly to improve the dissemination of company information to all employees. There is much to admire in the sentiment and values which lie behind these initiatives, but they amount to an approach which clearly sees communication as an end in itself. Who, after all, gives a damn that 'the value of the group's tangible assets have increased by 6 per cent in the last quarter' or that 'Frank Hackenbusch has moved from the Hong Kong office to look after sales in Kuala Lumpur'.[7] Not surprisingly, therefore, these initiatives, though beginning in an atmosphere of enthusiasm on the part of management and workforce alike, and though often supported by a considerable investment in training, almost invariably fail, like any other exercise in cultural noise. They usually fail not because the FLMs are inarticulate or inadequately trained but because, quite simply, *they have nothing to say*. There is no post-shift review; there are no team-based measures of performance.

When GK FLMs address their teams at the pre-shift briefing they do so as the captains of their sections, as the managers of their units, not as the conduit through which messages reach employees from on high. The briefing's function is not to hand down the decisions or views of management, a practice despised by the more capable and conscientious FLM and treasured only by those who would disassociate themselves from the responsibilities of management. Neither is it an exercise in selling those management decisions in order to make them palatable to the workforce.

The pre-shift briefing is a business meeting. Its function is to tell the team how it is performing and to start the shift on the right note. It has far more in common with the briefing of a junior or non-commissioned officer to his soldiers before going into action or with the words of a sporting team coach before an important game than it has with the slick rendering of company platitudes which often characterise 'team briefing' in many organisations, that is before the initiative inevitably expires through lack of purpose and the indifference of both parties.

NOTES

1. This aspect of GK disciplines, needed to maintain an ordered workplace, is often referred to as 'FiveS' or 'FiveC' activity. (See Appendix II.)
2. Otto Meikus and the achievements of the Eighth US Air Force featured in the March 1994 issue of *National Geographic* which contains a superb illustration of *Nine-O-Nine* with all its team performance adornments.
3. Though neither is it to assert that 'prudent cash flow management' should be allowed to encompass the despicable and, sadly, all too common practice of deliberately withholding and delaying payments beyond the time agreed with suppliers.
4. This is an example of the power of measuring real outputs and customer satisfaction but it is not, of course, what *should* happen in a GK organisation and indeed the technical department, the materials department and other support functions in this particular company now measure *their own* outputs and, every shift, check their performance with their customers.
5. Vilfredo Pareto's observation that 80 per cent of possible benefits are achieved by 20 per cent of possible efforts – or, negatively, 80 per cent of the damage or discomfort derives from only 20 per cent of problems.

6. A few GK companies none the less retain 'clocking in' for reasons associated with security and safety procedures. Honda's Swindon plant in the UK is an example and it should be noted that, consistent with its declared reasons for the practice, *everyone*, including the chief executive, 'clocks in' using the same system.

7. What concerns production teams most is how they themselves are performing and the impact this has on the company as a whole. Broader aspects of the company's business are best transmitted by other media such as an in-house magazine or by a direct and personal address given by the plant manager or CEO on a regular basis.

11 The Levers at Work

Here's tae us! Whae's like us?
Damn'd few and they're a' deid!

Traditional Scottish toast

This chapter illustrates how the principles described in Chapters 7 to 10 are applied by FLMs in GK organisations as they carry out their daily activities and respond to operational problems. Its purpose is to demonstrate how GK is not a disparate collection of 'Japanese tools and techniques', but a fully integrated manufacturing system comprising mutually reinforcing elements.

In drafting this example I have drawn heavily from my production experience at Nissan. This is a fictionalised account in which I have invented a facility and set of process problems which can be readily understood and therefore sustain the objectives of the exercise, without the lengthy and involved explanations which would otherwise be required of a more technically accurate account. I have, nevertheless, endeavoured to reflect faithfully the most important aspects, namely the production management systems, roles and responsibilities, production disciplines and working practices of a real and highly successful GK company.

THE SCENARIO: PALADIN MOTORS

This company, however, is called Paladin Motors and it makes pick-up trucks. About a third of its volume is for the domestic market; the rest is exported to some 30 other countries. The plant has most of the main components of automotive manufacture on its 700-acre site as illustrated in Figure 11.1.

Final Assembly is the setting for our story. They complete 4200 trucks per month on two production shifts. Day shift consists of five days per week from 08.00 until 16.45. Night shift is four nights, Monday/Tuesday until Thursday/Friday, each beginning at 21.00 and finishing at 07.00. Teams of workers, together with their FLMs and shift managers, rotate between day and night shift every fortnight. During production, a truck comes off the end of the

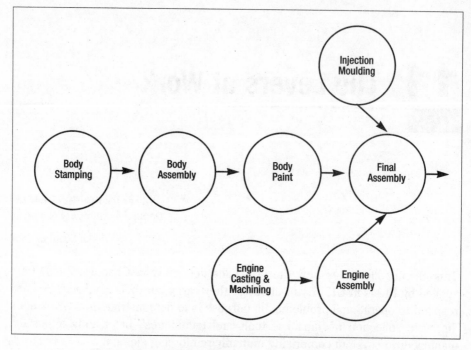

Figure 11.1 Paladin trucks: product flow through main facilities

line every four minutes, which means that every one of the direct workers on the factory has, in theory, a work assignment of four minutes per truck.

Although Paladin make only one model at this plant, there are seven body variants (including two-seat and four-seat options and left- and right-hand drive), six engine and transmission types, five levels of trim, ranging from basic to deluxe, and three colours for interior trim parts. Adding the differing commercial and legislative requirements for overseas markets means many different possible combinations of vehicle, each with their own specific problems at every stage of assembly (Figure 11.2).

The assembly line consists of body carriers which, when the system is full, hold 76 trucks. Finally, the trucks are dropped on to a twin-slat floor conveyor from which they are driven off the line for final inspection and test. The line is divided into seven geographical 'zones', each with its own production team, led by a 'supervisor'.

Zone 1 starts with a painted body, removes the doors (loading them on to a separate door line), fits wiring harnesses, sound deadeners, sunroofs, carpets, engine bay trim and so on.

Door Zone builds up complete door sets, fitting glass, locks, arm rests, door trim, speakers and so on, before the completed doors travel by overhead conveyor to be fitted again to their original bodies on Zone 5.

Zone 2 fits front and rear lamps, headliners, interior trim, pedal boxes, steering columns, suspension struts and so on.

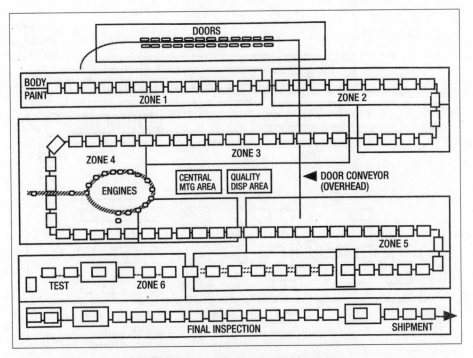

Figure 11.2   Paladin trucks: Final Assembly

Zone 3 sub-assembles and fits instrument panels, fits front and rear screens and bumpers and so on, and carries out a functional check on all electrical parts fitted up to this point.

Zone 4 carries out final assembly of and fits engine and other underbody components, including brakepipes, exhausts, steering racks, fuel tanks and so on.

Zone 5 fits road wheels, seats, steering wheel, makes final connections of wiring and hoses on the engine bay, refits complete doors, adds the fluids, fits battery and drives the truck off the end of the line.

Zone 6 is the inspection, test and repair line, where road wheels and headlamps are aligned, trucks are tested for water leaks, for all aspects of functionality ('roller test'), exhaust emissions and full visual inspection; there are areas to repair any defective trucks, including original paint and body faults and any secondary damage.

Alan Harper is the 'A shift' supervisor for Zone 5 (Figure 11.3).

Alan is *totally* accountable for everything that happens between Station 52 and the end of the twin-slat conveyor. He has the remit and range of responsibilities described in Chapter 7. Like his partner, Sean Flynn, who runs the zone on B Shift, he has 18 people on his team. This figure is derived from a standard time (averaged out on the basis of the best estimated mix of product variants) of 64.8 minutes. This gives a manning figure 'required to run' (RTR) of 16.2 people. Add to this a check operator plus an allowance for holidays, unplanned absence and

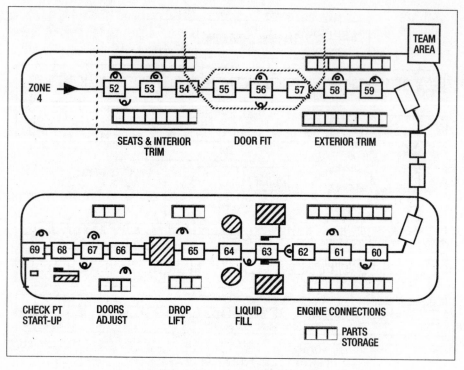

Figure 11.3 Final Assembly, Zone 5

other contingencies, and Zone 5 has a 'required on payroll' (ROP) manning figure of 18. Because of past productivity gains arising from *kaizen* improvements, Alan and Sean usually run their operation with only 15.5 people. Company-budgeted assumptions about standard time and budgeted manning figures simply have not caught up with them yet. They are both confident that, when they do, they will have already moved on to a practical need for an RTR figure of 15 or less. True to the best standards of GK training that they have received about lean production, Alan and Sean have concentrated all the slack time in one assignment on Station 66. In this way they have made all the inherent waste in the job distribution *visible*. They can also do something useful with this time: the half-assignment is usually given to one of the Team Leaders so that they have time to carry out the demands of the role.

Two team members hold the job title of 'Team Leader'. As such they are paid about 15 per cent extra, for which they perform the duties described in Chapter 8. The Team Leaders are respected throughout the team for their hands-on skill and job knowledge, as is the last team member in the line-up: the check and repair operator. This is the team's back stop, its goalkeeper, the zone's last line of defence in ensuring, as far as possible, that no defective trucks leave the zone. This person also has a very broad skills matrix and a comprehensive knowledge of all the product quality standards that apply to the zone's operations, together with the parts specifications for virtually every truck variant. The role is usually a stepping stone and proving ground for a future Team Leader appointment. Check and repair operators do not answer to a QA department or anyone other than their supervisor. They are a resource that belongs to the team, together with the data they collect on faults found within the zone. Although there is nothing secret about these data, they are primarily for team consumption – the information they need to identify and resolve process problems.

THE FIRST DAY

07.20–08.00

It is a winter's morning, a Tuesday, the second day of the second week that A Shift are working days. Alan walks through the Final Assembly plant towards Zone 5. He passes the central meeting area, where the two shift managers have their desks and where B Shift's post-shift review is still in session. He will clearly have to wait a while before his customary handover discussion with his opposite number. Alan looks in on the CSA display area.

CSA is customer satisfaction audit. It is the most important measure of quality, of *anything*, in the whole plant. CSA results are published across the whole of Paladin's organisation worldwide. Related in concept to the J.D. Power survey, one of the main independent evaluations of quality for the motor industry, CSA attempts to examine quality from the perspective of the customer.

A specialist team of CSA inspectors selects two vehicles at random from the end of the twin-slat conveyor, every shift. They submit the vehicles to a thorough inspection and mark up the vehicles where they find any item which could be a source of dissatisfaction to the customer, regardless of whether or not they meet Paladin's current quality standards or engineering specifications. (The latter *are*, however, vigorously applied where the vehicles are tested and inspected in Zone 6 and by similar 'check and repair' zones at the end of Body Assembly, Body Paint, Engine Assembly and the rest.)

Faults are numerically rated in terms of their seriousness, from a fairly minor 0.2 to an apocalyptic and virtually unheard-of 10. The higher the total score, the worse the truck. Paladin's average plantwide performance is currently 7, as opposed to 11 a year ago. During the same period the plantwide target has come down from 14 to 8. Of the 8, Final Assembly has a target of 4. The 4 is further broken down between the zones by a consensus of the supervisors and on the basis of past history and operational difficulty. Zone 5's current target for CSA is 0.7.

The CSA display area is brightly lit and highly visible. A two-by-four-metre board maintained by the CSA Team Leader shows a composite bar chart of average weekly CSA performance, in total and for the various production facilities, and reveals a steadily improving trend. Alan examines the two trucks which were audited on night shift. Sean's team might have had a clean bill of

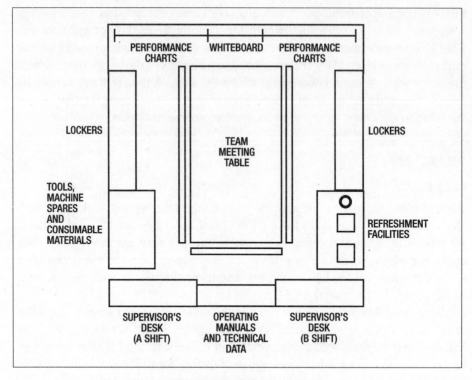

Figure 11.4 Zone 5 team area

health but for a stain of red liquid on the top of the engine – power-steering fluid. Alan suppresses a groan. He knows all about the problems of power-steering fluid.

Alan makes his way to the team area on his zone. This is the command post, where he and Sean have their desks. It is also the central focus for the team: where they assemble, where they hold their meetings, where they keep their tools and personal effects, where they take their coffee breaks, where they display and discuss their performance (Figure 11.4).

Alan begins to bring his performance charts and graphs up to date, starting with the team's off-line quality as measured by CSA, roller test, and final inspection. At the same time he makes a note of the things he wants to mention at his pre-shift briefing.

Alan's last shift was not a good one. To begin with there was the incident of secondary damage which was picked up in final inspection after leaving the zone: a small paint chip, through to the metal, near the rear corner of the left-hand door. A similar problem occurred last Wednesday and again during the night shift of last Thursday/Friday. Sean had to account for it at B Shift's post-shift review. Secondary damage is always a sensitive and difficult problem. The effort and cost of repair in Zone 6 is significant and any likely common causes are always difficult to pin down because of the relative infrequency of occurrence. Secondary damage to doors is especially embarrassing for Alan. Though no one actually points an accusing finger, only Door Assembly Zone and Zone 5 handle doors. Demerits on doors picked out on CSA audits are invariably shared between these two zones unless the cause can be pinpointed. Alan had exhaustive discussions with Ruth Perlmann, the A Shift Door Assembly supervisor, yesterday to no avail: too many possibilities and not enough hard facts.

Then there were six faults identified by Zone 6 relating to routing problems in the engine bay. Four of these were incidents of the temperature-sensor lead passing over the coolant expansion-tank hose: it should pass *under*, according to both the quality standard and the Standard Operation sheet which Alan himself has written and has frequently reinforced to his operators on Station 62. This is not a new problem. Every once in a while it rears its ugly head. This job, concludes Alan, is just too easy to get wrong.

Also, Alan had his worst CSA demerit in two years for a leftover seat-fixing bolt found on the floor of the truck: a silly, simple and costly error. As Alan draws in the graph line for his team's performance on CSA, he sees that this has significantly worsened.

Finally, there is the most frustrating problem of all. Paladin have recently invested in new equipment to fill the power-steering system with fluid (Figure 11.5). The equipment was successfully commissioned last week and a much tighter quality standard for the fluid level was introduced. The target level is 5mm below the 'max' line on the reservoir. (More than that and customers are thought to get anxious; less and they might think Paladin is being stingy with its fluid.)

Between 11.00 and 12.00 yesterday, final inspection found a dozen trucks to be

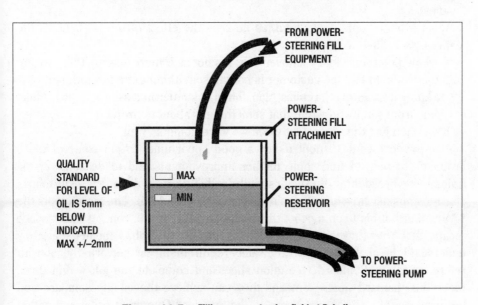

Figure 11.5   Filling power-steering fluid at Paladin

below the minimum tolerance for the level of fluid. Alan moved fast. He added the fluid levels to the checklist of his 'check and repair man', Nazim Aziz, armed him with a jug of fluid to top up any non-conforming levels and made urgent calls to Final Assembly's facilities engineer and maintenance Team Leader to examine the equipment. While their study was in progress, Dave Rosenthal, one of Alan's Team Leaders, had to fill the fluid by hand – an arduous task, involving the need to start the engine and turn the steering wheel back and forth to draw the fluid. The examination drew no conclusions. There was nothing obviously wrong with the equipment, although it was still underfilling. For the rest of the afternoon Nazim continued to top up the fluid. This was an almost impossible task to conduct with any accuracy. Another eight failures were marked down on final inspection before the end of the shift, mostly now because of *over*filling. Alan also asked Nazim to record the levels of fluid on each truck *before* topping up in the hope of accumulating data to solve the problem. By the end of Monday's shift, Zone 5 had experienced its worst quality performance for a long time (for whilst Nazim was struggling with power-steering fluid, other items were being missed): a total of 29 faults.

As Alan is marking up the charts, his first team members arrive. John Connel and Shaka Johnson live furthest from the plant, to the west of the county. They share a car and John likes to leave home early to miss the traffic, have some conversation with his team mates and read a newspaper before starting work. John slams a home-made bacon bap into the microwave while Shaka waters a rubber-plant named 'Norman'. Both these items were bought six months ago with money they were awarded to be spent on their team area in recognition of Paladin's 'most improved zone of the year' (as the brass plaque on the wall testifies).

'What a bitch!' comments John, as he sees the effect of the B1 fault on the team's CSA rolling average.

'A whole point for a lousy leftover bolt! It's not as if there was anything wrong with the truck. In fact the customer is getting something extra for nothing!'

'*We* know its a leftover', replies Alan, 'but a customer in a saleroom just thinks it's come from somewhere and that something is about to drop off.'

'It's a bitch just the same. Just when we were doing so well!'

Alan expects a full turnout today: a good opportunity to put some of these problems to bed, to find some further improvements and to do some cross-training for broadening the team's skill flexibility. He looks at the skill matrix chart to consider how he will deploy his team (Figure 11.6). The matrix plots the 18 members of his team against the 16 assignments in the zone. A blank space means that they have negligible competence in the job. ı means that they understand the quality standard and safety requirement, can perform the job with reference to the Standard Operation sheet and complete the job within three times the standard time. ∟ means they can achieve the quality standard and perform the job, without reference to the Standard Operation sheet and within

	52R SEATS INT. TRIM	52L SEATS INT. TRIM	53 INT. TRIM	56R FIT DOORS (RH)	56L FIT DOORS (LH)	58 EXT. TRIM FRONT	59 EXT. TRIM REAR	60 ENG. BAY (RH)	61 ENG. BAY (LH)	62 ENGINE BAY FRONT	63 FLUIDS FILL	65 BAT. FIT AND TRUCK BED	66 BADGES AND SIDE TRIM	67R ADJUST DOORS (RH)	67L ADJUST DOORS (LH)	69 CHECK AND START UP
Jim Armstrong								—								
Nazim Aziz							□*	□	□	□	□	□				□*
Mary Clarke																
John Connel	—		□*					□	□	□	□	□				□
Sandy Cutherbertson					□*											
Pam Easton (TL)		□		□	□	□	□	□	□	□	□	□	□			□
Gina Falcone								□*	□*	□						
Keith Fisher				□	□	□*	□	□*					□			
Tom Grey				—										—	—	
Jean Halloran	□*	□	□				□		□							
Matt Hedley				□*		□					□*					
Shaka Johnson					□								□	□	□	
Fergus Joyce			—							□*					□*	
Chris Lao	□	□					□									
Tosh McGregor	□			□	□									□*	□	
Elaine Robson			□								—	□*				
Dave Rosenthal (TL)	□	□	□	□	□	□							□*	□	□	□
Paul Taylor		□*														

*Indicates how Alan's team members were deployed on his previous shift

Figure 11.6   Zone 5 skill matrix

standard time. ⊔ means they can achieve the requirements of ⌞ and also train others. ☐ means they are experts on the job: they can contribute to improving the Standard Operation, troubleshoot operational problems (understanding acceptable deviations and appropriate corrective quality actions) and complete the job in 90 per cent of standard time or quicker.

The asterisks in Figure 11.6 do not actually appear on Alan's chart, but they tell us how his people were deployed on his previous shift. On that occasion, Mary Clarke was on holiday and Pam Easton was off the job carrying out Team Leader duties. Dave Rosenthal carried out the half assignment on Station 66 and therefore was able to fulfil the Team Leader role for much of the time.

By now more than half of the team have arrived, and Sean Flynn also makes his way to the team area to debrief Alan about what has happened on night shift.

'Still problems with power steering, I see', remarks Alan.

'I take it you've seen our little problem in CSA. Looks as if somebody's had a nosebleed right by the Paladin logo on the rocker box cover. A fortune has been spent on new equipment and we are filling oil with a jug! By the way, I managed to find a pipette for topping up with a bit more accuracy – it's on the bench at the end of the line. But I still copped six faults on test: three overs and three unders – and half a point in CSA for the spillage, of course. It's a good job it's only power-steering oil and not brake fluid. We'd have to hose down every truck to avoid paint damage!'

'What about the data on fluid levels?'

'Here it is, for what it's worth. All it tells us is that the damned machine's not capable. Either QA change the quality standard or we should just put a match to it! Even if the machine was recalibrated, you couldn't fit this spread of measurements into the tolerance band.'

'I don't know: it worked fine during trials and on Friday. Mary Clarke didn't have a problem with it at all.'

'Maybe there always *was* a problem. Maybe Zone 6 only started looking closely when they found the first one.'

'Maybe. But I still think it's method, not machine. Mary's back from holiday today and I want to look at it again. Any other problems?'

'A few: a couple of wrongly routed temperature-sensor leads, for example.'

'I mean to have another look at that one later today.'

'Before I go, there's something I want to fly by you. I thought about it most of the night. There are 640 bolts on the twin-slat conveyor. On the last Saturday morning of every other month, Maintenance bring somebody in on overtime to check and tighten every one of them. We also have to fork out from our own overtime budgets to have somebody stay back half an hour to drive or push every truck from the twin slat and somebody to come in half an hour on the Monday morning to put them back again.

'Now, how about this? *We* do the maintenance as a TPM exercise. We etch a number into the head of every bolt. Over two months 640 bolts is only eight bolts per shift. We put up a check sheet on the twin slat, and check the bolts as part of a rolling programme. We get the standard time, which helps our efficiency a little, we save 30 minutes' overtime a month and Maintenance save two hours. If you're game, maybe you can discuss it with Charlie Singh [Final Assembly maintenance supervisor]. He's on days this week. OK, I'd best be off: 18 holes and then bed for me. Good luck. See you tomorrow.'

By 07.59 17 team members are present. One more to go. Tosh McGregor is invariably the last to arrive. He has a simple philosophy: 'I refuse to spend any more time in this place than I have to', he says. But Alan has never known Tosh to be late. He is one of the team's skilled veterans: its expert on door and hood adjustment (perhaps the most difficult job to learn), and he has a dry sense of humour which amuses the whole team. Tosh strides briskly into the team area, sits down at his usual place and opens a can of Coke. He looks up at Alan with a wry smile as if to say 'OK, I'm here now. Let's get started!'

08.00–08.05

Alan begins his meeting by giving the full picture of how the unit and particularly how *the team* has performed on the previous shift. He uses the graphs and charts that he has just updated to illustrate this and reminds everybody of the specific problems that have contributed to such a disappointing result on quality. He asks the seat fitters to make a point of checking the truck floor for leftovers after every cycle. He asks everyone, especially those fitting and adjusting doors, to keep an eye open for anything which might shed light on the cause of the secondary damage. He calls for caution when routing hoses and cables in the engine bay, and mentions that, at yesterday's post-shift review, he promised a firm 'cut-off' of the temperature-sensor lead problem by lunchtime. He tells Nazim about the pipette for ameliorating the symptoms of the power-steering fluid problem. Nazim asks if he should continue to record the levels of fluid in each reservoir before topping up.

'No', is the response. 'Instead I want you to jot down the vehicle numbers of any that *don't* need topping up.'

'That shouldn't be much of a chore,' replies Nazim, drily. Alan explains that he wants to carry out an investigation of the problem as soon as the line starts. He will need Mary, Matt and Pam all on Station 63 to help him do this.

Alan hands over to Nazim at this point. Nazim takes the team through his own fault data from the previous shift. These were the faults 'cut off in zone' which he prevented reaching the downstream customer; but they still represent problems that the team must try to resolve at source. Heading the list is power-steering fluid levels. Fifty-one trucks needed to be topped up. Some other problems were:

- five misrouted temperature-sensor leads;
- four headlamp wash/wipers not reseating themselves after operation;
- three body side mouldings misaligned (1mm out of tolerance), all on the left;

- two bull bars misaligned to bumper;
- two screen-wash jets incorrectly set;
- one tool kit not fitted;
- one wrong steering wheel fitted.

Nobody becomes defensive or tries to rationalise away problems. This is a team which is proud of its achievements and genuinely concerned to try to find ways of adding to them. Although, as with any team activity concerned with performance, there will be disappointment or even a degree of embarrassment about individual failings, neither Alan nor Nazim tries to make team members feel uncomfortable about these items. They always stress *what*, not *who*, is the difficulty and what might be done about it. The last thing Alan wants is to introduce the kind of atmosphere which prevailed at his previous company, where fear of recrimination led workers to conceal problems.

Included in Nazim's list are also seven faults which originated in upstream zones:

- three automatic transmissions wrongly set (trucks not starting in 'park');
- two brake-system leaks (as detected by the fluid-fill equipment);
- two missing grommets on door-wiring harness.

These faults originated in Zone 3, Zone 4 and the Door Assembly Zone, respectively. The brake-system leaks were loose brakepipe unions which Dave Rosenthal fixed on the twin slat and then Nazim filled using the back-up brake-fill equipment. Zone 3 and Door Zone Team Leaders themselves came up to the twin slat to fix the other faults before the trucks came off the line. Of course, all three problems, and others, will be the subject of discussion in the pre-shift briefings of the upstream zones.

Alan's next subject is downtime. The only downtime on the previous shift was the 45 minutes lost while the power-steering oil equipment was being investigated.

Alan warns the team that there will be a higher than usual proportion of four-seat models on today's schedule. In particular there will be four in succession which will hit the zone at about 09.40. Because the zone is fully manned today, Alan has no plans to change the content of work assignments to overcome the problem. Instead, he simply tells Dave, the Team Leader with most experience on seats, to make himself ready to give support to Paul and Jean on Station 52 when required.

On materials, Alan tells of a problem with painted door mirrors on the upper-range models. Some doors may well arrive without mirrors. These will be retrofitted in Zone 6 when the supplier company has resolved its colour-matching problems. Alan confirms that no one on Sean's team is aware of any problems with lineside stock of any part.

Alan discusses today's team deployment. He proposes few changes from yesterday, especially until some of the team's pressing problems are resolved. Both Mary and Matt will be required on fluids for at least the first hour. Chris Lao, the novice on Station 62, will remain there, with Pam Easton giving coaching and support. Alan gives Chris an objective of reaching $\llcorner$ standard by the end of the shift. Chris seems cautiously optimistic but confesses to a lack of confidence on turbo diesel engines. Alan promises personally to look at the problem with him.

Alan tells the team that he will be meeting John Brickhill, the materials engineer, to discuss battery stillages. He takes out a drawing of the proposed stillage and pins it to the notice board. 'Any comments on this before 1.30 p.m. gratefully received: either write them on the drawing or tell me. Sean and his team have already seen it.

'Finally, while we have a full squad, let's start a full station-improvement exercise this afternoon on Station 59. There are a lot of materials, some awkward motions and too much walking, bending and stretching. I think we could take a good 20 seconds off the job. Pam, can you go to the central meeting area, book one of the camcorders and a monitor, then meet me on fluid fill?'

Alan pins up a copy of a newspaper cutting circulated at last night's post-shift review. 'This is an article about Paladin's recent entry on the Trans-Australian Rough Road Race: you may find it interesting. Also the annual five-a-side football competition is nearly on us again. If we want to enter a team we have to register it by Friday. Names to John Connel if you're interested.

'Any questions or problems?...

'OK, power-steering levels ... leftovers ... John, Gina, Chris, watch the routing – you *know* the Standard Op. ... and everybody keep an eye out for damaged doors ...' (Alan gestures towards the visual management boards.) 'Let's get back to where we should be! That's all.'

The team grab their working gear and move to their workstations. They take their work tools from cupboards and locations lineside. At 08.05 precisely the conveyors kick into action.

The full content of Alan's meeting, even though it only lasted five minutes, is too much to present concisely here. Alan's pre-shift briefing is only one of nearly 50 happening at the same time across the whole organisation. Not only are these direct operating teams like Zone 5, but maintenance teams, materials supply teams, teams of engineers, production controllers, purchasers, accounts people, HR people all follow a similar format, starting with and driven by a concrete understanding of how well they are currently meeting the needs of downstream customers and what they need to do about improving *this very day*.

08.05–10.15

Alan sets up his study of fluid fill. Pam is his most experienced Team Leader and has already undergone much of the off-the-job training to equip her for a supervisor's job. Alan wants Pam to take ownership of the problem as a development exercise, but he suggests a way forward.

'Mary had no apparent problem with this machine on Friday. Let her do the first three trucks, then Matt the next three and so on. Watch very carefully for any differences in method – not just *between* Matt and Mary but also any variation on what they do. Jot down who does which vehicle numbers with any observations next to each. It'll take about 20 minutes for Mary's first truck to reach Nazim; then I'll bring you some feedback on what's happening.' (The final, crucial level of oil cannot be measured immediately after filling; only after the engine has been started up and the oil is pumped through the system.)

Alan makes two visits in the meantime. He seeks out Charlie Singh, the maintenance supervisor, to discuss Sean's idea for the twin-slat maintenance. Charlie is enthusiastic. In fact Charlie's Team Leader on Alan's shift has already spoken to Charlie about it. Sean and Charlie's Team Leader will now jointly write a Standard Operation for the work and also pass over the tools to Zone 5. The new regime for twin-slat maintenance will begin after the next full weekend overhaul. Alan agrees to arrange for the transfer of the maintenance time to Zone 5.

He then calls on the Door Zone supervisor, Ruth Perlmann. No joy in tracing the secondary damage; there have been no recent examples and the trail has gone cold.

'Apart from the missing door grommet, is everything all right at your end from us?', asks Ruth.

'Fine at the moment. But don't worry, I'll call you as soon as you give me a problem!'

Alan then returns to his zone and touches base with Nazim. 'How goes it?'

'So far so good. First five trucks needed topping up with power-steering oil.' (The first five trucks were already in the system from night shift.) 'This pipette thing certainly helps. *Our* first three trucks are fine for oil level; the next one underfilled. Here are the vehicle numbers. The only other fault found is one accelerator cable which hadn't been adjusted correctly.'

Alan goes towards the fluid-fill station but a flashing light and buzzer tells him that Tosh McGregor and Fergus Joyce are having difficulties adjusting doors. They seem to be running out of time and moving further down the twin slat with every truck.

'Left-side fenders', grunts Tosh. 'Every one of them is too far inboard and we can't get a flush condition with the front edge of the doors. Dave has been on the phone to the paint shop.' (The Sealer Zone in Body Paint are responsible for setting fenders.) Just then Dave comes back to his station on the twin slat.

'George Thomson [Sealer Zone Team Leader] says he'll be here in about ten minutes', announces Dave. He sets about his own half assignment and then uses the spare time to adjust the fenders himself before they reach Station 67. Alan helps out by adjusting hoods on the next three trucks, so that Tosh and Fergus can work their way back to their own station and the point where Dave has already pulled out the fenders and secured them to their correct position.

Alan finally reaches Station 63. 'Mary's method seems to be effective but Matt's first truck is underfilled.' (Mary is now doing the job again and Matt and Pam are watching closely.) 'What have you found out?'

'I think we've cracked it,' claims Pam. 'Not easy to spot at first, but the main difference is that Matt both sub-assembles and fits the windshield wipers while the power-steering fluid is filling, whereas Mary can't fit the wipers so quickly. So she fits the nozzle, starts the fill cycle, sub-assembles the wipers, removes the nozzle, *then* fits the wipers.'

This means that Mary takes 0.3 minutes longer than Matt for the whole assignment but that the power-steering nozzle is in place for 10 seconds *less* after the filling cycle is complete.

'It didn't matter how long you left the nozzle in place on the old equipment', explains Pam, 'just so long as the truck didn't move more than five metres with it still fitted. But this new gear is like the brake-fluid fill. Ten seconds after the flashing light and buzzer indicate that the filling cycle is complete, the machine starts to suck back to remove any drops of oil from the nozzle. If the nozzle is still in position at this point, it actually starts to draw out small but sufficient quantities of oil back from the reservoir.'

'So, what do you propose?' asks Alan.

'First we get Matt to try out Mary's method and confirm the process at the end, as before. Then I'll get the Standard Op. sheet for power-steering oil fill and write on a critical point about the need to remove the nozzle within *5 seconds* after the cycle is complete. You sign it and pass it over to B Shift.'

'Is that all?'

'Then we make sure that everyone with an I or better on the job is taught the new method.'

'Then what?'

'Have I missed something?'

'Mary obviously has some trouble fitting wipers. We'll have to look at the Standard Op. for wiper fit and find out what her difficulty is, regardless of when we do it in the sequence. But that can wait. First I'd like you to go on to Station 60 and free up Keith Fisher. We need his help on Station 66, readjusting some fenders. We'll need Dave on hand at the front of the line in five minutes when those four-seater trucks arrive.'

Alan has mixed feelings about the outcome of the fluid-fill investigation. He is pleased with Pam's performance and relieved that the problem appears to be resolved. But he regrets having reacted to the problem initially in the way that he did, presupposing a machine problem and calling in Engineering. If, according to his more usual inclinations, he had studied the job first, he might not only have saved Engineering some time but also both Zone 5 teams a great deal of discomfort.

Alan notes the arrival of George Thomson, Team Leader from the Body Paint Sealing Zone. He has one of his team members with him. Dave is demonstrating the fender problem. Keith Fisher has moved to take over Dave's assignment.

Dave goes to help out with fitting rear seats on Station 52. George and his colleague set about checking and fixing every fender between the twin slat and their home base – some 130 trucks in all. Alan expects no less, even though nearly all the offending trucks will not have come from George's own team but from the night shift. Body Paint are simply looking after their customers.

Next, Alan moves down into Zone 6 to make his first visit of the day to his own customers. He seeks out the Team Leader on the 'tester line'. 'Anything for me, Mel?' he asks.

'Let's see', ponders Mel, looking at his board, 'two power-steering fluid overfills; first two trucks of the day ...'

'I think we've killed that one off now, Mel, but let me know straight away if you find any more.'

'... one accelerator cable slack: 2 mm overplay and ... and one "left-hand door gap rear", 1mm wider than tolerance.'

'We've had a few problems on doors this morning. I think maybe it was missed as a result. Nevertheless, I'll feed it back.'

Not a bad start, muses Alan. He meets Gary Pearce, a supervisor from Body Assembly, who is obviously also checking out the downstream.

'How goes it with you, Alan? Any problems with our end?'

'Not so far, but you'll be the first to know.'

It is 10.15. The line has stopped and the team has retired to the team area for morning coffee. Alan pauses to glance at Nazim's check board. Apart from the first few power-steering oil problems everything has gone well. The run of four-seat models has now been completed without problems.

10.15–12.30

There is little formal conversation over coffee. Alan feeds back his findings in Zone 6 and congratulates the team on a good start to the shift. He asks if there are any problems. Tom Grey requests a day off for the coming Friday. Alan checks the holiday planner. Since no one else has a holiday on that day he gives his assent. Tosh and Fergus confirm to Alan that the fender problem has been resolved.

At 10.30 the team are back to their positions and the line starts up again. Alan picks up the appropriate Standard Operation sheets and goes to watch Chris Lao perform his job. Chris seems to be coping fairly well but is flustered when he encounters the first of two turbo diesels. While fitting an air filter he drops all his bolts and washers on to the floor. Alan jumps in to connect the turbo harness and fit the top radiator hose in order to give both of them a breathing space before the next truck.

'OK, turbo diesel air filters ... three bolts in the right hand, three washers in the left.'

'But I'm left-handed.'

'Of course you are. So, when you've pushed the bolts through the washers they need to be in your right hand so that you can hold the air tool with your left. That way you don't have to switch hands, you save time and you're far less likely to drop them on the floor. Try it. It'll be strange at first but after three or four times you'll find it's a better method.'

Alan takes the opportunity to watch all three engine-bay assignments. He has already decided how to resolve his most common routing problem once and for all. He describes his solution to Pam, who is now again freed from the line after Keith Fisher has reverted to his usual assignment.

'We need to connect the temperature-sensor gauge *before* the expansion tank hose. That way it'll be correctly routed *naturally*. The only failsafe way of doing it is to move the sensor-gauge job up line to another station. Besides, if we simply switch the sequence on Station 62, it'll require an extra tool change. The most logical place is Station 61, but Gina already has a very full assignment. What can we take from Gina that is about 0.1 of a minute that can go down to Station 62 and doesn't need an air tool?'

'Radiator warning labels seems the obvious choice.'

'All right, let's make the switch. You won't need to reinstruct anyone on Station 61 since they all have at least ∟ status on Station 62 operations. All you need do is move the material, notify the line feeder that this is where we want it from now on and teach Chris to fit the labels. Make sure he understands the quality standard for the label position and also how the truck's build sheet tells which of the six different language labels go on which trucks.'

Alan then checks his intray. He finds full CSA reports from the previous week (which he pins to the notice board); a design change notification and new engineering specification for the introduction of bolts with captivated washers for engine mountings (he makes a note in his diary on the timing of the change and the time by which he needs to produce a new Standard Operation), and a note from process engineering telling him of a meeting on Thursday about the new CD player which the zone will be required to fit from next month on high specification models.

By now the first CSA vehicle will have been evaluated and Alan makes his way to the display area. Just before lunch the manufacturing director, quality manager and all the production managers will be making their own visit. Like most of the other supervisors at Paladin, Alan is keen to get there first. The truck scores 8.2 points overall; not so good. Main contributory problems are a paint run, 1.0; disc mark on the body, 2.0; protruding front screen finisher, 0.5; squeaking window winder on driver's door, 0.5; and an uneven gap between the radiator grill and left-side headlamp, 0.5. Zone 5, however, has a clean sheet.

Alan goes back to his zone. Pam is explaining to Fred Wilkinson, the line feeder, the changes she needs to the delivery location of the fixing for the temperature-sensor lead and the radiator labels. Fred is formally part of the linefeed team, works for his supervisor, Tom Murray, and naturally attends Tom's pre-shift meetings. But like the other linefeeders, Fred is assigned to a direct production zone and does everything he can to look after his particular customer.

12.30–15.00

It is lunchtime. About a third of the team opt for lunch in the company restaurant. The rest eat sandwiches in the team area. Alan tries to make a point of having lunch in the team area at least twice per week.

Alan mentions to those present the results in CSA but avoids too much discussion about work. Most of the team are talking about football, their plans for the weekend and such-like. John and Keith, however, are having a quiet but animated discussion in one corner and appear to be sketching and scribbling on scraps of paper.

'No, *you* show him', encourages John. 'It's *your* idea.'

Keith brings Alan a sketch (Figure 11.7).

Keith is a quiet, shy type who does not often come forward with improvement ideas. 'It's a tool for fitting the top engine mounting.'

'How does it work?'

'It's easier if I show you.'

'Fine. Now? ... or would you rather wait until after your lunch break?'

'Now's OK by me.'

'It's brilliantly simple', chips in John supportively, as Keith and Alan make their way to Station 61. 'Don't know why I never thought of it before!'

At Station 61 Keith demonstrates his idea. He shows how it is often awkward to line up the holes in the mounting bracket with those on the engine block (Figure 11.8).

'We have to start the first bolt by hand to line everything up', explains Keith. 'Sometimes we have to haul the engine over with one arm until we catch the

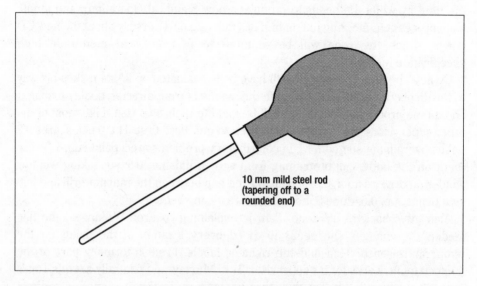

10 mm mild steel rod (tapering off to a rounded end)

Figure 11.7   Keith Fisher's alignment tool

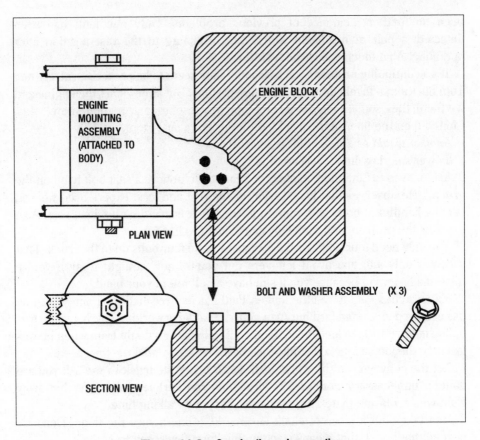

Figure 11.8   Securing the engine mounting

thread. What I'm suggesting is we just drop this tool down the middle pair of holes to align them all. We can then just gun in two bolts through the other two holes, take out the tool and gun in the third bolt. I reckon it'll save at least 10 seconds on every truck. All I need is some mild steel rod of different thicknesses to experiment with and a screwdriver or chisel handle or something; they'll have those in the *kaizen* workshop.' (The *kaizen* workshop comprises an area containing simple machine tools and welding and cutting equipment, for those certified to use them, and some basic materials such as box and rod steel, angle strip, steel plates of varying thicknesses, sheets of perspex, gravity feed rollers, plastic drainpipes and other materials. It is the common resource of all the production teams.)

'It'll only take me 20 minutes,' says Keith.

'OK, go and make one straight after lunch. I'll get Pam to hold your job down while you do it. Then we'll do some trials.'

13.00–15.00

Alan makes his second visit to Zone 6 to check his downstream quality. There has been no further incidence of previous problems. Only one fault has been detected: a pair of headlamp wipers not returning to the rest position after operating. Alan touches base with Nazim.

'It's a continuing problem', says Nazim. 'They seem to be properly seated when Tom fits them – firmly down on the rubber stops. But after I start the engine and try them, they sometimes rise up and I have to reset them. And then there's this. I found it on the floor of the truck.' He holds out a seat mounting bolt.

Another would be 1.0 in CSA, reflects Alan.

'Power-steering fluid levels are fine.'

Alan moves to Station 52 to observe seat fit. He notices a seat bolt lying on the ground. He observes that Paul Taylor, his newest and least experienced worker, takes a handful of bolts with him on to the truck every time he fits a seat. Alan explains the problem and the likely consequences in CSA.

'You only need four bolts for the seats; only take four bolts on to the truck. That way, not only will you avoid leftovers but you'll know straight away if you've missed a fastening because you'll still have a bolt left in your hand.'

Alan watches Paul for a little longer. Paul has just reached the point where he has achieved an └ standard but Alan notices that he is working nearly two metres upline in his efforts to 'get ahead of himself', a legacy no doubt from when he was learning the job and lacked confidence in his ability to hold the linespeed.

'Let the conveyor do the work, Paul. Let *it* bring the truck to *you*. All you are doing is unnecessary work. You're stretching your airline, walking further away from your tools and materials and increasing your walking time.'

Alan takes out a piece of chalk and marks a line across the floor. 'Don't go beyond that line. If that means standing idle for a few seconds, so be it.'

Alan returns to his desk. He takes out the Standard Operation sheet for fitting seats and composes an additional critical point about only picking up four seat bolts and the reason for so doing. He also finds on his desk the sheet which Pam has amended to record the new Standard Operation for fitting power-steering fluid. He signs both Standard Operations and puts them on Sean's desk for his approval. Tomorrow, Alan will make sure that his Team Leaders have thoroughly taught the new methods to all team members who carry out these operations.

He then goes to Station 60 to observe the progress of Keith's trial. It seems that he has already experimented with mild steel rods of varying thicknesses and degrees of taper until he has found one which gives the best result. By now Pam is confirming the new method. She has given her stopwatch to Keith who is timing her activity.

'OK,' says Pam, after torquing up the third and final bolt. 'How was that?'

'0.48 of a minute to fit the engine mounting.'

'0.25 faster than the old method, but I'm still 0.1 slower than you.'

'With this thickness rod I find you don't need to wiggle it; it just drops down and lines up the holes perfectly. I'll show you on the next one.'

'Would you like me to write up a new Standard Op. for this when we're through?' asks Pam of Alan.

'Just make some notes and leave me the tool. Sean's team can have a go at writing this one up. You'd better set up the exercise on Station 59 while we still have access to the camcorder. I'll join you there after my meeting with John Brickhill.'

Alan goes back to the team area to meet the materials engineer. After some discussion a conclusion is almost reached.

'So, if we delete the bottom shelf and fit this type of wheel, the contractors can go ahead?' asks John.

'Not quite', replies Alan. 'They can make *one* and we'll try it on both shifts.'

15.00–16.45

The team reassembles for its afternoon break. Alan reminds all of them to make a quick examination of lineside parts. Dave will be making a brief tour near the end of the shift to note any possible problems with materials.

After the break, Alan again visits Zone 6 to check the quality of the trucks leaving his zone and touches base with Nazim to find out if there are any other problems. He then systematically moves through the whole zone, station by station, carrying out an audit to ensure that the condition of the equipment, materials and the workplace is being maintained in good order. He usually does this at three varying times each week and uses the checklist (Figure 11.9) against which he marks the observations which he will feed back to the team at the next pre-shift briefing.

Alan spends two or three minutes on each station. Halfway through the exercise he goes into the team area to subject it, also, to these criteria. He collects the set of Standard Operation sheets for Station 62. When he reaches Chris Lao's station and has completed his audit, he observes Chris performing his assignment on three trucks. He checks that Chris is following the Standard Operation and also the quality standard of the trucks that Chris has completed. Chris's next truck is a four-wheel drive with a turbo diesel engine. Alan starts his stopwatch, observes Chris's performance carefully, and checks the finished result as before. Alan shows Chris the time of 3.88 minutes displayed on his watch:

'Well done, I think we have to give you an ⌞ standard.'

Alan continues his audit. While moving through the door fit area, he sees that Shaka has abandoned his own job and is helping Sandy, who is looking bemused, on the other side of the station. Three male electrical connectors are breaking out of the door cavity and only two female connecters are coming from the body of the truck. Sandy supposed that the wrong door had been loaded or the wrong door harness fitted. Shaka, kneeling on the floor with a roll of masking tape, is explaining which of the three door connectors is redundant for this model and how the Door Zone ought to have folded this back on itself, taping it up to stop rattles and tucked it back inside the door. Shaka is a ☐ standard on door fit. He

CLEAR OUT		
Litter and leaks	No. (includes oil, air, swarf, process liquids)	☐
Unnecessary items	No. of unnecessary items (e.g. unused and/or obsolete equipment and parts)	☐
Necessary but missing items	No. of equipment, tools and parts regularly required but not available	☐
Safety: access and operating areas	No. of items blocking or intruding into safety accesses, walkways and operational areas	☐
CONFIGURE		

Safety equipment	No. of safety items that are not:
	  – available
	  – operational
	  – identified clearly
		☐

Items not in correct locations	No. of items which have a set location but are not in it	☐
Lack of identification where signs or labels would help but are absent	No. of items (parts, switches, shelves and tools)	☐
CLEAN AND CHECK		
Equipment condition	0=Clean and professional 3=Some mess but operationally OK 6=Could affect operational performance (e.g. broken gauges, temporary fixes etc.) 10=Condition affects operational performance	☐
Floor and walls	0=Clean and professional 3=Some mess but operationally OK 6=Could affect operational performance (e.g. broken windows, peeling paint, leaking roofs) 10=Condition affects operational performance	☐
Routine maintenance	0=Comprehensive routine maintenace. Schedule up to date 3=Some routine maintenance. Schedule up to date 6=Some routine maintenance. Not all up to date 10=Breakdown response only	☐
TOTAL SCORE		☐

Figure 11.9 Zone condition audit

will have no problems catching up with his own assignment after helping Sandy out.

'How many of those are you getting these days?' asks Alan.

'Hasn't happened for a while. Mine was OK – somebody must have just been distracted. It's no trouble, really.'

'Let me or one of the Team Leaders know if you get any more. The trouble with "no trouble" is that, if we don't tell them, they'll keep on doing it.'

It is now 16.00 and the next truck in CSA should be completed. When Alan arrives at the display area he finds that his team have caused a 0.2 fault for 'unseated headlamp wipers'. These have raised up 3 mm from their rubber stoppers. Then there is a 1.0 fault for secondary damage to the left-hand door, rear corner. Alan's spirits sink. He had been having a good shift. Still, it had to happen sooner or later, since this problem has still not been solved. Alan and his team will share the value of this demerit with Ruth Perlmann's door assembly team.

As Alan moves back towards his zone he meets Ruth coming towards the display area.

'You don't look so happy, Alan.'

'Neither will you be when you see what I've just seen.'

'I already have, but I now know the cause. *It's a carrier.*'

'What makes you so sure?'

'These are the vehicle numbers of every truck with the problem during the last week, up to and including this one.' Ruth shows Alan a scrap of paper.

'There are 140 sets of door carriers in the system, some with doors on them, some now empty and making their way back to Zone 1. The gaps between the incidents of damage is always around 140 or multiples of 140. The offending carrier obviously doesn't damage a door every time – that's why I couldn't see a pattern at first.'

'So where's this rogue carrier now?'

'Looking at the time this truck came off line, I reckon it's now queuing up among the empties above Zone 1. We *could* get one of Tim Jackson's people to check each one as they come down.'

'No', answers Alan. 'I don't think we should risk it slipping through the net and going round the system again. Besides, its *our* problem, let's nail it now!'

Ruth and Alan climb up to the gantry which runs alongside the door conveyor return line. About 30 sets of door carriers are slowly making their way back to Station 1 at the very start of the main assembly line. Starting at opposite ends of the queue of carriers, they work towards the middle, carefully checking every left-hand door carrier, especially near where it would contact the door in the vicinity of the damage. Alan waves Ruth over on reaching the seventh carrier. He holds up a washer which he has taken from between the rearmost pair of rubber blocks which form a 'V' to hold the bottom edge of the doors. At the bottom of the 'V' are small tell-tale particles of paint.

'Here's our culprit. It must have fallen unnoticed between the blocks.'

'It's from a window winder – one of ours', acknowledges Ruth. 'I can arrange to have the CSA points reassigned.'

'It hardly matters now, does it? At least we've solved it. But let's check the others while we're here – just in case.'

Alan returns to the zone and checks its current status with his Team Leaders. Dave confirms that there are no problems with lineside materials and that there have been no breakdowns during the shift. Pam has completed a video recording of the operation at Station 59. She has rebooked the video monitor for the following morning so that the team members can watch themselves working and come up with improved working methods and an improved station layout.

At 16.40 the line stops and the team begins to put away their tools. Most drop in at the team area to collect their belongings. Alan thanks them for their efforts and for what seems to have been a successful shift. He is specific about contributions where appropriate. At 16.45 the team make their way home. Alan completes his shift report. This is used to calculate attendance figures, to record overtime and holidays taken, and also to calculate the efficiency of the plant.

16.50–17.15

Alan arrives at the Final Assembly central meeting area for the post-shift review. The meeting is chaired by Jim Henderson, the shift manager, Alan's boss. Five of the other six supervisors are also present. The supervisor of Zone 2 is on holiday and he is represented by one of his Team Leaders.

Also present are a number of key supplier representatives who do not work directly for Jim: Charlie Singh, final assembly maintenance supervisor; Tom Murray, material handling supervisor; Don Harrison, QA supervisor; Anju Patel, process engineer; Bill Casson, facilities engineer and Jane Holland, production control.

Item 1: quality. Don Harrison takes the meeting through all the demerits attributed to Final Assembly found on the shift's CSA audits. Obviously the door damage on the second CSA truck features prominently but Ruth and Alan are able to report on the action already taken and announce that this particular problem has now been eliminated. Tim Jackson, Zone 1 supervisor, also commits to introducing an additional check item for door removal. As part of their Standard Operation, his people on Station 1 will now make a visual check of the rubber blocks on the carriers before loading doors.

Alan also has to commit to action on the headlamp-wiper problem. He informs the meeting that he believes it might be addressed by finding a more effective setting standard and undertakes to carry out trials and report back by the next post-shift review.

The protruding screen finisher, squeaking window winders, gaps between the radiator grill and left headlamp and other problems are also discussed. Each item requires an *action*. Jim ensures that *someone* takes ownership of each and that all undertakings are recorded for future reference should the problem still exist at the next post-shift review.

Ian Robinson, the supervisor of Zone 6, then gives his own report of off-line faults found in his area: majors and repetitive minors. The items raised that concern Zone 5 are, of course, power-steering oil levels and temperature-sensor lead routings. In both cases Alan can report that action has already been taken to eliminate these problems.

Item 2: production schedule. At Paladin the production schedule is not a target, but a *standard*; not something to achieve if possible, but a *customer requirement*. As such it is virtually taken for granted and almost invariably achieved. In Final Assembly, a conveyor-driven facility, this is usually a simple confirmation that the production line has yielded the planned number of vehicles and that the same number have been shipped from Zone 6. Ian Robinson has a target of no more than 40 vehicles in Zone 6 at any time. He usually achieves this easily but at the moment he is feeling the effects of the painted door-mirror problem.

Jane Holland advises that she would like to enrich the model mix on tomorrow's shift and put down as many four-wheel drive vehicles as she can. Jim asks about constraints on the maximum percentage that can be handled. Joe Dixon, the supervisor of Zone 4, who has most of the additional work content for 4 x 4 vehicles, states that they can build 60 per cent 4 x 4s as opposed to the usual 40 per cent, provided that these are evenly spaced and that there are never more than two 4 x 4s in succession. Jane undertakes to load the schedule according to this constraint.

Jim advises that current forecasts indicate volume uplift to 5000 vehicles per month in seven months' time. This will involve a reduction in cycle time to 3.7 minutes. Jane issues each supervisor with a copy of the anticipated ratios of model derivatives. Jim has been asked to submit a manpower budget, based on this information, by the end of the month. He asks that each supervisor consider these implications, together with their current manning levels and further improvements and, having discussed these with their colleagues on B Shift, give an indication of their zones' hiring requirements by the end of the week.

Item 3: unplanned stoppages and machine downtime. For each stoppage or incidence of machine downtime Jim ensures that all further actions to be undertaken and all specific responsibilities for those actions, whether they be by any of the supervisors, Charlie Singh, or both, are faithfully recorded.

Item 4: parts and materials. The most pressing problem is that of painted door mirrors. Don advises that, according to the Supplier Quality Assurance engineer currently at the supplier's factory, a shipment of 240 sets of mirrors of an acceptable standard should reach Paladin by midnight tonight. Alan observes that both Tom and Ruth make a note of this, presumably to pass on to their opposite numbers. Jim asks Tom to ensure that his night-shift colleague gives top priority to shipping these mirrors out to the Door Zone and also that he liaises with B Shift's Zone 6 supervisor to establish his requirements for the unfinished trucks on his zone.

Item 5: other business. By now, their specific items of customer interest having been addressed, the various support representatives have departed, leaving Jim alone with his own team to discuss other matters. Jim has only one item for his team. He hands them a copy of a press release.

'Paladin has just won contracts to supply the National Parks Service and the Royal Canadian Mounted Police. This item will go out to the media the day after tomorrow: make sure your people hear it from you first.'

17.15–17.30

Alan makes one last trip to his team area to complete his zone 'log book' in order to update Sean with the salient points of the day's activity. The other supervisors, the representatives from the support functions and Jim himself are all doing likewise.

Alan briefly records the actions taken to resolve problems with power-steering fluid and leftover seat bolts and draws attention to the two amended Standard Operations left on Sean's desk. He mentions the changes he has made on the engine assignments for eliminating the routing problem and invites Sean's team to try Keith's new method for fitting engine mountings. He mentions the continuing problem with headlamp wipers. 'No shortages, no breakdowns', is his last entry.

THE SECOND DAY

07.35–08.00

Alan arrives a little later than usual. The roads are icy and there is a thin layer of snow. Sean is already waiting in the team area. Sean has had a successful shift and is in an ebullient mood. He confirms the success of the new methods and hands back the Standard Operation sheets, drafted by Alan and Pam, which he has now countersigned.

'It now takes us a little longer on Station 63, of course: we should fit the wipers somewhere else. It doesn't make sense to sub-assemble and fit them separately: it's double handling. We should be able to find another operation to carry out on Station 63 to exploit the power-steering fill time.

'We're also happy with the new assignments on the engine bays and Keith's method for engine mountings is bloody superb. I've made a stab at changing the Standard Op. to incorporate it. Maybe you could check it out and make sure it's consistent between the shifts and with what Keith originally had in mind.'

'What we need to do now to exploit it', observes Alan, 'is to pull in another 20 seconds of work, either directly or indirectly, from our half-assignment on Station 66. We'll get down to a 15-man RTR in no time at this rate. That's already one less person we need to hire for the volume uplift.'

'We should spend an hour or two together some morning and get our act together on that.'

'Not now. You'd best get home. The weather's turned a bit nasty. I think our shift will have a problem or two this morning.'

'I'd noticed your two hillbillies haven't arrived yet. Looks as if you'll be having some fun. A couple of gifts before I brave the elements. This is a Standard Operation sheet for the maintenance of twin-slat conveyor fixings and this ...,' Sean announces with a flourish of his arm, '... is a new improved method for setting headlamp wipers. Have a look at it and give it a try; but basically it means setting and torquing up the wiper blade approximately 3 mm *below* the rubber stoppers; and then lifting the wiper blade over the stopper. *That way*, it seems, after the headlamp wipers have been activated, they sit back on the stoppers as they should.'

John and Shaka have still not arrived. Alan can ill afford to be without them. They are among his most experienced and capable people and he has already granted Gina Falcone a day off to attend her great-aunt's funeral. Most of the other team members are present. Alan will have to think very carefully about how he deploys his people. He examines the skill matrix, considers his options, then updates the performance graphs before his meeting. By 08.00 all the team have arrived except John, Shaka and Gina.

08.00–08.05

Alan begins his meeting by drawing attention to yesterday's performance, referring to the Visual Management graphs for CSA and Final Inspection items (Figure 11.10). He pays particular tribute to Pam for resolving the power-steering

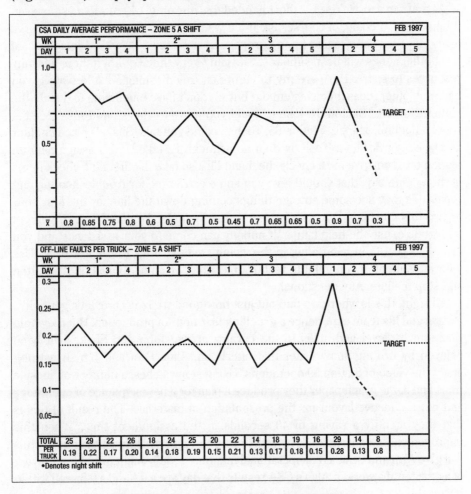

Figure 11.10 Zone 5's off-line quality performance

oil problem; Chris, for achieving └ standard on engine bay front; and especially Keith, for his improved method for Station 60. Alan mentions that all Station 60 qualified team members must make themselves familiar with the new method at the earliest opportunity if they hope to retain their current skill rating.

Nazim then runs through the results of his own checklist of faults found 'in zone'. Of particular note are two accelerator cables which needed readjusting and three headlamp wipers not properly seated. Alan mentions Sean's provisional Standard Operation for setting headlamp wipers and hands the sheet to Tom Grey.

'Try this out, Tom, and I'll touch base with you later about it.

'You may be interested to learn that we have just secured two prestigious contracts: one to supply the National Parks Authority and one for the Royal Canadian Mounted Police. It will all be in tomorrow's paper but, as usual, we wanted to tell you first.' He pins the press release to the notice board.

'As you can see, we're a bit short-handed this morning' (*A gross understatement*, thinks Alan). 'I could, of course, ask Jim if we can borrow some people but we've never done that before and I don't propose to start now. Besides, I imagine that most other zones will be in similar straits and I very much doubt if there'll be any resources to spare. Here are my thoughts on this morning's battle plan. If you have any other ideas then sing'em out but we don't have much time to debate the matter. Nazim ... Station 61; Pam ... could you move to check and repair; Matt ... stay on fluid fill; Mary ... Station 65; Tosh ... could you take Shaka's place on door fit; Dave ... back fill for Tosh on door adjustment. I'll take Dave's assignment on Station 66. Pam, give me a check sheet and I'll also take the first nine check items in the engine bay; that should give you some extra time for troubleshooting and repair. We may see some strange things coming down the line for the first hour or two this morning. Don't suffer unnecessarily under Pontius Pilate. If you get into trouble, use the help lamps. If nobody can come to your assistance and you can't fit a part then hang a tag in the vicinity and we'll try to catch it back. Use your judgement. If you get into real trouble, don't be afraid to push in the button and stop the line. Any questions?

'All right, this is where we find out just how good we *really* are; let's get to it!'

Alan and his team experience a gruelling first hour of production. But they hold their quality level and at 09.15 the cavalry arrive. John and Shaka had been delayed by drifting snow. Later that afternoon, Alan, Pam and Jim Armstrong study the video of Station 59 operations. Using stopwatches, a number of lineside trials and some graph paper they produce a plan for a new sequence of operations and more effective layout for the presentation of materials. The result of this is that they identify a saving of 40 seconds in the assignment time. When this improvement is consolidated, by redistributing more work from Station 66, this will give Alan and Sean a real operational manning requirement of 15.25 – a saving of a quarter of a worker. Alan's CSA results that day are a 0.4 and a 0.2: well within his target.

	TIME	%	CUM%
Observing working methods	3 hrs 00 mins	17.1	17.1
Solving problems, making and encouraging improvements, standardisation	2 hrs 40 mins	15.2	32.3
Checking quality of outputs with customers and test/audit areas	2 hrs 10 mins	12.4	44.7
Liaison with colleagues and suppliers (includes post-shift review)	2 hrs 10 mins	12.4	57.1
Training and coaching	1 hr 50 mins	10.5	67.6
Reacting to problems (includes giving practical assistance on the line)	1 hr 20 mins	7.6	75.2
Liaison and communication with opposite shift	1 hr 10 mins	6.6	81.8
Checking internal quality performance	50 mins	4.8	86.6
Maintaining/auditing condition of the workplace	50 mins	4.8	91.4
Giving feedback on team performance (includes pre-shift briefing and preparation)	40 mins	3.8	95.2
Administration	30 mins	2.9	98.1
Maintaining visual displays of team performance	20 mins	1.9	100
TOTAL	17 hrs 30 mins	100	100

Figure 11.11   **Breakdown of Alan Harper's time**

Alan and his team, like most other people at Paladin, go to work to earn a salary and, like most other people, would not trouble themselves to do so given a timely and sizeable inheritance or a win in the state lottery. But all of them end their shift on a 'high'. Alan reminds himself, however, of a popular saying among Paladin's managers and supervisors: *You're only as good as your last shift*. Indeed, fate has other trials in store for Alan during the remainder of the week, including transit-damaged steering wheels, sticking seat-slide mechanisms, a mysterious squeaking noise which seems to come from the vicinity of the door check link arm and some bodyside mouldings that fall off in Zone 6. Three of these problems will be solved by Alan and the team by themselves; the fourth with the help of a process engineer. But all that, as they say, is another story.

SUMMARY

Nobody fills out 'timesheets' at Paladin: they are a device of remote control management and serve no profitable purpose in a GK company. But if Alan were faithfully to record how he spent his time at work during these two days it would look rather as in Figure 11.11.

What has this achieved in just one small production area in a GK manufacturing company in just two of its 228 working days in the year? The following:

- the permanent resolution of four debilitating process problems;
- quantifiable improvements against the company's two main measures of off-line quality;
- the removal of 24 hours of annual overtime paid at premium rates;

- a real productivity improvement of 1.6 per cent.

All this has been attained by a self-motivating, self-sustaining production team as a normal part of their job, without the direct participation of middle or senior managers, without involving technical specialists, without submitting 'suggestions' and without the involvement of 'moderators' or 'facilitators'.

Part IV
Managing Productive Work

12 The Meaning of Lean

Much attention has been focused in recent years on so-called 'lean manufacturing', and there is a wealth of literature on the subject. This chapter, therefore, confines itself to the relationship between GK principles and the highest standards of productivity and cost-effectiveness and to discussing the underlying causes of waste which are inherent in conventional approaches to the management of productive work.[1] Nothing in this chapter has anything to do with 'downsizing' or any other euphemism for lay-offs. Forced redundancies and lack of employment security severely impair the implementation of all GK principles (see Chapter 16).

Many associate 'just-in-time' and 'lean manufacturing' with reduced inventory levels and working capital requirements. But this is only one aspect, and it is very much prone to the law of diminishing returns once historic excesses have been purged. True lean manufacturing is simply concerned with the constant and never-ending elimination of waste. Waste takes many forms: overproduction, waiting, transporting, WIP and finished inventory, unnecessary motion, defective parts and products.

Lean manufacturing in its purest form requires only two ingredients. The first is a passionate and overriding concern for the needs of the customer – both the commercial client and the downstream process. This is not only important for high levels of product quality and service but also as the key to leanness, since the needs of the customer provide the template for identifying waste; for distinguishing between fat and muscle. Waste is all activity or expenditure which does not add value to products or services or contribute to customer satisfaction.[2]

The second ingredient is to adopt GK operating disciplines which *make waste visible*. This demands courage and discipline, for it can often be a disconcerting and disruptive experience. Compare putting antifreeze into the coolant mixture of an old car before the onset of winter. The antifreeze searches out every crack in the radiator. Seeping from split hoses and loose connections, it drips on to the driveway outside the house and makes an appalling mess. This makes what ought to be a simple winter preparation an onerous chore. But the action provides a clear indication of the state of the cooling system and the areas that need attention. There is nothing comfortable about lean manufacturing. The discomfort felt is its inherent virtue. System failures become manifest rather than hidden; but at least we are then in a position to address these problems. The concept may seem strange at first, but if we really want high productivity, the very first thing that needs to be established is a climate which encourages both people and machines to stand blatantly idle if idle they truly are.

THE NEED FOR LEAN THINKING

Let us turn again to our two fictional manufacturers of diesel engines: Alpha Corp. and Omega Inc., first encountered in Chapter 9.

Ten years ago the executives of Alpha Corp. learned about something called 'lean manufacturing'. They were sufficiently excited by the concept to engage the services of a highly prestigious and expensive firm of international business consultants to help them introduce it.

As a result of this initiative, Alpha reorganised its production management structure along product lines. Instead of having production managers responsible for casting, machining and assembly, all processes were combined under two managers, each responsible for a product group of engines. By combining this change with a reorganisation of the factory layout, such that invisible curtains between stages were removed, the internal buffer stocks of cast and machined parts were drastically reduced. Senior and middle managers were sent on training courses and seminars to learn about just-in-time manufacturing. A bar coding system was introduced for stock control and improved scheduling, and delivery mechanisms for dispatching engines reduced the stock of finished units. The company became more vigorous in demanding smaller batch quantities and more frequent deliveries of materials from vendors.

The result of these changes was that Alpha doubled its stock turns, halved its inventory levels and working capital requirements and created a much more effective layout and product flow throughout the plant. Alpha believed that by achieving these worthy things, it had truly become a lean manufacturer. It was mistaken. It had not changed the deeply ingrained thinking of managers, supervisors and workers about production, productivity and profitability, whose outlook remains much the same as it had been in the era of Macmillan and Eisenhower, but Alpha's top managers either do not understand this or do not think it important. They attribute their company's remaining failings to historic labour-relations constraints and a shortfall of positive attitudes among some of its workforce. Alpha has yet to realise that its biggest problem is a singular inability to make and ship the right parts, in the right quantities, at the right time.

Alpha is sensitive about the fact that its rivals, Omega Inc. (a GK company), appears to be able to make a similar product range and volume with what appears to be only two-thirds of Alpha's workforce – even though their respective levels of technology and the main processes appear to be quite similar. Most crippling of all is the overtime which seems to be an endemic feature of the way that Alpha operates, even during those periods when demand is relatively flat. (Some managers believe that supervisors and workers are deliberately creating overtime to maintain the incomes to which they grew accustomed in previous years, but a tradition of remote control management deprives them of the practical understanding which would enable them to prove or disprove their suspicions.) Material flow is a big headache. Shortages of both internally and externally supplied parts are a way of life, even though the company has invested heavily in the latest systems, software and technology for the management of materials and scheduling of production. After this, the biggest contributor to lost production time is machine breakdowns; and the word on the streets is that these are *five times* as common at Alpha as they are at Omega.

We could understand the reasons for these problems if we were to visit Alpha and talk to the production managers, superintendents and supervisors to establish their perceptions of what the company demands of them. What are their key objectives and what, in their experience, constitutes a successful and satisfying day's work? We would find that their task, as they see it, is simply to keep the operators working and to keep machines running:

'That's what pays our salary; that's how the company makes its brass.'

'We're here to make product: we're here to *make our score!*'

'A good day is when the machines don't stop and nobody stands about idle.'

Nobody talks about satisfying the downstream customer or reducing real manufacturing costs. Nobody talks about delivery time, or about meeting the schedule. (Occasionally somebody feels sufficient need for political correctness to mention the word 'quality', but they are far from specific about what their responsibilities for this amount to.)

This lack of internal customer awareness and a relatively low regard for the requirements of downstream processes cause the non-fulfilment of the production schedule in some areas and wasteful and disruptive overproduction in others, poor workflow, soft shortages and misplaced materials. At Alpha, seven staff are permanently employed simply in counting and recounting parts on the shop floor. Supervisors and shift managers regard machine changeovers as an anathema. The need to change over a machine is resisted and postponed as long as possible.

'Changeovers harm our efficiency.'

'When we change over we are not producing. When we are not producing we are not making money for the company.'

'Only an hour left in the shift. Not worth changing over. Let the other shift do it. Meanwhile, knock off a few more of these instead. It's not as if they won't need them eventually.'

In Machining, the shift manager finds a production operator reading a newspaper. His machine is not running. The expected parts have not arrived from the upstream machining section. The manager takes the supervisor to task immediately. 'Get some work on that machine!' he snarls. 'We're not paying people to read newspapers. No wonder we're working so much overtime!' The supervisor runs around until he manages to find some partly machined components which can be processed on the machine. They were designated for a different machine process and for another job, to be undertaken on the subsequent shift – but he takes them anyway.

Plant and equipment are poorly maintained and breakdowns are frequent. In Assembly, a technician arrives at the appointed time to carry out some preventive maintenance activity. He is turned away.

'Pity you couldn't have been here this morning. The machine stood idle for the best part of an hour waiting for the right machined parts. Can't let you have it now – we'll probably have to work overtime as it is.' Forty-eight hours later, the equipment breaks down. Half a shift's production is lost; more overtime ensues.

Alpha is trying to satisfy a demand for production efficiency at the expense of the downstream customer and thus ends up satisfying neither. Ironically, were the 'productivity' measure less pre-eminent, the real productivity actually achieved would be far higher. When it comes down to it, there is only one imperative at Alpha and that is *volume*: volume, which can 'justify' existing headcount and machine capacity and is expressed as *labour efficiency* and *machine utilisation* ratios. Alpha's approach is dominated by a hostile disposition towards unexploited resources of manpower, machinery and materials. This is the very antithesis of lean manufacturing in the true sense of the concept illustrated in Chapter 1 (Figure 1.1), which established that to maximise profit, in a slow-growth economy with restricted demand, is to increase the value of outputs and *reduce*, not increase, the consumption of inputs. This failing lies at the heart of most of Alpha's operational problems and accounts for most of the disparity in real productivity between our two companies.

At Omega Inc., a different set of assumptions prevails and, as a GK organisation, it benefits from the reinforcing mechanisms outlined in Chapters 9 and 10. All supervisors and their teams are permanently aware of the requirements of the downstream: the standard of service they require in terms of quality and delivery and also how that service will be measured. In addition, each of these teams in turn is able to give prompt and meaningful feedback to their 'supplier' teams on the degree to which they are receiving the level of support expected. These requirements are the driving force behind *all activity* at Omega. All functional teams are judged *primarily* on their ability fully to supply the requirements of the customer and, *thereafter*, improve their performance by doing so with *minimal* consumption of resources: man, machine, materials. Omega's visual management systems enable every production team continually to assess its performance in terms of its outputs to customers and its progress in reducing the costs of providing those outputs.

The attainment of the production schedule, that which specifies the precise requirements of the downstream customer, is of paramount importance. Should there be a conflict, the requirements of the schedule always override the desire to maximise the utilisation of resources. In this way Omega's production teams address themselves to and measure their performance on eliminating the stoppages and maximising the efficiency of *their customers'* operations. Materials Control measures and displays lost production time due to shortages and delays in supplying raw materials to Casting and Machining, and vendor-supplied parts to Assembly. Casting teams measure themselves against any lost time by machining teams; machining teams do the same for assembly teams. It is the task of assembly teams to meet the plant's delivery schedule *precisely* – no more, no less. FLMs and Team Leaders, from both production and support functions, make frequent enquiries of their downstream customers to ensure that the latter's priorities are being addressed.

THE EVILS OF OVERPRODUCTION

Of all forms of waste, overproduction remains far and away the most crippling. It is particularly poisonous because, as well as being wasteful in itself, it serves both to create and to conceal other forms of waste. Taiichi Ohno condemns overproduction as 'a crime against society'.[3] Of course there can be very few industrial managers who are now unaware of the maxim of producing exactly the right quantities at exactly the right time. But this understanding seems to be tainted with a hefty measure of incredulity. It is as if there is a reasonable amount of acceptance by hearts and minds, but the bowels still need to be convinced. *Surely this is a 'guiding principle', a theoretical but unattainable ideal (a bit like the Sermon on the Mount).* No, it isn't. *Surely, if Matsushita or Toyota achieve the schedule with an hour of the shift to spare, they don't really stop production, do they?* Yes, they do. *Ah well, they're probably like us, then. The problem hardly arises because we never hit schedule: we're quite chuffed if we manage 90 per cent.* No, they always make schedule. The schedule reflects customer demand. It is an imperative, not a target.

Exceeding the downstream requirement is simply waste: of materials, energy, effort, fuel and space, quite apart from its tendency to create more inventory and increase working capital costs as well as cause disruptions to workflow and a longer throughput time. Once a GK production unit or team fulfils the downstream requirement, production ceases *immediately*, without a single superfluous part being manufactured and machines shut off accordingly –

irrespective of the amount of time remaining in the shift. Where there is surplus time in the shift, emphasis is directed towards training, carrying out preventive maintenance and the resolution of process and product quality problems, thereby perpetuating the right conditions for a similarly successful performance on the following shift. GK companies understand that it is far better to run at full efficiency and effectiveness for only part of a shift than ineffectively and inefficiently, with breakdowns, poor workflow and part shortages, for a full eight hours (and perhaps overtime). In the former case the surplus capacity is *highly visible* and *quantifiable*, and is demonstrably there to be had as and when work can be reallocated or when sales increase.

PERFORMANCE MEASURES AND PRODUCTIVITY

Why is overproduction still endemic in so many Western companies? Because, in spite of all the investment in literature, education and discussion about the merits of 'just-in-time' and 'lean manufacture', their main measures of daily operational performance – which so powerfully determine the priorities and behaviours of everyone in the factory – are much the same as those in place 50 years ago at the height of the postwar boom. As a consequence, production, for most middle managers and supervisors, is still about maximising volume, which is to say maximising the consumption and cost of resources – keeping workers working and machines running.

Sadly, the most common and most influential performance measures in many conventional firms are, at best, the least useful and, at worst, the most harmful. They have no bearing whatsoever on our ability either to satisfy the needs of customers or to reduce real costs. Nor can they be said to tell us anything about productivity or efficiency.

LABOUR PERFORMANCE

Let us begin with the time-honoured calculation by which a ratio of hours achieved is taken over hours available to give a percentage figure which we may call 'efficiency', 'productivity', 'volume' (if we are honest), or 'output' (if we still retain a moribund concept of outputs). Some companies measure the percentage shortfall rather than the achievement, and call it 'losses'.

What exactly are we measuring here and what does it tell us? Suppose, over a three-month period, we make concerted efforts for improvement: new equipment, better methods, better layout, faster changeovers, fewer stoppages, less scrap or rework. The results are shown in Table 12.1.

From our starting-point we have improved real productivity by 30 per cent (8.5 units per person in month 1; 10.55 units per person in month 3). But this is not shown in the conventional way of measuring labour performance, which has

	Persons deployed	Units actual	Units possible	Efficiency ratio (%)
Month 1	10	85	100	85
Month 2	10	95	111.8	85
Month 3	9	95	111.8	85

Table 12.1   Real productivity gains and conventional efficiency ratios

remained at a static 85 per cent throughout. Such a measure cannot inspire anyone in a company to improve real productivity. The reverse is also true. To expend time and effort on productivity improvement in many companies must be regarded as a waste of time or, at best, an occupational hobby, since it clearly has no influence on the main operational measure of performance. This should not be too much of a surprise. Chapter 2 indicated that there is simply no long-standing tradition of method improvement, of *kaizen*, in Western companies. This measure is just a very slightly more sophisticated way of measuring production volume; it is the vestige of a unique epoch, when demand almost always exceeded supply, when profit meant achieving economies of scale and marginal costs, when *volume*, not quality, not cost reduction and not productivity, in any meaningful sense, was king.

Of course this measure does, after a fashion, show the extent to which production has been disrupted in any given shift. But this amalgamated ragbag of disorders is not of much practical use if our purpose is to take action to resolve problems. Everyone is familiar with the causes of lost production, the components of this ratio. They are very few and are common to all processes. They consist simply of failings in our three factors of production: man, machine, materials. The two most common are material shortages and machine breakdowns. If the denominator for the ratio includes everybody on the payroll and not just those who are actually at work, then absence might also be a significant factor.[4] If these are the factors that are hindering us, then these are the *specific* factors we must measure and take action on.

In 1995 I gave a presentation to the production management team at a European car plant. Their main daily performance measure was 'losses'. I expressed grave doubts about the helpfulness of this measure, having experienced its destructive influence on the effectiveness of another manufacturer. Nobody could understand why I had a problem with something which had clearly become such an important and cherished aspect of their daily lives.

Two hours later, the subject was the post-shift reviews and pre-shift briefings described in Chapter 10. There was much positive interest in this approach – so much, that they seemed on the brink of introducing it in their plant. Then I received two questions. One manager wanted to know how it would be if only the team leaders attended the supervisors' pre-shift briefings. Was it strictly necessary to include the other members of the production teams? Another asked if they really must occur immediately before production begins. How about midway through the morning – coffee break, for example? With a growing feeling of depression I explained that, for the approach to work, team members must be aware of the team's performance and its problems so that they can focus on achieving the needs of the downstream. This could not be a voluntary activity; they would have to invest some production time.

'It's only five minutes', I lamely tried to assure them.

'Don't you realise that on our cycle time, that means we *lose* four cars?'

Of course I did. But what more could I say? (Dare I be so flippant as to ask if they had checked their pockets recently?) Had I the heart to tell them how astounded I had been by the hundreds of cars held in their final area and the scores of people permanently employed in repairing the faults on them? Could I confess how singularly unimpressed I had been with the standard of quality and productivity that I had witnessed in their factory: absurd and wasteful work assignments, cramped and restricted working conditions arising from excess lineside stock, everything in cardboard boxes, production parts spilling into dirty aisles to be trampled upon? (This was a reputable worldwide car manufacturer, a household name.) Why rub their noses in it? So what, if I convinced them to introduce the new approach? What would be the main item on the agenda at the post-shift review? Progress on a target to reduce the daily volume of fault-ridden vehicles in their repair shop? No. It would be 'losses'.

MACHINE PERFORMANCE

The equivalent folly in capital-intensive plants is an undue obsession with machine utilisation, either especially measured as such or else revealed in a tendency to regard and measure as 'downtime' simply any occasion when a machine is not producing. A Dutch company, visited in 1995, was achieving utilisation ratios on its plastic injection-moulding machines of better than 90 per cent at its manufacturing plant. At the same time, although it was struggling to meet the delivery needs of many of its clients, it had over 27 million US dollars' worth of finished stock in its warehouses (by cost of production, not sales price value). In common with so many companies adopting a 'build for stock' approach, the production department was unable to develop a profitable identity with the downstream customer. The warehouse was simply a repository for the physical result of their efforts to maximise the utilisation (consumption) of resources. Finished inventory was then in the domain of sales and marketing who regarded it as a honey pot. Finance regarded it as an asset on the balance sheet, though recognising that 20 per cent of it was *aged* and unlikely to be sold. Also, like most manufacturers who 'build for stock' (usually on the universally ephemeral basis of sales forecasts), it sought to justify this in the name of responding quickly to commercial clients. Some of these were seeking lead times of less than a week;

the normal expected transaction and process time, from receipt of order to dispatch, was about five weeks. But processes simply do not come any shallower than injection moulding, where it should be possible to complete even moderately large requested volumes within *hours*. Obviously shorter runs and smaller batch sizes are the key. Yes, this may adversely affect the utilisation ratio, but who cares? In this particular business, *materials* were by far the most significant element of the costs structure – and how many spanking-new injection-moulding machines could be bought with even half of 27 million dollars?

There is only a problem if a machine is not performing when we require it to do so to meet customer demand. 'Downtime' must be strictly defined as 'planned production time lost due to breakdowns'; that is, the machine is unable to function to produce the scheduled parts at the time they are required to be made – no more, no less.

Even this is not always sufficient. Consider the case of an aluminium extrusion plant in the South of England. In marked contrast to Alpha's problem, production were virtually begging maintenance (part of the engineering division in this organisation) to shut down and carry out corrective work on machines which were unable to run at full throttle without causing defective quality. Maintenance often argued that there was nothing much wrong with the machines and that the problem was actually poor operational skills on the part of production personnel. Significantly, though the production director's main performance objective was to *achieve schedule*, that of the technical director was to *eliminate downtime*. Downtime was not incurred so long as the machine was actually running – even if unsatisfactorily.

In such cases a useful measure is overall equipment effectiveness (OEE). This is a holistic measure of machine performance which is becoming increasingly attractive to capital-intensive industries. This brief example shows how it is calculated.

A machine is required to be operational for 6 hours	(100%)
Because of breakdowns it is only operational for 5 hours	(83%)
Short stops (*ad hoc* adjustment, slow running or changeovers) account for 30 minutes	(92%)
Out of 230 parts produced, only 198 meet the quality standard	(86%)

83% x 92% x 86% gives an OEE rating of 66%. The other 34% is waste.

There are, however, some important aspects to consider in making full use of this performance measure:

- Establishing hard data on *ad hoc* adjustments and slow running requires constant and close monitoring by FLMs and/or Team Leaders.
- The measure should be owned or at least shared by production teams and not simply given over to maintenance or plant engineering functions.
- The 100 per cent we start with should not simply be 60 minutes an hour, 24

hours a day. It must equate to no more than that required to meet schedule if we are to avoid overproduction.

- The main thrust of actions taken to reduce time spent on changeovers should involve improvements in methods of resetting (using SMED techniques or similar), not simply avoiding the need to reset by opting for longer production runs.

Machines are not customers. They are simply tools that we use to meet the demands of customers. When they are not required for that purpose, what could be more logical than switching them off? At least that way we save on energy costs. The propensity that so many have of seeking to justify capital expenditure *after* purchase rather than before is a curious phenomenon. Suppose I were a keen gardener and, after a prosperous month of business, decided to treat myself to a fancy new lawn mower. Maybe the next month's business is not so hot and I am beginning to regret my purchase. But this does not mean that I will be cutting the grass three times a day in some vain attempt to justify my earlier recklessness.

One of the silliest plant performance measures that I ever encountered was at a factory near Atlanta. They actually measured 'output' as a ratio over machine depreciation. The machines were subjected to absurdly long production runs and were flogged almost to death; they received very little maintenance. Massive stocks of unsold products coexisted with failed deliveries and frustrated clients (as they almost invariably do). Some accountant, somewhere along the road, had forgotten what the concept of depreciation was supposed to be all about. Few would treat their car this way. Of course one of the reasons is that the market value of a used car is largely affected by its condition and its mileage. Perhaps if meters, indicating the number of cycles performed, were a more common feature on equipment, and if our finance people profiled their depreciation calculations accordingly, this might make a very positive contribution both to ensuring that machines were properly looked after and to enforcing lean disciplines.

MONTHLY TARGETS

If 'efficiency' and utilisation ratios are the bane of the big corporations, the monthly financial photograph is often the curse of smaller companies, particularly those which are part of a holding company.

Astarte was the Phoenician goddess of fertility and of the moon. To the Greeks she was Artemis; to the writers of the Old Testament she was Ashtoroth, capricious and cruel, demanding constant human sacrifice. She was always portrayed crowned with the horns of the lunar crescent, whence our traditional way of depicting devils is derived. Legend also held that the moon was the treasure house of everything wasted on the earth: misspent time and wealth, unfulfilled dreams and intentions, broken promises, unanswered prayers.

Like, I suspect, most people starting out on a career in industry, it did not take me long to notice the strange and compelling influence of the calendar on the behaviour of managers: how otherwise prudent and level-headed people gradually submitted to some kind of psychosis as each month neared its end. They became increasingly disposed to overturning the disciplines that they themselves had previously insisted that everyone should follow, while foremen, engineers and workers shrugged their shoulders at one another or else made twirling motions at their temples with their index fingers.

After two months with my first employers, I finally summoned up the temerity to ask my boss about this. Why were we ignoring the clients' clearly expressed shipment priorities and only making and dispatching the high-value products – especially since one of them had sent stuff back last month, at our expense, because it had been shipped too early? Why were we laying on extra shifts and copious amounts of overtime when next week's material would be so exhausted that we would probably have to pay people to sit at their benches doing crossword puzzles?

'You have a lot to learn', he replied. 'Do you really think you're the only one who thinks this is crazy? We do these things because my backside gets kicked *this* week, not next. Next week only affects my fate in four weeks' time. Right now, that's a long way off. And, in answer to your next question, *yes, he does*. Not only that, he *expects* it because this is *his* week for being kicked too!' Small wonder that from the moon comes not merely the practice of reckoning days into months, but also the word 'lunacy'.

The president of a holding group, comprising about a dozen similar-sized companies, was enthusiastically pursuing 'World-class manufacturing' practices. He particularly wanted to see evidence of reduced levels of inventory in all his companies. This became a key item in the monthly report submitted to the president by each individual CEO. One such company, making electrical equipment in the American mid-West, regularly had serious problems with material shortages and disrupted workflow in the last week of every month. Why? Because, in order to make the report on inventory look good, the procurement department simply stopped placing orders after the second week of each month. The same company took a similar approach to measuring and achieving its delivery performance. It made sterling efforts to clear all its arrears at the end of each month before submitting the report and, against this measure, it seemed to be performing very well. But how does this augur for a customer placing an order on 26 June on the basis of a five-working-day delivery promise?[5]

Monthly aggregations and month-end 'freeze-frame' positions are of no operational relevance or utility in the *genba*. There, we must have pertinent and meaningful measures which put *daily* emphasis on fulfilling customer needs and identifying and eliminating waste.

Of course the difficulty for many production managers and directors, and not a few chief executives, is that the priesthood of Astarte is often well represented in high places: in boardrooms, banks and among those who advise commercial shareholders. That they themselves may some day find enlightenment is perhaps the best hope for Western industry. All right, so many of us have to accept that, ultimately, gorillas will sit wherever they like. In such cases, where we are constrained by the performance expectations of our superiors, then we must find the courage to argue the rationality of our case. Meanwhile, perhaps, we must render unto Caesar that which is Caesar's. The important thing is to ensure that we do not pass on the disease; that we, at least, give to *our* people performance measures which truly measure performance; which are relevant to the world that we now inhabit; that focus primarily on the needs of the commercial client and the downstream; and that help show us where the waste is, not conceal it from us.

NOTES

1. 'Lean manufacturing' is, of course, a Western epithet conveniently applied to features which are perceived to characterise the operational practices of Japanese and other GK organisations. 'Lean' is in some respects an unfortunate word since it carries with it a tang of the gaunt and consumptive rather than portraying something which is above all strong and healthy, streamlined and efficient. 'Sleek' would be better, evoking an image more akin to a natural predator than to a scarecrow. Nevertheless I shall employ the term which is now in common use.
2. A feature often noted in GK companies in Japan is the degree to which, both in training literature and in conversation, everyone in the organisation is exhorted to ensure that they provide themselves with a 'profitable job'. A 'profitable job' is one which gives value either to commercial clients or downstream processes.
3. T. Ohno (1988), *Toyota Production System* (p. 129). Portland, Oregon: Productivity Press; originally (1978), *Toyota Seisan Hoshiki*, Tokyo: Diamond Inc.
4. If we are honest, we feel deep down that there is another component: how *hard* people are working. This, I suspect, is the real reason for the continued prevalence of this particular measure of 'efficiency': it remains as surreptitious evidence that many managers still set greater store by physical effort on the part of workers than they do on process improvement.
5. Thorn Lighting PLC at its plant in County Durham is one of the best British examples of a non-Japanese company working to GK principles. Its approach to measuring delivery performance is radically different: hard, uncompromising, reflecting performance against unadulterated customer requirements and completely free of contamination by the monthly photograph. The measure they use is called simply 'hit rate'. Say a customer sends in an order for a variety of different items, each with required quantities and a delivery date. If the order can be met *in full* by the due date, then it is logged as a 'hit'. If just one item cannot be delivered in full quantity by the due date, regardless of how unreasonable that date might be and irrespective of Thorn's current lead time capability, then *the whole order* is treated as a 'miss'. 'Hit rate' is simply the percentage of 'hits' achieved of all orders received. It is measured and displayed daily.

13 Paying for Waste

> *It is a true proverb, that if you live with*
> *a lame man you will learn to limp.*
>
> Plutarch, *Morals*

PIECEWORK AND WORK QUOTAS

Of all the plagues and blessings to have escaped from the Pandora's Box of Scientific Management nothing has so poisoned manufacturing performance as piecework and 'productivity' bonus. With Deming, I am disinclined to distinguish between the two.[1] The various manifestations, individual or group-based, differ only in degrees of harm; none has beneficial ends.

Space forbids discussion of the moral, psychological and motivational arguments against piecework; anybody unmoved by Abraham Maslow, Frederick Herzberg or Deming himself will certainly not be swayed by me. But this hardly matters any more. Today, the practical arguments are enough. Piecework and bonus schemes are an encumbrance to managers in meeting standards of quality, cost reduction and customer delivery. They distract FLMs and workers from a view of production based on a more profitable concept of outputs determined by customer needs. They are extremely costly to administer and sap an undue proportion of managerial time and energy. Far from adding any value to products and services, they serve rather to exacerbate operational difficulties, disrupt workflow, reduce flexibility and encourage waste. They are, moreover, irreconcilable with the requirements of modern, competitive manufacturing. Should we need to complete and dispatch 143 units, then 143 units is what we must make and ship. Production of 142 units means a disappointed customer; 144 units means *waste*. How can such a precise imperative coexist with a payment system which tacitly invites the production of *more* or *less*; which acknowledges, accepts, panders to and further promotes variations in 'skill', energy, appetite or motivation on the part of the workforce?

The most damning indictment of all, however, is that piecework and bonus schemes reinforce the association of increased productivity with increased physical effort: which is endemic in the minds of both workforce and management in the overwhelming majority of Western companies and stalks like a virulent plague through their factories. This flies in the face of a concept which we so desperately need to instil in our organisations: that real productivity improvements come from improving the *process*.

Improvement means making the work *easier*. It means expending *less* physical effort. It means finding a method which involves using only the hand or fingers rather than the whole arm. It means ensuring that methods eliminate bending and stretching and needless consumption of shoe leather. It means that if someone can perform a job sitting down, then we find them a comfortable chair. It means, above all, that in seeking the best from our people, we get them to think more and sweat less.

I was once caught up in a long debate with the manufacturing director of a renowned producer of fine English porcelain. His view was that the removal of piecework would decimate his production volumes by 'demotivating' his more highly 'skilled' workers. Such 'skill' he primarily attributed to natural ability and dexterity.[2] I gave my view that there are only slight differences between individuals in terms of their innate capability to perform specific tasks. He replied that, on the contrary, there was one person who could decorate 120 plates per shift while another could only manage 70. The removal of piecework would cost, in this instance, 50 plates per shift. My response was that, if such was the discrepancy, then someone ought to be fired (perhaps quite literally somewhere else in the process). I was not referring to either of the plate decorators. Such a difference could only be attributed to variation in method. Piecework and the failure by management to identify and teach the better method was *already* costing the company 50 plates per shift – quite apart from its contribution to waste.

Bogus altruism is usually the last refuge of the die-hard defender of 'productivity incentives': 'What is so wrong about rewarding workers or with yielding them a share of the fruits of their endeavours?' What indeed? But there are innumerable choices open to companies if such is truly their intention, including equity options, profit sharing and of course the good, old-fashioned method of giving a pay rise.

Mercifully, in most Western countries during the past decade, piecework and productivity bonus have now become the exception rather than the norm. A few industries, such as clothing and tableware, have clung to their cherished practices a little longer than most, but, even there, things are beginning to change.[3] Only in Germany, the strongest of the Western manufacturing nations during the latter part of the fast growth era, and therefore the last to feel the bitter winds of Asian competition, are piecework and productivity bonus still the most common way of paying the direct workforce. That, too, is changing fast.

Measured day working (MDW) is now by far the most common method of payment for production workers. It is so prevalent that it is simply assumed to be a natural, normal way of paying people – a flat rate, no bells and whistles, no bonus: *the* alternative to piecework. What else is there? But, in reality, MDW is not much of an improvement on piecework since it preserves two of its most debilitating ingredients: 'hourly pay' and 'work standards'. The 'work standard' is what Deming condemned with such persistent vigour. It is the 'rate for the job' – a quota. What MDW says to an employee is, *'This is what you must achieve* per hour, per shift, per week, *to earn your pay.'*

When we institute MDW in our organisations we land ourselves with a big problem. Once established, such quotas or 'work standards' become difficult to change and, until we change them, we come up against the problem highlighted by the example of the power press operator in Chapter 3. 'Hourly-paid' workers, having met the criterion for payment, regard the fruits of any productivity improvement as their own *fairly earned* free time, and we cannot harvest the improvement on the bottom line. Managers in such companies are sometimes given to complaining that the 'hourly paid' always insist on 'hanging a price tag' on improvements. But it is management who, by their quotas, hang the price tag. The workforce are simply responding in kind and playing by the rules set by management – rules which apply *uniquely to them* as part of their 'hourly-paid' status.

As a consequence, the onus is now on management to *prove* that improvements are the result of better methods and involve no additional effort. They must develop unimpeachable mechanisms for doing this. The resulting cumbersome apparatus and procedures choke off most potential improvements. This is why piecework still survives. For some managers it allows the hope that, *just maybe*, some people, some of the time, *might* share some of the benefits of their improvements with us by using the free time generated to make more products – without any effort from management. In other words, those who retain piecework erroneously believe that it provides a partial solution to a problem for which MDW clearly has no solution at all.

Rates and quotas and 'work standards' are the common currency of both piecework and MDW. Both are devices of a sedentary approach which permits managers to stay at arm's length from the actual work while expecting workers to establish detailed methods for themselves. As such they are a poor surrogate for the effective management of the process and the provision of real leadership, guidance and direction in the *genba*, where the work is actually carried out.

This is why GK companies, possessing the world's most efficient and productive factories, function without operational performance incentives or quotas of any kind: they simply pay, to all of their people, a *salary*. It is why, in terms of *performance in the factory*, Ford, General Motors and the indigenous European car makers will never be able even to enter the same league as their Japanese-owned rivals until such time as they are willing to abandon their cherished practices of 'hourly pay' and MDW. If and when they do, *all things become possible.*

THE ROLE OF INDUSTRIAL ENGINEERING

Two workers are filling 5-litre cans of paint for the aerospace industry. (Another pair performs the same task on night shift.) These are mainly low-volume products and the company has decided that automation would not be a worthwhile investment.

The first worker fills the cans. The second worker checks the weight and fits the lid, a spring-loaded seal and a label, before stacking the filled cans on a pallet some four metres away. The time taken to perform the second worker's tasks is less than the time it takes to fill a can. The second worker stands and works on a high bench. The first worker squats, *actually sits on an upturned bucket:* he does this because the tap at the bottom of the vat of paint is only some 30 cm from the floor. He puts an empty can under the tap and turns it on. He watches it fill to the required level and turns off the tap. He then, still in his squatting position, stretches out his arm upwards and outwards to put the full can on his colleague's bench. With optimised working heights one worker could perform both tasks with greater comfort and less physical effort than that currently expended by both of them. A child could see the absurdity and yet this is happening in a blue-chip international chemical corporation. Does nobody in management observe and notice these things? Is nobody angered by them? Does nobody care?

If Western industrial performance has suffered because managers and supervisors have backed away from observing and managing the work, is there not at least one function that can be relied on to fill the void? Do not our industrial engineers spend time in the *genba* studying and improving working methods, identifying and removing waste? Sadly, too often the answer is 'no', although this is not the fault of the IEs themselves. Their role has also been distorted by the legacy of piecework, the introduction of work quotas and the assumptions of remote control management. This was once a noble calling. Whatever else may be laid at their door, the doyens of scientific management, so many of whom were also the pioneers of industrial engineering (Emerson, Gantt, the Gilbreths, Taylor himself) genuinely believed themselves to be making a real contribution to the well-being of mankind. Now, however, the prime function of so many IEs is neither to make the task of the production worker easier nor to find real productivity gains for the company. They are more concerned with measurement than with method.[4] Despite whatever some may have been taught in college or technical school, once in a company they are charged not so much with identifying and eliminating waste as with finding acceptable and equitable means of distributing it and paying for it. Frequently, this serves only to legitimise waste, cementing it into production operations and thereby making its extraction even more difficult.

Suppose a workteam of five people for whom there is currently only sufficient productive work to occupy four-and-a-half of them. Figure 13.1 shows three possible approaches to distributing the work. Which is best?

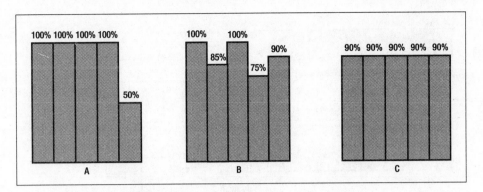

Figure 13.1 Three alternative work distributions

Many would plump for option C, which gives the most even distribution. For the same reason, option B would be seen as the worst: it appears random, arbitrary and totally irregular. But from a GK perspective, only option A is acceptable. Here, by concentrating the waste in one person (or one operation or one machine), it is rendered highly visible. Everyone is aware of it, including all members of the team. It offers far more scope for adding more productive work should we be able to find it. Option C is far more susceptible to Parkinson's Law.[5] Anyone working according to this distribution would soon become unaware of the waste. It would be very difficult to come along at a later date to try to fill up the assignments. The difference between 90 and 100 per cent is too slight. Team members would already feel themselves to be working at 100 per cent. Option C is actually the *least* acceptable. Option B is practically no worse than C but has one important saving grace: it is *obviously* bad and cries out for improvement.

Figure 13.2 illustrates the workplace as it pertains to the assembly and fitment of just one part in a factory making four-wheel-drive vehicles. The example about to unfold is all too easy to dismiss as farce. It is important to concentrate on the reasons for the absurdity since it is only one manifestation of a broader underlying tragedy.

The part in question is a plastic interior trim, about 80cm square, with a cosmetically textured finish. Scratched and chipped trims are a major corporate quality concern following unfavourable feedback from clients.

The cycle time for this production line is 140 seconds. The man on Station J has 80 seconds of activity, fitting components to the roof of the vehicle, and so works on a raised platform accessed by a flight of 14 iron stairs. Since 80 seconds is far less than the cycle time, he works progressively upstream – further and further away from his tools and components. By the fifth vehicle he is actually fitting his components on Station H.

He then walks the length of the platform, down the stairs and down line to the vicinity of Station L (congestion of materials prevents trims from being brought any closer). Trims are delivered in very large, compartmented boxes, each

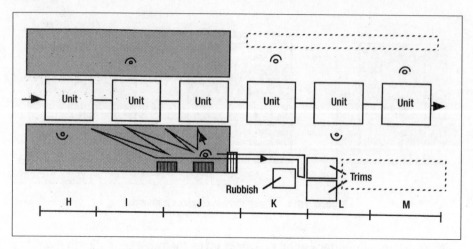

Figure 13.2   Case example: legitimisation of waste

holding 20 pieces. Such is the level of sensitivity attached to these parts that the vendor has individually wrapped and protected them so well that it seems almost possible to drive a tank over them without doing too much damage. Our man takes out five trims and strips off the wrapping, putting it in the bin provided. He then stacks the five naked trims up to the level of his chin and, pizza-delivery style, picks his precarious way back up the stairs to his station. He puts the pile down on a bench and to each fits heater and air-conditioning switches. He transfers the trims to a nearby shelf which holds a stock of between five and ten assembled trims. After completing his other work on each vehicle roof, he literally launches one of these trims down into the cabin of each vehicle. It is finally fitted to the vehicle by a man working on Station L where the parts were delivered in the first place.

The IE, for in this company it is he and not FLMs who determine work assignments, has a clear and simple rationale for this bizarre performance. 'It was the best way I could manage to make an even distribution of work; I have to make sure that everybody is topped up to 140 seconds.' Indeed, our man's activity related to the trims amounts to five minutes every five cycles: 60 seconds per cycle, which, added to 80 seconds of platform work, gives 140 seconds. But it only takes 15 seconds per trim to fit the switches. The other 45 seconds, 28 per cent of the whole work assignment, is waste. Putting to one side the quality and safety implications of this job, our man walks more than 1.4 kilometres per shift fetching trims. (The round trip from platform to lineside stock is 40 metres and daily volume is 180 vehicles.) Negotiating the stairs equates to both climbing and descending the Eiffel Tower every one and a half shifts. What kind of industrial engineer would be associated with such idiocy – would either forget or abandon the principles of his discipline? The answer is, simply, one whose concerns and actions have been trammelled by the operational business practices of his employers. One whose attempts to achieve an equitable distribution of effort too often bring about a situation which, to borrow a phrase from Winston Churchill, merely results in 'equal misery for all'.

There is a final twist. The main performance measure in this plant, the one that everybody gets hot under the collar about, is 'losses'. What would happen if the IE or the FLM were to remove this 45 seconds of waste which 'tops up' the work assignment? Unless and until alternative, ideally *profitable* work can be found to replace it, 'efficiency', as measured in this way, would actually *worsen*, since the ratio's denominator denoting available labour time would increase. In this situation, the more waste that can be legitimised as necessary production activity, the better the labour performance (the 'efficiency' measure!) will appear.

Is it simply advocated, then, that IEs redeem their profession by spending most of their time searching out waste and making real improvements to production methods? Not entirely: it is rather too late for that now. The world has moved on. It is no longer enough. Such is the volume and frequency of productivity improvements now enjoyed by GK companies that, in order to become one or to compete with one, the whole production department and especially its FLMs and Team Leaders must themselves become IEs. This still leaves a vital role for those already in the profession. Aside from advising management on costing, capacity and manpower-planning issues, they act as internal consultants in GK companies, giving training, coaching and support to FLMs, enabling them to learn and regularly practise basic IE techniques and providing practical specialist advice and assistance with some of the more complex or difficult aspects of their operations.

But how can we expect FLMs and Team Leaders to go out and search for waste? How do they know where to look, especially if there are no glaringly obvious problems? The pursuit of truly lean manufacture requires that all our people are encouraged and expected regularly to ask a number of questions of each and every activity and in due sequence. The 'Five Ws and One H' is a much-emphasised device in Japanese-owned companies but, like so many other aspects of GK, its roots lie in the Western tradition. In this case the source is Rudyard Kipling:

> I keep six honest serving-men
> (They taught me all I knew);
> Their names are What and Why and When
> And How and Where and Who.[6]

Foremost among these is *why*. Why is the activity being done? (What does it contribute to quality, delivery, safety or cost-effectiveness?) Do we really need to do it? Does it add value to our products and services? Would there be any adverse consequences of not doing it? If the answer to the last of these questions is 'no', and this has been confirmed with the downstream, then the activity must cease immediately and we need go no further.

Otherwise, the next step is to consider *where, when* and *who*. Where and when is it done? Where and when else could it be done? Where and when does it make most sense to do it? (What is the most reasonable and rational operational sequence?) Who is doing it? Who else could do it? Who has the skill, tools, time, opportunity to do it? Who *should* do it?

Finally, all that remains are *what* and *how*. What is being done, or should be done? How is it being done; should it be done? How can we establish the best available method? What shall be our *Standard Operation*?

NOTES

1. 'Incentive pay is piece work.' Deming, *Out of the Crisis* (p. 72); see Select bibliography.
2. Which, if it were true, would indicate piecework to be inherently unfair, since the less 'skilled' would be condemned to lower earnings in spite of their best efforts and through no fault of their own.
3. Coats Viyella and Josiah Wedgwood in the UK are notable examples of such companies which have found that the removal of piecework actually improves productivity and real operational efficiency.
4. Measuring employee 'work rate' is a waste of time and counterproductive. It is invariably a feature of low-productivity companies, a vestige of piecework design which now serves no purpose. How does it avail us to judge that 'this person is working at an 80' whereas 'that one is only managing a 74' when we ignore the fact that both assignments probably include at least 25 per cent of redeemable waste? Not surprisingly the practice is not found in GK factories.
5. 'Work expands to fill the time available for its completion. General recognition of this fact is shown in the proverbial phrase "It is the busiest man who also has time to spare"'. See C. Northcote Parkinson (1965) *Parkinson's Law*, London: Penguin, originally published in the USA (1957), Chapter 1.
6. R.M. Kipling, *Just So Stories*: The Elephant's Child.

14 The Standard Operation

So let it be written, so let it be done.

Appended to the edicts of the Egyptian Pharaohs

Chapter 7 explained the central role and responsibilities of GK FLMs for securing and sustaining continuous improvement. Chapters 9 and 10 described the mechanisms by which GK companies create the necessary hunger and desire for improvement, together with a clear expectation for the rapid and permanent resolution or containment of process problems. The next chapters set out the *means* by which FLMs and their teams are able to do this; how they are capable of making swift, unilateral changes in a controlled way to effect improvements and resolve problems without having to invoke cumbersome, time-consuming procedures.

The key to all this is the clear ownership of the detailed work process by production and the FLMs' unequivocal responsibility for it. The Standard Operation remains Japan's best-kept and most invaluable secret. It is *the* medium of process control and improvement and is the manifest recognition that neither quality nor productivity can be managed by remote control – only by direct leadership on the shop floor. (Standard Operations must not be confused with so-called 'work standards': see Chapter 13 and the glossary entries for 'work standards' and 'standard time'.)

The Standard Operation is the foundation of customer satisfaction and profit since these spring from our ability to control and improve the manufacturing process (Figure 14.1). The Standard Operation can be defined as follows:

The best currently available method capable of sustaining the specified quality, cost and delivery requirements and of securing operational safety.

The best current operation eliminates waste, ambiguity, irregularity and irrationality from productive work and contains all sufficient relevant details to ensure that the method is easy, quick, inexpensive and safe.

'Currently available' is a key phrase. Standard Operations are perpetually changing in response to process problems and in pursuit of improvements. There

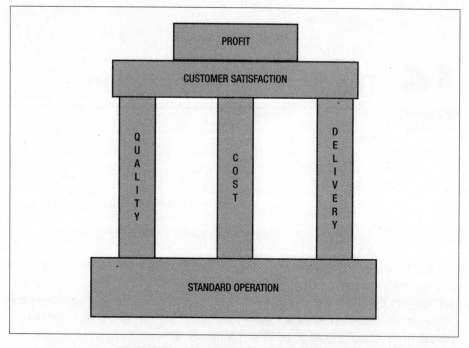

Figure 14.1   Importance of the Standard Operation

is no *best* method, for now and for ever. There is always a better way that we simply have yet to identify and define and it is for FLMs, with the help of their team members, to be looking continually for improved means of performing productive work. Another way of putting this is to say that the Standard Operation is the very worst way that the job will ever be carried out. It is satisfactory for now inasmuch as it provides a benchmark beneath which we shall not allow ourselves to fall and a secure platform from which to pursue a better way.

Chapters 6 and 7 made it plain that in a GK company the responsibility for and ownership of the manufacturing process is that of the FLM and the team and not the discrete preserve of the engineering or technical department. Indeed, in such a company, the tasks of compiling, instructing, observing, enforcing and of continually improving and revising Standard Operations accounts for some 60 per cent of FLMs' time and efforts. Many managers in conventional companies baulk at this level of investment: *how can they possibly find the time*? But what else would they, *should* they be doing? What else can possibly be as important? This activity is the very core of production management itself and the source of all discipline and improvement.

In this way the FLM and the team define, sustain and improve their production processes, including those for quality actions, machine set-ups and changeovers, basic maintenance and diagnostic actions.

Standard Operations are applicable to all activities in all manufacturing companies. A GK company has Standard Operations for fitting components, for delivering those components on a forklift truck, for charging a battery on a forklift truck, or for purchasing a battery for a forklift truck. Standard Operations, devised jointly by direct production FLMs and maintenance personnel, are a vital ingredient both for any programme of total productive maintenance (TPM) and for achieving and maintaining quick changeovers on machines.

Neither are Standard Operations only of value to short-cycle assembly operations or capital-intensive process industries.[1] Some companies rationalise their reluctance to standardise on the basis that they produce long-cycle, 'bespoke' products: industrial equipment, switch gear, ships, power generators. All the more reason why recording the best method is important. Standardisation was the weapon of Shigeo Shingo which enabled first Japan and later Korea to devastate Western shipbuilding. Where there is a gap of months or even years since overcoming the problems of specific applications, painfully earned knowledge and experience must be recorded and preserved.

I recall one long-established, traditional heavy engineering company that I worked with. 'We only make one-offs. Besides, we only employ skilled men who can all read an engineering drawing.' The company, nevertheless, was often constrained to bring former employees out of retirement for short periods and at great expense because no one else knew how to build the product. However, one manager, himself a veteran with over 40 years at the company, was sufficiently impressed with standardisation to want to do something about it. In setting about the task of devising as complete a set of Standard Operations as possible, people cheerfully opened up lockers, tool kits and pockets, and out spewed ancient notebooks, scraps of yellowed paper and scribbled cigarette packs yielding a wealth of process knowledge that the company did not know it possessed. Clearly the workforce of this company had for many years understood and valued some of the merits of standardisation even if the management had not.

The Standard Operation cannot be defined and written from the comfort of an office, only in the *genba* itself: by actually performing the job and, where possible, encouraging the involvement and contribution of the workteam. Moreover, only production FLMs can ensure compliance with the Standard Operation and they will only do so if they own responsibility for it and have taken the trouble to establish it. They will never display any great enthusiasm for enforcing a purely engineering-owned method. Rather, in many conventional organisations the denial of production ownership of the process affords a ready-made excuse for underperformance and the failure to address problems.

This is not of course to say that, in GK companies, FLMs and production teams can ignore the product specification or overturn quality assurance procedures or key technical parameters. In GK organisations the central role of the FLM for defining the process *augments* rather than jeopardises process integrity by adding missing details and rendering the process practical and meaningful.

A succinct description of most twentieth-century devices for process control

OPERATION: FIT HUMIDISTAT AND SOLENOID								
PARTS REQUIRED								
ITEM	PART NO	DESCRIPTION	QTY	ITEM	PART NO	DESCRIPTION		QTY
1	3081074	3/16 RIVET	4	11				
2	1132200	HUMIDISTAT	1	12				
3	2131128	STAT BRACKET	1	13				
4	3081058	CSK RIVET	2	14				
5	3030422	SOLENOID	1	15				
6				16				
7				17				
8				18				
9				19				
10				20				

OP NO	PROCEDURE
1	SECURE MOTOR BRACKET TO FAN HOUSING USING ITEM 1
2	SECURE ITEM 2 TO ITEM 3 USING ITEM 4
3	POSITION ITEM 5 ONTO SOLENOID VALVE
4	CABLE TIE ITEM 2 TO MOTOR BRACKET

DRAFTED W. Brewer	ALPHA	ISSUE	1	2	3	4	5	6	7
		DATE	1.12.96	7.1.97	15.1.97	1.3.97			
CHECKED H. Hawke	UNIT PART NO. 1131100		WORK STATION 9		SHEET 11 OF 38	DRG NO 5050110			
APPROVED U.T. Cobbley	UNIT DESCRIPTION ACME SERIES 5								

Figure 14.2 Typical process instruction in conventional companies

could well be modelled on what Giacomo Casanova is supposed to have said of eighteenth-century condoms: they tend to afford an impenetrable barrier to improvement and a sieve against the risks of process error. Figure 14.2 shows how process sheets or 'work instructions' are frequently written in conventional companies. It is a real example taken from a domestic appliance manufacturer which had recently been admitted through the hallowed portals of ISO 9000. The next chapter will provide further revelations about its problems and how they were overcome.

The bottom part of this sheet testifies to the strange but common conviction that quality is achieved by making things difficult to change and that the degree of process control is somehow proportional to the number of signatures on a document. Suppose that in the interests of quality, safety, efficiency or ease of working the FLM wants to change the sequence or move the job to another workstation. He or she must seek the approval of the three signatories: must *suggest* and cannot *do*. Improvements to this 'method' will consequently be most

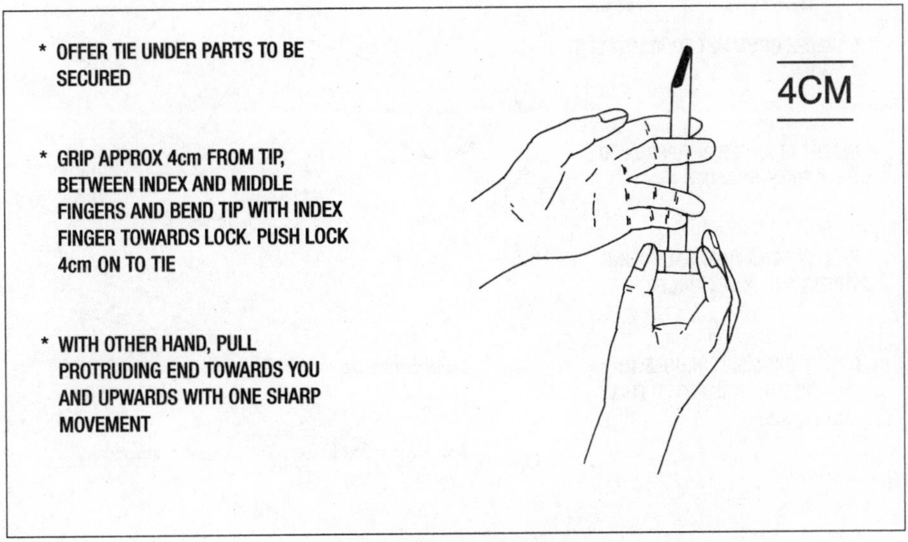

* OFFER TIE UNDER PARTS TO BE
  SECURED

* GRIP APPROX 4cm FROM TIP,
  BETWEEN INDEX AND MIDDLE
  FINGERS AND BEND TIP WITH INDEX
  FINGER TOWARDS LOCK. PUSH LOCK
  4cm ON TO TIE

* WITH OTHER HAND, PULL
  PROTRUDING END TOWARDS YOU
  AND UPWARDS WITH ONE SHARP
  MOVEMENT

4CM

Figure 14.3   Fitting cable ties

exceptional. Few will be deemed worth the trouble.

The four revisions shown were all the result of what appears at the top of the sheet. The practice of putting part numbers on this kind of documentation is a superb means of keeping people, mostly valuable engineers, busy. What do part numbers do? They *change*, and, when they do, the document has to be passed by all the signatories.

And what do we have in the middle to justify this effort? Something so vague and vacuous as a means of specifying how work should be done that a bus could be driven through it. *How* do we 'secure item 2 to item 3 using item 4'? What is the most reliable, safest and most efficient method? *How* do we 'cable tie item 2 to the motor bracket'? The answer is, of course, that workers are expected to fathom these things out for themselves.

Incidentally, Figure 14.3 shows us how to fit a cable tie. It is taken from a Standard Operation in a GK company and was written by an FLM with the help of one of his team members.[2]

Or how about fitting a humble grommet? Certainly we need a technical specification for where to fit the grommet and for precisely which grommet to fit. But then what? Figure 14.4 provides an answer. Again, it is taken from a real GK production-owned Standard Operation.[3]

Chapter 6 explained how GK distinguishes between the unique and complementary professional disciplines of engineering and production. Engineering must supply the *what*. But only production has sufficient detailed knowledge and familiarity to provide the *how*. Figure 14.5 shows a simple engineering specification, adequately describing *what* is required from production.

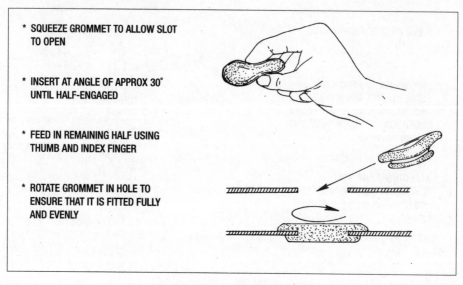

* SQUEEZE GROMMET TO ALLOW SLOT
  TO OPEN

* INSERT AT ANGLE OF APPROX 30°
  UNTIL HALF-ENGAGED

* FEED IN REMAINING HALF USING
  THUMB AND INDEX FINGER

* ROTATE GROMMET IN HOLE TO
  ENSURE THAT IT IS FITTED FULLY
  AND EVENLY

Figure 14.4   Fitting grommets

Figure 14.6 shows what emerges when this is turned into a fully fledged Standard Operation by the GK FLM. The *what* of the engineering requirement has been fully restated and all the essential details of the *how* have been provided in order to ensure the best current method for attaining quality, cost, delivery and safety.

On the whole, the countries of the British Isles brew good-quality tea and make unpleasant coffee. In most other Western countries the reverse is often the case.

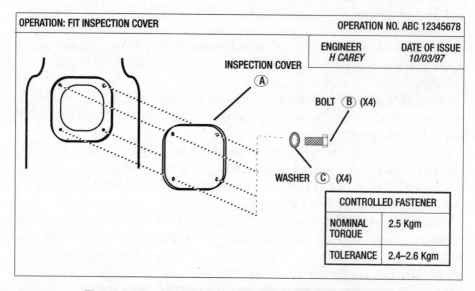

Figure 14.5   GK engineering specification for fitting inspection cover

STANDARD OPERATION SHEET

No.	REVISION	DATE	INITIAL
1.	Sequence of torque check	12/8/95	WB
2.	Handling of cover plate	17.8.96	WB

ZONE	3	SHEET	1	OF	1
DEPT. Final Assy		DATE 24/7/95			
AUTHORISATION					
		W. Bond			

OPERATION No.	OPERATION NAME
ABC 12345678	Fit inspection cover

No.	MAIN STEPS	KEY POINTS	REASON FOR KEY POINT, SKETCH, ETC.
1.	Fit four washers to four bolts	* Pick up four bolts with leading hand and simultaneously four washers in other hand	– Simultaneous motions save time
2.	Insert bolt assembly into air tool socket	* Hold remaining bolt assemblies with 3 fingers as shown	– Frees up thumb and forefinger for next step – Makes for easy insertion into air tool socket
3.	Attach cover to casing with bolt and washer assembly through upper right hand hole using air tool	* Hold cover in position with thumb and forefinger * Squeeze trigger gently at first until bolt engages * Ensure bolt and air tool are at 90° to cover surface * Do not fully secure bolt – half fit bolt only	– To align holes – To avoid cross threading bolt – Otherwise cover will spin out of alignment and subsequent bolts will be impossible to fit
4.	Secure cover to casing with remaining bolts and fixings	* Follow the sequence as shown * Hold cover in position with thumb and forefinger until second bolt is fitted * Ensure bolt and air tool are at 90° to cover surface * Remember to complete the fastening of the first bolt	– To make for a repeatable and regular operation – To secure alignment – To avoid cross threading bolts – Otherwise torque wrench operation will take longer
5.	Check torque spec on each bolt with torque wrench	* Torque spec is 2.5 Kgm +/– 0.1 Kgm * Use wrench on bolts in sequence shown * Ensure wrench is calibrated at start of shift	– Engineering spec to avoid leakage – For a regular operation and to avoid missing a bolt – To guarantee achievement of quality standard

PROTECTIVE CLOTHING	JIGS/TOOLS	REQUIRED CHECKS	TRAINING COMMENTS
Standard	Air tool 2354/78 Wrench A45/20	Torque calibrate 1 per shift	Approx 20 cycles needed

Figure 14.6 GK Standard Operation for fitting inspection cover

STANDARD OPERATION SHEET

No.	REVISION	DATE	INITIAL
1.	Swirl water in pot	14/2/97	PA

OPERATION No.	OPERATION NAME
XYZ 7654321	Make Tea

ZONE	Beverages	SHEET 1 OF 1
DEPT. Restaurant		DATE 20/12/96
AUTHORISATION		
	P. Armendirez	

No.	MAIN STEPS	KEY POINTS	REASON FOR KEY POINT, SKETCH, ETC.
1.	Fill kettle with water and connect to power	* Half fill kettle * Ensure lid is firmly replaced * Align plug to socket before inserting (see sketch)	– Is enough to fill teapot: saves time and electricity – Escaping steam slows boiling and could scald fingers – Saves time and fumbling Notch uppermost
2.	Warm teapot with hot water	* Using either piping hot tap water or small amount of water from almost boiled kettle * Ensure free hand is clear of water being poured * Swirl hot water in pot (see sketch) * Discard all water from teapot after warming	– Warmed pot is essential for good quality tea – To avoid scalding – Speeds up warming process – Teapot should be dry before brewing
3.	Place tea and water in teapot	* Place teapot on trivet * Three heaped teaspoons of tea for full pot * Ensure water is actually boiling: (listen for the boiling sound and wait for steam jet) then disconnect kettle and pour immediately * Cover pot with tea cosy * Leave to brew for between 4 and 7 minutes	– Prevents heat damage to table or work surface – Optimal strength and flavour – Only boiling water produces good tea – Improves brewing and retains heat – Optimal time for flavour and freshness

PROTECTIVE CLOTHING Wash hands before touching food or drink	JIGS/TOOLS Kettle, teaspoon, teapot, cosy, trivet	REQUIRED CHECKS Nil	TRAINING COMMENTS 5 Brews

Figure 14.7   Standard Operation for making tea

Figure 14.7 is my humble contribution to one half of the problem. Following this Standard Operation makes it very difficult to make a bad job of brewing tea.[4] Its other purposes are to demonstrate how just about any process can be standardised and to illustrate an appropriate amount of detail for Standard Operations.

CONSTRUCTING THE STANDARD OPERATION

Constructing Standard Operations is not so difficult for FLMs as some may suppose. They need not be conjured from thin air. Standards which attempt to govern process systems and procedures already exist in most organisations and many of these are in written form.

It is a popular misconception that the United Kingdom lacks a written constitution. The British Constitution is the aggregation of many written statutes and documents including Magna Carta, the Bill of Rights, the Act of Succession and thousands of others. Unlike the US and many other Western democracies, however, it is not defined and codified in a single document. Because of this, constitutional issues in Britain are frequently ambiguous. Such an act of codification is exactly what we are requiring our FLMs to perform when constructing the Standard Operation. Their task is to pull together all the various aspects of existing company standards, as they affect a particular job of work, and then to supplement these with their own knowledge and experience and that of their team members, derived from the actual performance of the job in the *genba*.

In any reasonably competent manufacturing company we would expect to see the basic standards in the top half of Figure 14.8 – although they may exist in a variety of formats and indeed two or more of these items might be combined into one. For every specific operation the GK FLM uses these standards to produce a sufficiently detailed document which, if thoroughly instructed and faithfully carried out, should itself be sufficient to guarantee the required standards of quality and safety in accordance with established company procedures. However, in the GK organisation, there are other contributory sources which are regarded as of comparable value in securing the most effective manufacturing methods, the highest level of skill and the most efficient means of production. These appear in the lower half of Figure 14.8.

FEEDBACK FROM THE DOWNSTREAM PROCESS

GK FLMs are acutely conscious of the status of all downstream processes as their customers, and of the fact that the final product specification may not of itself be enough to meet all downstream process requirements. Consequently, it is their duty to ensure that their Standard Operations guarantee that product is produced

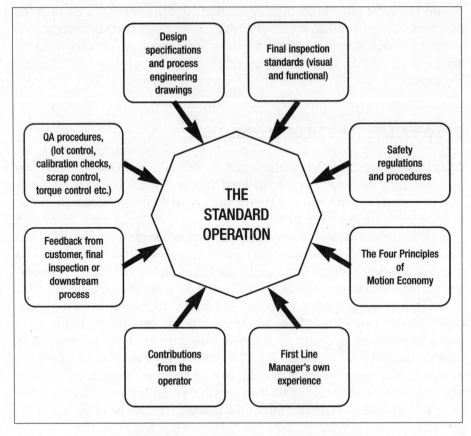

Figure 14.8   Sources of the Standard Operation

and shipped to their downstream colleagues in such a way that makes subsequent operations as easy as possible. To this end, FLMs, Team Leaders and occasionally team members will spend a significant proportion of their time out of their own section, visiting their downstream customers and continually appraising and reappraising their performance and their Standard Operations in the light of such requirements.

CONTRIBUTIONS FROM TEAM MEMBERS

Of course the person who knows most of all about the job is the team member who regularly performs it. Even when drafting Standard Operations for new processes or new products, it is wise to involve the designated job holder or holders whenever possible. Once drafted, the Standard Operation must be rigorously adhered to. Conformance is much easier to achieve if the affected parties have had ample opportunity to make a full contribution to its construction.

Occasionally some companies adopt what they presume to be an enlightened and progressive approach which, on the face of it, seems logical and reasonable. They propose that the workers themselves draft and construct the Standard Operation. In so doing, they demonstrate that they do not fully appreciate some of the most important principles of GK and of job standardisation. There is nothing wrong as such in inviting a production worker to construct a Standard Operation. In fact, this may constitute good practice as a development tool where the intention is to enable the production worker or Team Leader to learn and acquire process management skills. But if the fruits of job standardisation are not to be diluted, then we cannot and must not absolve FLMs of their *responsibility* for ensuring that the Standard Operation is sufficient to guarantee quality, cost and delivery time. Nor must FLMs be allowed to become remote from and ignorant of the processes and production activities for which they are responsible. One of our central principles here is that management and Western companies have over the years retreated from the task of managing the process. If that tendency is to be reversed, then we must make sure that our FLMs have a thorough grasp of all their operations.

THE FOUR PRINCIPLES OF MOTION ECONOMY

The four principles here are simple and basic industrial engineering maxims which can be readily and easily taught to supervisors, team leaders and production workers alike. They are:

1. Reduce the number of motions
2. Perform motions simultaneously
3. Shorten motion distances
4. Make motions easier.

A table showing examples of the detailed application of these principles is provided in Appendix I. They are valid for all products and processes since they apply not only to detailed manual activity, but also to the efficient operation of machinery and to the transport of materials. Specific applications will, of course, vary. For example 'reduce the number of motions', as applied to the movement of hands and fingers to take valuable seconds from each short cycle of bench assembly work might equate, in a long-cycle, heavy machining plant, to finding a sequence that minimises the requirement for slinging and lifting and the hours of delay often associated with dependence on craneage.

FLMS' OWN EXPERIENCE

GK FLMs, experienced in the existing processes and practised in the art of constructing Standard Operations, will be in a good position to be able to avoid a whole host of potential quality problems even before a new product is manufactured in production conditions. They will be able to draw on awareness of historical quality problems associated with similar processes and similar products.

Furthermore, bearing in mind their responsibilities for *instructing* as well as for writing the Standard Operations, they have an unequalled ability to express requirements in simple, practical language which is devoid of technical jargon and can be easily taught to and acquired by team members. This language might not impress a high court judge or be capable of winning a Pulitzer prize, but it is far more likely to give the worker a clear indication of what is required. Anyone who has struggled with the written accompaniments to self-assembly furniture will understand the value of this. GK FLMs entreat their trainees not simply to rely on their visual sense. Touch and hearing can also be important. In describing the requirement for fitting a part which is attached by five spring clips, not clearly visible after the part is fitted, an engineer might specify:

'Make sure the part is fully secure,' or '... pushed fully home'.

A GK FLM might state:

'Start at the top left and move round clockwise, pressing down with the thumbs – make sure you hear five clicks!' There is no argument about that. We hear five clicks and can be confident that we have performed a quality job.

GK FLMs must devise methods which eliminate *waste, awkwardness* and *variability* in the job,[5] and create robust working methods which are *easy to get right* and *difficult to get wrong*. This is what is meant by the phrase 'building in quality'. Some erroneously think that the pinnacle of quality control is reached when workers inspect their own work. This is not so. All inspection is wasteful, adding nothing to the value of products, no matter who does it. A common last item on many work instructions entreats the worker to 'check quality'. What do the authors think this will achieve and what colour is the sky in their world? Do we truly imagine that, as a result of such an entry, workers, on completing a unit or a batch, have time in production conditions to gaze fondly at their produce until faults jump out and hit them in the face? In GK companies quality checks are always specific and temporary activities pending the solution of known difficulties of supply, either from upstream processes or commercial vendors. The real goal is to provide processes which obviate the need to inspect and in which workers can have complete confidence. This confidence lies at the heart of both quality *and* productivity. Contrary to popular belief, slowing down or taking pains does not give better quality. If we are uncertain of what we are doing it makes no difference to quality whether we spend two minutes or two hours doing it. Any worker or any line manager in any factory will confirm that a bad day for quality is usually also a bad day for quantity. Both depend on the effectiveness of manufacturing processes and adherence to them. Robust processes give confidence, which brings rhythm and regularity. Regularity enhances productivity and aids concentration.

STANDARD OPERATION MAINTENANCE AND IMPROVEMENT

The Standard Operation is a live document. Its purpose is to maintain and improve operating methods. However well it is written, it will not perform this function if, like the 'work instructions' and quality manuals found in so many companies, it merely collects dust on a shelf or is interred in a filing cabinet. However much time and effort has been invested in its construction, it is worthless unless it accurately and precisely reflects how the work is actually performed in the *genba*. Even veteran, experienced team members therefore must be reinstructed when their actual methods start to drift from those laid down by Standard Operation – except when such changes constitute improvements (quicker, safer, more stable and conducive to good quality) and can form the basis of a new Standard Operation for all to follow.

Enforcing a Standard Operation can be a difficult task but it cannot be avoided if we are serious about achieving world-class levels of quality and productivity. The Japanese, when teaching their own people about quality, are fond of quoting Dr Joseph M. Juran who, they claim, taught them that: 'If a man will not follow the Standard Operation, let him go home!' Nevertheless, this is not the oppressive kind of conformity that it might at first appear. All members of the GK production team are expected and encouraged to contribute to establishing and subsequently improving the Standard Operation. Genuine method improvements, which are either pursued deliberately by individual team members or else evolve unconsciously from the acquisition of new working habits, immediately become the new way of working for everyone. It is my own experience that it is often the most self-willed and headstrong of team members, frequently found among the most knowledgeable and experienced, who generate the most improvements. Faced with the need to conform to a standard, they cannot resist the challenge which runs: 'All right then, find and prove a better method and we will all do it your way!' Sheer cussedness and tenacity usually drives them to do just that. Moreover, in a GK company, it is infinitely more likely that their contribution will be taken up – and quickly. The only person who needs to be convinced, the only process guardian, works with and alongside them every day. GK FLMs cannot avoid responding to the contribution by passing the buck to engineering; nor would they wish to do so.

Nor is there anything inherently virtuous about the current fashion for pinning process documentation on walls, notice boards or machines. These may impress the less discerning visitor but are simply another species of the 'wallpaper' described in Chapter 10 and are usually indicative of poor training and poor process control.[6]

Suppose we jump into a taxi. As we lean forward to give our destination we notice a square of paper fixed to the right-hand side of the windshield. It says: 'Always follow this sequence: 1, mirror; 2, signal; 3, manoeuvre.' Over at the left side is another sheet proclaiming: 'Remember: green = go; red and amber = stop.'

Down on the dashboard are a couple of sheets stapled together and headed: 'Procedures for roundabouts and four-way stops.' We do not hang around to read any more. Panic overcomes us and we start to wrestle with the door handles to let ourselves out. Why? Because we only have confidence in a driver who *knows how to drive* without prompting; because we expect him to be concentrating on his driving and watching the road, not reading cue cards.

'What's the matter with these people?', mutters the cab driver as we run off in search of the nearest bus stop. 'Don't they know I'm the only driver in the city certified to ISO 9000?'

Our workplace is no different. Anyone who has performed a real job of work in a factory, to any reasonable standard of productivity and quality, knows this full well. Our workers must know the job. If they do not they must be properly trained and instructed. It is not enough simply to stick a crib sheet in front of them and expect them to get on with it.

OBSERVING THE REAL SITUATION

Once it has been taught, there is only one way to make sure that the correct method, the Standard Operation, is followed, and that is to apply the almost forgotten technique of *observation*. FLMs must watch the performance of the work using their own knowledge of the process, which can be buttressed by reference to the Standard Operation sheet beforehand if necessary. Any deviation from Standard Operation must be corrected there and then *on the spot* by guidance and instruction. This dual role of the FLM as both process manager and trainer lies at the heart of *Genba Kanri* and of the venerable old Western industrial tradition which spawned it. Nothing can ever be an adequate substitute for this.

What I have written here is not an appeal for Western companies to regress to a primitive style of management which is untrusting of the workforce and requires them to be *overseen*. The opposite is the case. A former colleague of mine once visited a car plant in Sweden and, in spite of the host company's espoused humanitarian values, he was appalled by what he saw. Supervisors in this company inhabited little offices which were raised up some 2.5 metres from the factory floor and were accessed by a flight of steps. The walls of the offices were constructed of big panes of soundproof glass which afforded a commanding view of the workplace and of everyone working in it. Rarely did these sentinels venture forth from their crystalline enclaves, other than to enquire as to the causes of stoppages or to admonish anyone perceived to be slacking on the job. There was no clear interest in the actual methods being carried out; nor could there be, from such a remote outpost. There are now businesses offering worker-surveillance equipment to industry – surely the most vile and cowardly tool yet devised in the furtherance of remote control management.

By contrast, the starting assumption of GK organisations is that their members are honest, conscientious and diligent. Management must be prepared to assist their efforts to ensure that they have the best methods to follow and the ability to follow them. They must get close to the work and close to the worker. But it is the method that is being observed and evaluated.

The GK FLM observes the actual performance of Standard Operations for the following reasons:

- to ensure conformance of actual methods in the interests of stable processes and consistent quality;
- to identify and capture method improvements that better satisfy quality or make the job safer, faster or easier;
- to avoid potential problems by looking for trends and abnormalities evident in the performance of the job;
- to find causes and countermeasures to known and current problems.

Figure 14.9 shows how the PDCA cycle lies at the heart of the GK FLM's approach to establishing, maintaining and improving Standard Operations.

All elements of this cycle are of course the FLM's responsibility. The best people to make changes to methods are those who have observed, studied and

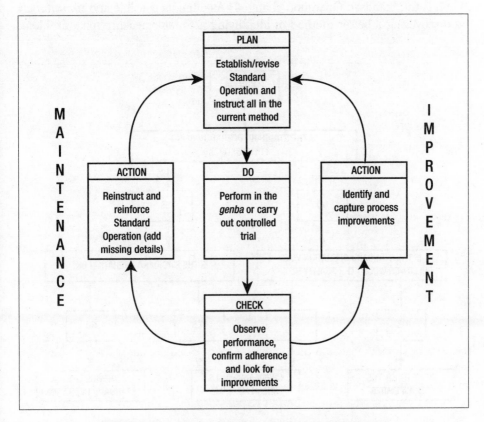

Figure 14.9　Standard Operation maintenance and improvement

performed them (and are accountable for their outputs). The best people for observing the performance of the methods are those who have responsibility both for defining them and for teaching them. This is a very powerful combination both in terms of process and quality control and in terms of grasping the fruits of improvement quickly and easily.

Thorough observation of the work corresponds to the CHECK phase of the cycle. The purposes and the outcomes of the observation shall determine the appropriate ACTION or countermeasure to be taken and whether to proceed with the appropriate sequence for *maintenance*, shown on the left; or with that for controlled *improvement*, shown on the right.

The simplest of algorithms depicted as Figure 14.10 shows how standardised operations assist FLMs by bringing a systematic approach to diagnosing the causes of process problems, but again it relies on analysing the real situation in the workplace.

REVISING THE STANDARD OPERATION

When is the Standard Operation changed? As often as possible and *immediately* on discovering a better method of identifying a countermeasure for a problem.

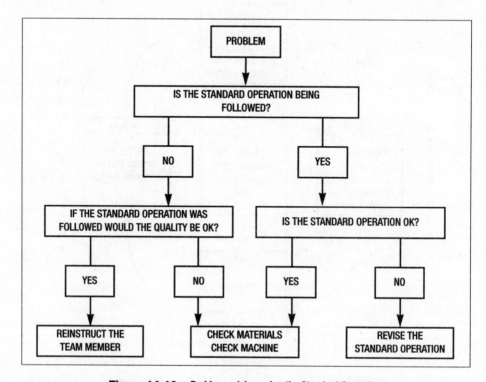

Figure 14.10 Problem solving using the Standard Operation

The Standard Operation has to be a *live* document. It must be regularly amended and updated such that it accurately reflects the work as it is currently being carried out, and fully captures the benefits of any process improvements as they happen. For this reason the document defining the Standard Operation should not be difficult to change. There must be no procedural hurdles placed in the path of changing it: not for having it approved by whomsoever nor even for having it typed or produced on a word processor. Any difficulties or delays are not only a disincentive to improvement but also a temptation to ignore creeping disparities between the Standard Operation and what is actually performed in production conditions. The only signatures that should appear on a Standard Operation document should be those of FLMs. They are the process owners and no other authority for changing it is required. In a GK organisation FLMs take a Standard Operation document from their desk, cabinet or shelf in or near the team's work area. They observe the job to check for conformance and make improvements. If they make improvements, they carry out trials to confirm the effectiveness of the new method. If these are successful they revise the document, ensure that everyone is trained in the new method and put the revised document back in the place from which they took it: end of story. It only becomes slightly more involved and time-consuming when there are multiple shifts. In such cases, since methods must be standard across shifts, all corresponding FLMs on other shifts must approve and sign the change. The synergy which comes from such necessary dialogue and consensus building often provides the impetus for yet more improvements.

I recall one clothing manufacturer midway through its struggle to attain BS 5750 and ISO 9000. It had just reached the stage where quality assurance personnel, working together with operators, had produced a fine set of word-processed 'work instructions'. (Significantly the supervisors were not invited to take part in this exercise; nor did they show any enthusiasm for it. They were too busy with the 'real work': catching up on missed deliveries, worrying about unresolved quality problems – that kind of thing.) I asked the QA manager what she would do next. 'Now, we'll get them laminated to keep them nice and clean!' she replied proudly. I urged her not to do that and, for good measure, further suggested that the 'work instructions' should be written in pencil so that they could be subsequently erased and updated regularly and easily. From the look on her face, she was clearly wondering whether I was joking or had newly arrived from another planet. Yet most of my supervisor colleagues at Nissan did just that. My own preference was for a ball pen and copious amounts of correction fluid. Those who are horrified by these disclosures simply do not fully appreciate the purpose and importance of this document.

Standard Operation sheets are like the standards once carried into battle, whose glory was ever greater the more stained and tattered they became. I have no doubt that, before too long, a point will be reached when all FLMs have their own PCs on their desks in their team areas to create, store, revise and print out their Standard Operations. Meanwhile, which of these two examples yields most evidence of both improvement and the highest standards of process control? A neat, untarnished, centrally produced process document which is rarely referred to in production conditions, whether it is in a filing cabinet *or* stuck on a machine, and which may or may not reflect what actually happens? Or a hand-written sheet containing details which betoken real job knowledge: dog-eared and decorated with greasy fingermarks and alterations, testifying to a history of frequent reference in the workplace and numerous improvements?

NOTES

1. In fact, their contribution is not limited to the manufacturing sector at all. We have recently been privileged to be associated with standardisation programmes for the regular maintenance of railway trains and rolling stock and for the production of eyeglasses and contact lenses for a chain of opticians. Both programmes brought about massive gains in productivity.
2. Not everyone, of course, has a talent for clear, freehand sketches (although Toyota, at their plant in Derbyshire, actually give training in these skills to their Group Leaders and Team Leaders). A photograph can be an adequate substitute. Companies wishing to pursue and secure the benefits of GK principles should ensure that all their FLMs carry a serviceable industrial stopwatch and have ready access to an instant stills camera and a camcorder. This will, in all probability, prove to be a more worthwhile investment than training in the latest exotic, fashionable and expensive techniques in problem solving.
3. A whole volume could be devoted to examples of production-written methods from a wide variety of processes. These few assembly examples are to illustrate the level of detail which is both necessary and attainable and which can easily be understood by those familiar with any process.
4. Figure 14.7 is based on a prototype first devised by Steve Milner, a former colleague now at Real Time Consulting.
5. Frequently referred to in Japanese companies as the 'Three Mus: *Muda, Mura* and *Muri*' respectively.
6. A distinction should be made between process documentation (work instructions or Standard Operations) and simple visual aids which are genuinely referred to during the execution of the work, such as those which distinguish between outwardly similar parts or materials or critiques which give a clear and unambiguous standard for visual quality. These have a specific, value-added purpose and can truly be regarded as tools of the job.

15 Benefits of the Standard Operation

Method goes far to prevent trouble in business; for it makes the task easy, hinders confusion, saves abundance of time and instructs those who have business depending what to do and what to hope.

William Penn

A SECURE PLATFORM AND LAUNCHING PAD FOR FURTHER IMPROVEMENT

The Standard Operation fulfils both a maintenance and improvement function. It is the tool which is used to effect the perpetual helix of sustained improvement shown in Figure 2.4. When combined with the application of the PDCA cycle, it is the means both of ensuring that the benefits of previous countermeasures and improvements are fully retained and do not slip away from us over time, and of propelling us towards further improvements and ever higher levels of performance in quality, productivity, delivery and worker safety.

Most of us are familiar with the frustrations of the following situation which is more or less endemic in many conventional companies. After much time-consuming effort we at last resolve a disruptive or debilitating process problem. This may perhaps have adversely affected our clients; maybe we had to visit their premises in order to eat humble pie and promise, with a show of confidence that we did not truly feel, that the problem has now been truly buried and will certainly not recur. Perhaps the problem did not reach our client, but cost us dearly in terms of scrap, rework, overtime, disrupted schedules and stress for all concerned. The relief and satisfaction we feel on solving the problem seems a just reward for our efforts and previous discomfort. But, six weeks, three months, or a year later, it returns to haunt us with depressing familiarity.

There are only two possible reasons for the recurring process problem. The first is that we made a wrong diagnosis and did not pinpoint the true or underlying cause. The second, however, is much more likely (otherwise we would not have benefited even from a temporary respite). It is that the countermeasure or corrective action was *not standardised*, not consolidated, not effectively captured and preserved. No written definitive record was kept of the improved process, or perhaps it was not thoroughly taught to or assiduously acquired by all who might be called on to carry out the work.

Elsewhere on a production line improvements are introduced to methods and to the layout of materials, tools and fixtures, which means that the work can be performed by deploying only 15 people as opposed to 18. Six months later the line is revisited. It now needs 16 people to run it, even though volumes and product ratios are unchanged, there are no apparent new process problems and all seem to be working just as hard, if not harder than when only 15 team members were deployed. Sixteen is better than 18 but it is not the same as 15.

Machine changeovers are a common example of the same phenomenon. Working together with supervisors and workteams and using simple SMED techniques, we might reduce the time required to change over a given machine, say, from 3 hours to 20 minutes, with an indication that this might be brought down even further for the cost of a few low-value fixings. Months later, at a return visit, it becomes clear that the expected time for changeover is 40 minutes. Forty minutes is better than 3 hours but it is not the same as 20 minutes.

'Oh, we had one chap who could perform a changeover in 18 minutes but he left us recently and no one else seems to have the knack. Actually, we can sometimes manage 25 minutes, given a fair wind and if everything just happens to be at hand.'

So what exactly is 'the knack' (whatever that is supposed to mean) and why is everything not 'at hand' every time? Where is our Standard Operation for carrying out the changeover?

My friend and colleague, Tim Waddington, is an enthusiastic mountaineer. He described his ascent of Kilimanjaro some years ago. Like so many volcanic mountains, Africa's tallest peak is an arduous but not technically difficult climb. Its conical sides slope gradually upwards to a height of some 6000 metres. The ascent takes three or four days; it starts on the fauna-filled Serengeti plain, rising through jungle, scrubland and then a barren, almost lunar landscape. The last 1000 metres are the most difficult. The air is thin and starved of oxygen. This is the steepest part of the mountain, the outside of the volcanic crater itself. The ground is calf-deep in volcanic ash. The feet fail to find satisfactory purchase and the ash slips away with each step. It is like climbing a gravel heap or a dune of soft sand.

There is a drastic but effective countermeasure for this. The party turns in early on the eve of the last day of climbing. They are roused by their guides at 02.00 to make their final assault in darkness and in severe sub-zero temperatures. The surface of the ash has become encrusted by the cold to produce a firm foundation for even the weariest limbs. When the dawn comes, to give a magnificent view of the surrounding vista, the ash quickly melts again. Everyone has a hard time for the last few hundred feet but by now the party is close to the snow-capped summit, and of course coming down afterwards is comparatively easy. The Standard Operation eases our upward journey to ever higher levels of performance in a similar way. By 'freezing' the progress attained with each hard-won step it stops the benefits from slipping away from us and gives us a secure platform from which to make further progress.

THE STANDARD OPERATION AS A FILTER

To be assured of a firm foundation from which to propel ourselves to ever higher levels of performance, we must be confident that the same detailed working methods are being faithfully carried out on every single product and by all who may be required to do the work. This, moreover, vastly improves consistency of performance and reduces process and product variation.

A simple and worthwhile experiment to ascertain the degree of genuine standardisation in any workplace can be carried out by any manager in cases where there are two or more production shifts. All that is required is to ask each shift manager or FLM, or whoever is responsible for the production unit during a given shift, to list their problems in order of severity (by whatever criterion, be it frequency of occurrence, cost or lost production) and compare the results. Assuming that each shift uses the same equipment to make the same range of products with workteams which possess a comparable level of generic skill, then, if processes are standardised, the outcome ought to be two identical lists. The amount of difference is inversely proportional to the degree of standardisation and also indicative of the gains to be made by using a standardised approach to optimise working methods. Suppose the subject of such an experiment is an electronic assembly section and that the findings are as follows:

Shift 1	*Shift 2*
A. Missing components	F. Dry joints
B. Short circuits	E. Reversed polarity
C. Contamination	A. Missing components
D. Excess solder	G. Damaged circuit boards
E. Reversed polarity	B. Short circuits

The disparities shown indicate non-standard working. Were this to be resolved by observing and capturing best practices to formulate and maintain Standard Operations or best current methods, then problems C, D, F, and G would be eliminated from the plant and problems A, B, and E would be much improved.

Tim Waddington and another of my colleagues, David Redpath, delivered part of a programme in manufacturing management run by the Universities of Cambridge and Durham for some of their undergraduates. The undergraduates were learning about job standardisation by studying the production methods at a Japanese-owned host company which manufactured microwave ovens.

The designated liaison, a senior production engineer, was asked to identify a difficult process for the undergraduates to study – one which was associated with quality problems or which was in some way awkward or difficult to perform. Without hesitation he described a problem with the oven doors on one of their high-volume products. Some of these were not 'a good fit'. Leakages were found at test and required subsequent repair and retest.

'But they won't solve anything', the engineer cautioned. 'It's a design problem', he added confidently. 'They have the same problem in Japan.'

The workplace was configured into two parallel assembly lines feeding into a testing area. The first line was permanently engaged in making the same high-volume model in question. The second line made a variety of products according to variations in demand but, on this particular day, was also making the same model as the first line. The undergraduates examined the fault data for the product on both lines. They discovered that 'leaking doors' affected 14 per cent of the ovens from the first line but only 0.6 per cent of ovens from the second line. They then carefully observed the two workers who were fitting doors on each of the lines. They soon noticed slight but significant differences between the methods of the two workers, although both methods were compatible with the parameters of the specified 'engineering process'. The worker on the first line held the door in place from its top edge while he secured it with screws using a power driver. The worker on the second line used the same equipment but placed her arm around the front of the door and held it by the side edge, opposite the hinges. This had the effect of pushing the hinged edge more closely into the recess of the oven and achieving a better seal – although the worker was unaware of the beneficial consequences of her method. Each worker was simply performing actions which 'seemed natural' to them. The undergraduates then produced a Standard Operation based on the second worker's method and successfully transferred it to the first line. As a result the problem, which had affected 11 per cent of this model, now had a much reduced occurrence of 0.6 per cent. The new method was adopted within the plant; it was also exported to Japan.

It is in the nature of any regularly performed task that we drift away from the methods that were first taught to us. It is sometimes said that formal driving lessons do not teach us how to drive: we only *really* learn to drive *after* we have passed our driving test. It is certainly true that, as we gain experience in driving, our methods change. Gradually over the passage of months and years we reach a point where there is very little resemblance between the way we drive now and the way we drove on the day we passed our driving test. We acquire new habits. Some acquire good habits; many it seems acquire bad ones. Most of us probably accumulate a mixture of good and bad.

So it is with the performance of any job of work. As our experience increases and our confidence grows, we develop new habits, often unconsciously. Some will be refinements which enable us to perform the job faster, more easily or to a more consistent quality standard. Others will be bad habits which may be detrimental to product quality, cause us undue fatigue or, in the worst cases, jeopardise our own safety or that of our co-workers. The Standard Operation is a filter which enables us to benefit from the development of good habits and yet sift out the bad. FLMs check the work which is being performed against the Standard Operation. Good practice becomes the new standard as everyone is instructed in that technique. Deviations from the standard which are not beneficial are dealt with by reinstructing team members to bring the work back to the current existing standard.

Good working habits are not difficult to acquire and maintain. They soon become routine and may actually be difficult to shake off. As a schoolboy, I had a part-time job serving fuel in a filling station. The owner of the station had once been a banker. He insisted that the banknotes should always be oriented the same way – Queen's head facing up and to the back of the till. This made them quick and easy to count up at the end of the day. I quickly developed the subconscious habit of sorting the notes out on my brisk walk back to the kiosk to get the customers' change. After all these years I still cannot hold cash in my hand without making the notes all lie the same way, especially if I am about to give them to somebody else.

SKILL AND THE STANDARD OPERATION

Job standardisation and the other GK principles force a reconsideration of what is meant by the term 'operational skill'. I once observed a CNC lathe operation in a heavy engineering plant, together with some of its managers.

'You should be aware that this is a highly skilled job', they told me. As I watched with whetted anticipation, the machine operator took a casting from a pallet and loaded it into the chuck. He closed the sliding doors on the machine and pressed the start button. He watched the machine perform its cycle. (Yes, I wondered why too.) Afterwards, he opened the doors, removed the piece from the chuck, placed it on a different pallet and picked up another casting. One of the managers read my thoughts.

'It isn't *always* that simple', he pronounced. 'The machine doesn't work as well as it should and sometimes he needs to thump and tweak it. Also, sometimes the castings from our foundry are slightly oversize. If he doesn't spot this and make adjustments, not only will the piece be scrapped but the cutting tool may be damaged.'

The other managers nodded in earnest assent. I got the distinct impression that they were rather proud of this arcane tinkering which they were pleased to call 'skill'. Skill in this company clearly equated with an ability to cope with unresolved management problems and the failure of upstream processes. Others think of skill as innate ability (where people spring from the womb as natural born welders, machinists or assemblers), the inevitable consequence of indentured servitude ('time served'), the ability to make some sense out of the vaguest and most ambiguous of engineering drawings or simply a difficult-to-define, 'black art' (the secret preserve of initiates on whom managers gaze in paternalistic wonderment because they are simply too far removed from the work to understand what the hell is going on. *Thump and tweak?*).

Expressions such as 'bad workmanship', 'human error', 'a one-off' all are examples of system and management failings to resolve non-standard working. Deming makes a distinction between two groups of people in organisations: those who work *in* the system and those who are responsible *for* the system: namely management.[1] It is unfair to blame the worker for the failings and vagaries of the system. Although it makes obvious sense to secure the involvement and contribution of workers, the burden of *responsibility* for devising processes which contain sufficient detail to guarantee quality, cost, delivery and safety must fall on the shoulders of management and particularly on FLMs who work in the *genba*. That is what production management is supposed to be all about.

Skill, therefore, in a GK organisation consists simply and starkly in demonstrating the full acquisition of the Standard Operation and following it meticulously. This definition will appear sterile or unsatisfying only to those who cherish a Pre-Raphaelite ideal where industry chiefly comprises activities such as shoeing horses or carving original designs on Queen Anne legs.

Companies which fail to standardise, who give to their workforce only broad parameters and expect individuals to work out the missing details for themselves as they think fit, must expect an equally broad distribution of performance in terms of efficiency, quality and safe working practices. In such conditions managers become trapped into assumptions that such distribution is a natural consequence of variations in individual ability and levels of effort or motivation. Figure 15.1 demonstrates the consequences of this thinking. Figure 15.2 shows how, by identifying, capturing and disseminating all the necessary details which

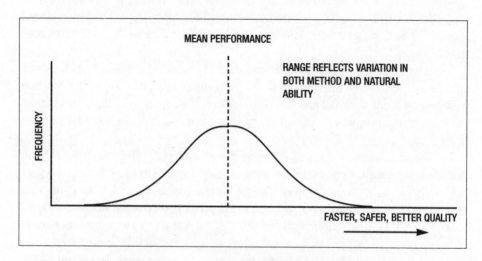

Figure 15.1 Performance without standardisation

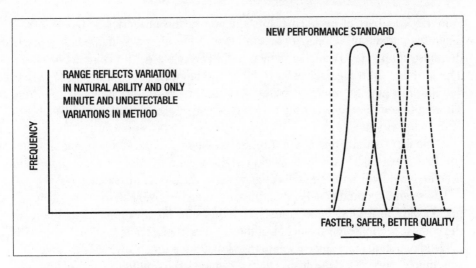

Figure 15.2   Performance after standardisation

comprise the most efficient current method of safely meeting quality standards, the Standard Operation at once drastically narrows the distribution curve (which now spans only the relatively minor variations in individual ability) and shifts it sharply to the right. Further moves to the right will be brought about by subsequent improvements to the Standard Operation.

Taiichi Ohno makes a provocative contribution to our understanding of this concept.[2] Suppose we wish to establish a standard time for a given operation and we record the time taken to perform the job, say, seven times. What should our standard time be? Most people in conventional organisations would answer that it should either be the slowest time or some mean or mode of all the times recorded. But in a GK organisation, the standard will always be the *fastest* time. Far from being either unfair or too demanding, this time must reflect the *easiest* method. If we can closely observe this method and pinpoint and record those aspects which make it so easy then we can standardise it and ensure that the job is performed that way, every time, by everyone.

Real unfairness is to apply a mean standard time where there is variation in method, as shown by the vertical broken line in Figure 15.1. Here, everyone using methods to the right of the line would achieve the standard. Some would surpass the standard easily (although they would soon drop their performance once the standard was introduced). Some to the left of the line would never achieve the standard while others would only do so at the cost of undue fatigue and strain on muscles and joints.

The fact that in Figure 15.2 we have raised the true level of skill by ensuring that all follow detailed and optimised working methods means that we can apply a seemingly much more demanding standard which, paradoxically, *everyone* can achieve comfortably given appropriate training and practice.

In 1985, as part of my formal introduction to the mysteries of the Standard Operation at Nissan's Oppama plant in Japan, I was shown a simple but effective demonstration video recording which had been made by the Oppama foremen. The foremen, who themselves introduced the item, had used a Japanese coffee-vending machine for their purposes. At that time a cup of coffee cost 80 Yen. Three different methods of obtaining coffee with eight 10 Yen coins were shown to us in the video.

In the first method, one of the foremen walked up to the vending machine and reached down into his trouser pocket eight separate times for the coins. Each time he moved his hand the full distance up to the slot to insert each coin.

The second method consisted of the same man removing all the coins from his pocket with his leading hand, transferring the coins into his other hand, lifting all the coins to within some six inches of the slot, and then picking out each coin with his leading hand, inserting each into the slot one at a time. Obviously this method was much more effective: it drastically reduced the amount of movement and effort of the leading hand and involved far less fumbling. Not surprisingly, it took only about 20 per cent of the time of the first method.

Method three portrayed the same foreman again taking out from his pocket all coins in his leading hand but then immediately lifting his hand, with all the coins, to the level of the slot and with dexterous manipulation of this thumb and all four fingers, slipping each coin into the slot in rapid succession. This looked very impressive, and took less than half the time of the preceding method.

We were all primed to give our answer when the inevitable question was asked. 'Which do you think is the Standard Operation?' We unanimously replied that it should be the third method. 'You may be right,' came the response. (Japanese find it difficult to tell people that they are wrong – especially foreigners.) 'But we have found that, even after considerable practice, people using this method usually drop some or all of the coins on the floor every fourteenth or fifteenth time. The time then taken to pick the coins from the floor more than destroys the time advantage of the third method. Method three we therefore feel is less secure and less stable; we think that we would prefer the second method to be the Standard Operation.' Clearly, then, the demands made on the dexterity of the worker by the Standard Operation should be no more than that all could reasonably acquire, given appropriate training and the required amount of practice.

However, we must not underestimate the level of dexterity that can be brought about by thorough, on-the-job Standard Operation training throughout the whole workforce. Some time ago, I was explaining these concepts of skill, quality, productivity – and their due acquisition through the medium of the FLM teaching the Standard Operation – to a group of production managers and quality engineers from a leading, established, Western motor manufacturer located in the UK. I was having some difficulty in portraying the magnitude of what we were talking about in terms of company-wide productivity and performance. (I had already used the penny saving per car model, but I wanted something more impacting that they would all recognise.)

In motor manufacturing, in common with many other assembly industries, many nuts and bolts are fitted. Naturally, virtually all of these are assembled using power tools of various strengths and sizes, depending on the application.

'In your company', I asked, 'do you hand-start all your nuts and bolts?'[3]

A quality assurance engineer immediately misjudged the purpose of my question. '*Mea culpa*', his shrug seemed to say to me as he conceded: 'We're supposed to, but there are always one or two people who don't. A few operators seem to have the skill to get away with it. Production managers and foremen turn a blind eye because it's quicker.'

'In a GK car plant', I replied, '*nobody* hand-starts nuts and bolts, apart from on a very few designated critical fixings. Only a new recruit could fit nuts and bolts with their fingers without being ribbed by their team mates.'

'Don't they strip rather a lot of threads?' came the response.

'Very few', I replied. 'Production workers are *taught* how to fit bolts with an air tool without stripping threads.'

New operators are *taught* how to hold an air tool while fitting and securing fixings. They are taught how to position the socket squarely over the head of the bolt, and the threaded end of the bolt squarely over the hole; how to ensure that as they begin to fit the bolt their head and eye positions are focused on the fixings and nowhere else; how to use the variable speed trigger on the air tool to start the tightening process slowly at first and building up speed thereafter. These aspects appear on the Standard Operation sheet as critical points specifying the 'how' of the method. FLMs are particularly attentive to making sure that this method is fully acquired and consistently practised by all production workers, novices and veterans alike.

Thus we have a situation where what is regarded as clandestine and unorthodox 'corner cutting' practised by a few in one organisation is considered as a *company standard* equating to a level of *skill* in another, and is practised *by all* in a controlled way. When we consider the quantity of fixings involved in the assembly of a motor vehicle, then this simple example tells its own story about quality, skill and productivity, contrasting GK and other motor manufacturers. But, of course, this is only one example among many. It is not the mere practice of 'gun starting' as opposed to 'hand starting' which accounts for the yawning productivity gap between GK and conventional car makers, but rather the completely different approach to skill, quality, control of the process, on-the-job training, and *real* productivity that it represents.

MAKING IT EASY TO IMPROVE

The Standard Operation, as owned by production teams and managed by the GK

FLM, removes the most common difficulties of conventional manufacturers described in Chapters 3 and 4. It resolves the 'empowerment paradox' by establishing real quality and process control *at source*, reinforcing manufacturing accountability, improving consistency of performance and minimising product and process variation *while at the same time* increasing the speed and volume of improvements by shortening the process change loop. The Standard Operation thus genuinely empowers FLMs and their teams. It allows for the rapid introduction of quality countermeasures and process improvements by unilateral action at FLM level and below, since the only constraint in this area is the need to secure consensus with other shifts and to comply with the overall engineering standard and product specification. The Standard Operation is therefore not an imposition but an opportunity, not an impediment to improvement introduction but a releasing agent. It overcomes the wicket gate of conventional process management systems and lowers the value threshold for a myriad of small, incremental (*kaizen*) improvements by reducing the hassle factor associated with the capture – so that small value improvements become worth the effort of process change.

At this very moment production teams in GK companies are generating ideas for improved productivity or to resolve quality problems *as they engage in production activities*. These will not be submitted to engineering, a 'continuous improvement committee', senior management, a 'suggestions officer' or moderator. FLMs are themselves determining the value and feasibility of improvement ideas, assuring their compatibility with process and specification parameters, making any necessary changes to the Standard Operation (carrying out controlled trials where appropriate or necessary), and ensuring a re-instruction of all affected operators in the new method. In most cases this will be done and the company will be enjoying the fruits of improvement *within hours* and nobody other than the FLMs and their teams will have been involved: they are *totally* responsible for their processes.

This key responsibility also serves to take the grind and pain out of ISO 9000, BS 5750 and other certified quality systems, thereby releasing technical staff from clerical drudgery to spend more time on product development and more specialised improvement activity. In so doing, it clarifies and encourages a positive, supportive and profitable relationship between engineering, quality assurance functions and manufacturing. Engineering can spend less time struggling to keep process documentation up to date and more time carrying out real engineering work. Quality assurance can escape the ignominious label of being 'blockers' or as those employed 'to catch manufacturing out' and can be truly regarded as valuable allies in the drive to add value to products. Manufacturing ceases to be the victim of change and becomes the very vanguard of improvement.

Many conventional companies appear to be organisationally incapable of meeting the demands of their own quality systems. They are barely able to keep pace with externally imposed changes, much less contend with a flood of small process improvements. For many of these companies the achievement of a nationally or internationally recognised approved quality system is a basic commercial necessity. Yet so often the approach taken to achieve these accolades is costly to administer and unwieldy, stifling initiative and adding nothing of real value. This need not be so, as the following example illustrates.

Let us return to our company making domestic appliances from which the example of a conventional process control document (Figure 14.2) was taken. The company displayed all the classic symptoms of a small to medium-sized manufacturer having just attained an internationally recognised standard of 'quality control'. It was choking on its own newly acquired systems which were fermenting an antagonistic and unsupportive relationship between its three key disciplines of production, engineering and quality assurance.

Quality assurance saw their role as being merely to police the system; to audit what was actually happening on the shop floor against established procedures, and especially against the engineering process documentation. Workers who did not clearly have the correct and up-to-date documentation physically in front of them were judged, as were their supervisors, to be in breach of procedure. QA also had responsibility for housekeeping and conducted regular audits of the orderliness of the shop floor. They rarely if ever became involved with real product quality problems; nor did they place any emphasis on the importance of downstream process requirements or help compile meaningful data on the quality of finished products. They were the guardians of the company's new status as an ISO 9000 manufacturer, which they saw as being under constant threat by the indifference and indiscipline of the other two functions.

Production, not surprisingly, rather despised the quality assurance department. The latter, it was felt, took smug pleasure in highlighting problems, yet offered neither solutions nor constructive support. Production saw themselves as the company's achievers, its front-line battalion who struggled to make schedule and overcome the real production problems in spite of, not because of, the efforts of the other functions.

'It's not our fault if we have out-of-date process documents. If QA want to do something useful they should go upstairs and lean on those laggards in Engineering who are supposed to get it to us on time. Even when we get it, it's often wrong. If we tried to build everything exactly to the engineering process we'd never ship anything! And we've just about given up on the tooling and design changes we've asked for.'

But QA *had* now started to lean on engineering, adding their voices to the complaints of the production managers. For engineering the problem was one of resources. This company designs and markets its own range of products. In spite of an increase in the number of engineers employed, the list of outstanding projects continued to expand – some of it was vital development work for new products. Almost a third of the engineers were merely dedicated to issuing and

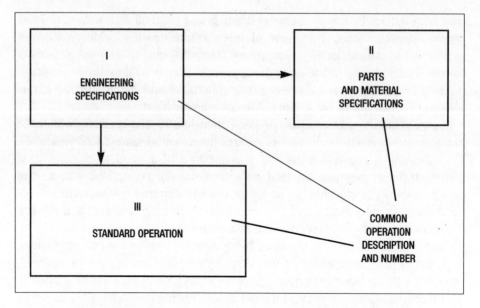

Figure 15.3   Robust approach to process and parts control documentation

updating process documentation and yet they still failed to keep up with even minor alterations in specification, many of which involved simple changes to part numbers on 'process sheets'.

'OK', they acknowledged, 'so ISO 9000 is important for us. We accept that. But senior management must recognise the need to recruit more engineers.'

Who is to blame for this counterproductive and unprofitable relationship? Nobody in the functions concerned. It is merely the symptom of a manufacturing company being organisationally *incapable* of meeting even the maintenance demands of its own quality systems.

The domestic appliance company found salvation in its pursuit of GK principles and the introduction of production-owned Standard Operations. The established format for process documentation (Figure 14.2) was abolished and replaced by three new documents, two of which were compiled and managed by engineering, and the third by production supervisors. This tripartite set of documents is shown in Figure 15.3. All three documents are cross-referenced using a discrete operation description and operation number.

The trigger document is the *engineering specification*. This is a simple sketch of the assembly and parts associated with the operation, supplemented only with the relevant dimensional, functional and process parameters (similar to Figure 14.5). Part numbers do not feature on this document. Parts are merely referred to as 'bolt A', 'bracket B', 'capacitor C' and so on. The process specification is generated according to the design drawing and it is issued to the production supervisor.

The *parts specification sheet* is a printout which identifies 'bolt A', 'bracket B' and 'capacitor C' with part numbers and specifies the quantities required of each and the specific products to which they relate. This again is issued from engineering to production (and also to materials control). Significantly, changes which simply relate to parts and part numbers do not necessarily affect documents I or III and can be swiftly and easily actioned with minimal disruption.

The *Standard Operation* is, of course, owned by production. Its authorship is triggered by the issue of document I and it must reflect its requirements. But it is written, monitored and enforced by FLMs, and any changes they wish to make to it which do not conflict with the requirements of the engineering specification concern nobody but themselves.

FLMs must revise and change their Standard Operations in respect of reissues of the engineering specification but, since again part numbers do not feature on Standard Operations, they are not necessarily affected by changes to the parts specification sheets. FLMs are responsible for holding up-to-date sets of documents I and II and for destroying outdated issues, but the working document on the shop floor is the Standard Operation. FLMs train their team members and observe their actual methods against this, *their* standard.

Our domestic appliance company quickly discovered that, in addition to the other benefits of introducing Standard Operations, it was able to preserve the integrity of a viable quality system, sustainable and maintainable in full, without additional engineering resources. It allowed the QA function to adopt a more profitable and satisfying role in terms of contributing meaningful product-quality data which enabled engineering and production to focus on the vigorous pursuit of real process problems. This brought about an atmosphere of mutual respect and co-dependence between the functions and eliminated the disruption which was endemic in the old system.

Nevertheless it was with some trepidation that the ISO auditors were invited into the plant so that the management team could explain their proposals for changing their procedures and the benefits they would expect to derive from them.

'Sure', was the response, 'so long as you describe the procedure in your quality manual. Actually we always did think that your system was rather bureaucratic.'

'Why didn't you tell us?'

'That's not our job. You are responsible for developing your own systems and procedures. We are only here to check that they are clear and unambiguous and that they are being followed.'

Quality certificate auditors are rarely the problem. They are usually reasonable, practical and highly perceptive people. They know what real quality control looks like. The high price that so many companies have to pay for their certification is usually caused by the system they have unnecessarily saddled themselves with. I sometimes think that the root cause of the problem is the lucrative severance packages offered during the recessions of the 1980s and early 1990s. Many quality managers saw an opportunity to accept a golden handshake and then to exploit a growing market for certified quality systems. Setting themselves up as BS 5750 or ISO 9000 consultants, and laden with the erroneous assumption that the surest and quickest way to gain acceptance was to produce a weighty tome of complex procedures, they simply sold an approach which was modelled on the one they had taken at their erstwhile employers, and they thereby successfully disseminated bad practice.

HARVESTING THE FRUITS OF PRODUCTIVITY IMPROVEMENTS

By filling the void between management and the detailed execution of daily production work, FLM-written Standard Operations, in all their detail, capture *for the whole company* the full value of productivity-based improvements. As such Standard Operations overcome the fourth of our problems with *kaizen* (described in Chapter 3) and also bear directly on the difficulties of what Deming described as 'work standards'.

As we have seen, work standards are historically linked to piecework, bonus and similar 'productivity incentive' schemes and are now a common feature of measured day work (MDW). Like piecework, MDW goes hand-in-hand with the status of 'hourly pay' for direct workers and all that this implies concerning the mutual obligations of management and workforce. Let us restate the old problem.

What is it that we tacitly say to an 'hourly-paid' employee when we operate a system of work standards and measured day working? We say to such people, 'This is the work we have calculated that you should be able to perform: in a 5-minute cycle, in an hour, in a 39-hour week.' When they find for themselves the means of performing the assignment in: $4^{1}/_{2}$ minutes, 54 minutes, 35 hours, they enjoy the benefits of more relaxation, more cups of coffee, more cigarette breaks or a slower pace of work. What else do we have a right to expect? They have fulfilled their obligations *as the company has defined them.*

In this situation it is very difficult to introduce small continuous productivity-based improvements which may involve a change in the 'work standard'; for when we try to do so we are changing the contract of employment in a very real sense. In large and in highly unionised organisations this is a particularly difficult matter. In the UK, Ford's 'Work Standards Agreement' and General Motors' agreement 'We Sell our Time' (a title which tells its own story) are examples of the sort of custom and practice which conspire to make the time and effort required to improve methods prohibitive.

Nissan's plant in the North-East of England makes an interesting contrast. There, they have hundreds of different work assignments and thousands of discrete Standard Operations across a full range of automotive processes: stamping, plastic moulding, body assembly, paint, aluminium casting and machining, engine assembly and final assembly. Scarcely a shift goes by without each and every small production team improving its Standard Operations and/or reassigning work between team members to capitalise on the benefits. Orthodox methods of controlling such a massive volume of improvements would require *hundreds* of industrial engineers: yet at Nissan they have about half a dozen. How do they keep up with the pace of improvement by re-establishing and, if necessary, renegotiating 'work standards'? The answer is, of course, that they do not. Invoking a procedure whereby new methods are retimed and formally endorsed by all parties would delay the implementation of the most valuable improvements and deter all the others. Standard work times in GK companies are purely a budgeting and manpower planning tool for product or facility launch or commercial 'what if?' models. They are not part of an immutable contractual agreement between a mutually suspicious management and workforce, but *targets* which FLMs and their production teams *expect to demolish*. In anticipation of this, the company will make across-the-board, percentage reductions in *all* standard times on a regular basis and factor these reductions into its future budgetary assumptions. Small, productivity-related method improvements are not measured individually by management – only by the truck-load. This not only avoids a potential logjam of would be improvements, but also spurs FLMs and their teams to further increase real productivity.

There is only one sure, *once-and-for-all* way of ensuring that companies can fully benefit from spontaneous worker-generated improvements, and it has two components. First, the practice of paying workers by the hour must be abolished so that all employees are paid a *salary*, thus destroying the basis of MDW and depoliticising the 'work standard'. When a GK company pays someone a fixed salary to work an agreed number of hours, and takes action to remove a measurable quantity of unnecessary work and effort, replacing it with the same measured quantity of *productive* work, who can regard this as unjust?

Second, management must *get closer to the work* by introducing full FLM responsibilities for job standardisation. In this way, work methods can be improved and work assignments reconfigured at production-team level, without the burdensome and time-consuming need to invoke cumbersome company-wide procedures designed to revise and re-establish 'work standards'. FLMs' detailed knowledge of processes enable this to happen easily and without acrimony or mistrust. People only debate, barter or seek to negotiate work times when they are aware that the other party understands significantly less about the job than they do, and yet GK FLMs are able to demonstrate the Standard Operation *personally* to their team members.

Detailed, recorded Standard Operations, as the product of the job knowledge of the FLM and of the team, ensure that *nothing is hidden*. The full detail of how work is performed becomes part of the company domain. All improvements are automatically captured on the bottom line. There is no private discretionary 'black art' concept of skill or knowledge. This is a trusting relationship where everything is transparent: team workers know that FLMs would not require them to perform tasks which they could not perform themselves.

In such companies, direct workers have discarded their traditionally perceived right to 'mystique' in the way they carry out the detail of their work in the interests of a more disciplined approach to process control and more consistent and reliable working methods which reduce product and process variation. They recognize that this enables them to be among the world's most productive, profitable and stable companies. They give up this discretionary knowledge partly because of the comfort and security this brings, partly in exchange for the opportunity to have a far greater involvement and influence on the way their team (their business unit) is run, but mainly as their contribution to an unwritten covenant which ensures that they are accorded far greater respect as people and individuals than in more conventional organisations. That is why the following chapter is so important.

NOTES

1. Deming, *Out of the Crisis* (pp. 315–18); see Select bibliography.
2. Ohno, *Workplace Management* (pp. 151–3); see Select bibliography.
3. The term 'hand starting' refers to a practice whereby assemblers apply the nut to the bolt (or the bolt to the threaded hole) by hand, and then turn it a thread or two to ensure a clean contact between the threads before applying the power tool. The alternative, 'gun starting', is to use the power tool for the complete duration of the assembly and here the nut or bolt head is often inserted into the socket of the power tool before the part is even pre-positioned. Hand starting takes workers a little time – a great deal of time if they have a lot of nuts and bolts to fit – but it can reduce a tendency to 'cross-thread' fixings which might otherwise be a frequent occurrence. 'Cross-threaded' nuts and bolts are extremely disruptive to the operator's workflow, and obviously some considerable time and money is lost with the need to retap threads or make repairs. For this reason gun starting is a proscribed activity in most assembly companies who demand a hand start for virtually all fixings as a formal process requirement.

Part V
Making the Transition

16 Breaking down the Barriers

Yatha Raja, tatha praja. (As is the king, so are the people.)

Hindu Proverb

GK operating principles demand a new covenant of understanding between management and workforce. Not the empty platitudes seen on so many company mission statements (such as 'people are our most valuable resource'), but solid and tangible standards of treatment and behaviour which bring about mutual trust and confidence. Sony's president, Akio Morita, stated that the most important secret of making a business successful is to create 'a feeling that employees and managers share the same fate'.[1] Words and platitudes are not enough to create this feeling. Loyalty and commitment must work in both directions. To demand more of people we must *provide more:* not merely 'hygiene factors' of a financial, material or environmental nature, but especially organisational practices which reflect a respect for human dignity.

Table 16.1 lists catalysts for and barriers to commitment loyalty and effective teamworking. Most of the catalysts are captured by the seven GK elements. This chapter is concerned with four characteristics of GK organisations concerning people management which enable those elements to function effectively.

SECURITY OF EMPLOYMENT

The first characteristic is the extent to which GK organisations bend over backwards to give job security to all their employees. This is a prerequisite for continuous improvement, especially as it pertains to enhanced productivity and the elimination of waste. Nobody would willingly improve themselves out of a job. I shall never forget the bitter rhyme that I often heard at my first employers:

Who works hard and does his best
Gets paid off just like the rest.

Japanese management orthodoxy declares redundancies to be a failure of

Catalysts	Barriers
• Regular feedback on and recognition for team and individual performance	• Piecework or 'productivity bonus'
• Flexibility (responsibilities understood but not prescribed in detail)	• Restrictive practices (management or union)
• Clearly understood and challenging company-wide and team targets	• Written job descriptions
• A sense of company and team identity	• Job grading and job evaluation
• Common terms and conditions of employment	• Alienation from company aims (them and us)
• Positive peer-group pressure ('we can all do it; we expect the same from you')	• Negative influences from peers ('don't suck up to the suits')
• Personal loyalty to the team	• Limited responsibility, limited capacity for action
• Job security	• Insecurity (fear of redundancy)
• Pride in the job: skill, quality, versatility ('people are relying on me')	• Little sense of being valued ('if I stay in bed I won't be missed')

Table 16.1   Teamwork, flexibility and commitment: catalysts and barriers

management, pure and simple. Recession does not cause companies to fail; failing companies cause recession. While I have some sympathy with this view, try telling these things to a Western company making bricks and tiles during a building slump. Japan's economy does not pitch itself around the cycle of boom and gloom half so violently as do those of Western nations. When a critical mass of Western businesses are also GK organisations, then things might change. But, until then, what is the minimum that GK employees in Western economies have a reasonable right to expect of their company? They have a right to expect that, short of jeopardising its survival, it will do everything it can to avoid compulsory lay-offs, even if that means a temporary moratorium on the payment of shareholders' dividends or the freezing of senior managers' salaries.[2]

Superfluous advice on budget presentation for existing departmental managers in GK companies might run as follows.

1. *Expenditure*: make a rational and well thought out case. Make sure it's watertight.
2. *Capital*: as for expenditure, but be prepared to do it two or three times. Expect a real grilling and fresh objections on each occasion.
3. *Manpower*: as for capital, but also indicate and *prove* that the direst calamities will befall your business objectives if your needs are not met. Then chalk up a victory if you are granted even half of what you think you need.

Does this seem Draconian? It is only the workings of a company that genuinely treats labour as fixed cost and not as a consumable item to be frivolously incurred and just as frivolously disposed of. Such companies deliberately buck the trend of corporate behaviour during both boom and recession. Their stringency and vigorous pursuit of productivity improvements during the good times reduces their cost base and enables them to be much more protective of their people during the bad. The best of them may even welcome recession, for it kills off competitors and increases market share. And of course the benefits gained in terms of loyalty, dedication and continued commitment to continuous improvement are inestimable.

ABSENCE OF RESTRICTIVE MANAGEMENT PRACTICES

A city policeman came across a drunk on a busy street corner, waving his arms around and grunting loudly. As many of the passers-by appeared to be somewhat intimidated by this, the policeman decided to take action. Cautiously and unthreateningly he approached the drunk.

'Don't you think you should be running along home now, Sir?' he said. 'Where do you live?'

The drunk leaned very close to the policeman to let him in on his big secret. 'I *can't* go home yet,' he hissed. 'I'm scaring away the giraffes!'

'Come along now, sir', said the policeman. 'There are no giraffes around here.'

' *I know*', replied the drunk, grinning, 'I'm doing a good job ain't I?'

Since the 1980s, which witnessed a transformation in the attitudes of unions and a greater recognition by all of the economic realities of the worldwide slow-growth economy, most practices which restrict flexibility and commitment of employees have been those of management. For the most part they are the remnant of a bygone era, of a less competitive world. They were the product of a desire to make the job of managing easier but are now cumbersome and expensive, add nothing to the value of products or services and detract from real operational discipline.

The problems of piecework, bonus and measured day work were discussed in Chapter 13. Most of the other restrictive management practices are vestiges of piecework or other aspects of remote control management: systems, procedures and devices which, though honoured by time and familiarity, are no longer serving any useful purpose and simply get in the way of teamwork, interfere with the FLM's responsibility for managing people and hamper our ability to reinstate real leadership in the workplace.

Detailed written job descriptions are one example. They serve no purpose other than to create employment opportunities for personnel officers. It is argued that they enable employees to understand their prime function and focus on clear goals, but Chapter 10 established that GK organisations in particular have much more effective methods for doing this. Moreover, I have never known a case where a job description has been pulled from a filing cabinet to help someone understand what their job *is*. Usually it is only demanded by a job holder who, in a pique of rebellious conformity, wants to demonstrate what it *isn't*. We talk of teamwork but we don't find written job descriptions in team sport even when, at a professional level, clubs might spend millions on a player. All that the members of a successful team need to know are the rules and objects of the game and where the goal posts are. Specific individual roles are spelled out by the captain or the coach and, if the run of play demands that these change, then they simply make it happen. Nobody complains: that's what teamwork is all about. (See page 10 for the only profitable, *universal* job description.)

The biggest giraffe-scaring exercise of all is 'job evaluation'. The first thing we do is form a committee, usually comprising personnel people, production managers and worker representatives. We bring in a consultant to train the committee in 'JE techniques'. They set about developing a set of 'JE criteria', such as *skill, knowledge, responsibility, physical effort, working conditions*, and a complex numerical rating system for each. Armed with this, they establish a set of 'benchmark jobs': three or four for each of maybe four or five payment grades. Then they observe every discrete work assignment in the factory, read the job description and give it a grade by comparing it with the benchmark jobs. Whenever a new operation is introduced or an existing job changed, it goes before the committee. The ensuing inflexibility is a great irritant for our better production managers and supervisors. And *for what?* So that, ultimately, we can 'justify' paying one person maybe 50 pence per hour more or less than another.

But for all its meticulousness, what does job evaluation *not* take into account? It ignores conscientiousness, a good attendance record, quality of work, creativity, the contribution of ideas for improvement, the capacity to maintain a good relationship with other members of the team – in short everything that is important. The idea of job 'worth' as applied to production operations is one that GK organisations find difficult to understand. All processes need to be completed, all parts need to be fitted, and all support activities undertaken to make a finished product. What does it matter that some jobs take longer to learn than others, that some are more varied, more repetitive, more uncomfortable or more physically exacting (and of course it is the duty of all GK managers to make them all *more* comfortable and *less exacting*). Consequently they have only one basic grade of payment for all their direct workforce, covering not only production workers but inspectors, laboratory testers, forklift truck-drivers and so on.[3] The benefits that accrue are those of complete flexibility. We know the alternatives. Speculate on the implications of JE for a cricket captain: 'Stop the game a minute, umpire, while I complete this temporary grade change note and pop it across to personnel. I want to move Fred from square leg to silly mid-off for the next couple of overs.'

The time clock is a marvellous device for those organisations which are largely indifferent to the need for punctuality from their workforce. This is ideally suited to organisations in public administration when the nature of the work only requires a given amount of time and can be performed in a pattern best suited to the personal needs of the individual employee. However, it is particularly *ill-suited* to the demands of most manufacturing organisations, which require production workers to be at their place of work by a fixed time. Time-recording devices and their associated 'clock cards' survive as one of the most pernicious artifacts of a style of management which appears to ignore everything common sense tells us about human nature.

As managers we fondly think that, by requiring 'hourly-paid operatives' to register their time of arrival and departure at the plant with a central monitoring authority, we are enforcing a disciplined approach to punctuality. Nothing could be further from the truth. In addition we delude ourselves into thinking that penalising a late arrival by a proportionate or even disproportionate deduction of wages will bring about better performance in terms of prompt arrival. What we are actually doing is tacitly instituting 'flexi-time' in our factories. We are making an implied contract with our employees which allows them to redeem their lack of punctuality by sacrificing a part of their earnings.

Let us return to our two model companies, Alpha and Omega. An Alpha employee lies in bed listening to the sound of his alarm clock. He knows that if he fails to rise from his bed within the next two minutes he will not beat the rush hour and will not arrive in time for the start of his production shift. He knows further that, if he does not succeed in sticking his clock card into the time-recording machine before eight o'clock, then he will pay a financial penalty. This may take the form of losing *the* first 15 minutes of his wage or perhaps the first hour of his wage, or it may mean that he forgoes any opportunity to work overtime during that week. He quickly calculates the value of the imposed penalty. He listens to the driving rain against the bedroom window. Perhaps his spouse is displaying a degree of physical affection he has not experienced for some time. Perhaps he overindulged himself the night before, after his club won the bowling championship. If he stays in bed another hour it might cost him as much as £10–£15. Right now that sounds like *a very good deal*.

Of course, thinking itself to be a stringent and highly disciplined company, Alpha has *rules and regulations* concerning incidents of lateness. Our hero knows that, if he arrives late for work more than four times in a three-month period, as reflected on his clock card, then he will automatically be summoned to the personnel department to be given a formal disciplinary warning. But he also knows that he has only clocked in late twice during this quarter; and therefore concludes that he is still entitled to two late appearances in order to meet the company standard.

Nearby lives an Omega employee. He is undergoing a similar experience and finds himself in the same dilemma. At Omega there are no time-recording devices and no clock cards. Moreover, Omega operates on the principles of common terms and conditions of employment for all its employees. He is paid a salary and enjoys full sickness benefits. Not only is he freed from the demeaning obligation to 'clock in' but, should he choose to stay in bed all day after phoning in 'sick' he will nevertheless receive his full salary and not be penalised at all.

Nevertheless, it is the Omega employee who drags himself wearily out of bed and makes his way to work by the appointed time while his neighbour of Alpha Corp. opts instead for a comfortable morning in bed, untroubled by a conscience which has been successfully bought off by the forgiveness of the time-recording machine and its supporting company-wide centrally driven 'disciplinary' systems and procedures.

Why is the Omega employee more conscientious about arriving at work by the appointed time? I would venture to suggest that the answer is that he works *as part of a team*, and not as part of an impersonal system, and also that he is *managed* by the leader of that team, namely the FLM, and not by a machine and a rule book. Our employee knows that he is obliged to attend his team's pre-shift briefing. (This is in stark contrast with what happens in Alpha, where employees, having made a mad rush for the time clock and successfully registered the required time, then casually saunter off in the direction of a drinks-vending machine with no apparent urgency or enthusiasm for reaching their place of work – *and they call this discipline!*) Omega FLMs can tell *immediately* if any member of their small teams of no more than two dozen is missing. They do not need a time-recording device to tell them this and they are pleased to be without the chore of signing off clock cards and brokering queries and arguments between their team members and the personnel department.

Unlike the time-recording device or the personnel department, FLMs *know their team members*. Should there be any occasional problems with lateness or casual absence, *they* will determine the appropriate action to be taken – or, indeed whether any action should be taken at all. Following an incidence of lateness, FLMs establish the reason for that lateness, irrespective of whether it amounted to five minutes or five hours. In all probability they will choose to ignore even a very late appearance, given a reasonable and plausible justification from the employee and a previous record of good timekeeping. On the other hand they may well take a far more severe line, involving a deduction of salary, or even consider formal disciplinary action against frequent incidents of casual lateness of only two or three minutes. In either case, it is the *FLMs* at Omega who determine whether or not to take disciplinary action. If they decide not to, then the personnel department does not become involved at all. The FLMs are the managers and leaders of their teams, not the personnel department and not a time-recording device.

There are other reasons why the Omega employee will make every effort to attend and do so promptly. Omega is a GK company and therefore a *lean* company. The size of the team is sufficient to carry out the tasks required of it during the production shift plus only a moderate allowance for holiday cover, cross-training and a reasonable degree of absenteeism (no more than 1 or 2 per cent). Omega employees are fully aware that their fellow team members depend on their support and that, if they fail to appear, someone else will have to do their work for them: maybe one of the Team Leaders, maybe the FLM, maybe one of their colleagues who was otherwise hoping to learn a new job on that day. Omega's workteams have a 'work hard, play hard' mentality as an inherent part of their outlook. In many respects the FLM scarcely needs to manage the situation at all. Peer group pressure at Omega is a *positive* rather than a negative force. Far from being accused of 'sucking up to management', the Omega employees know that if anybody is going to make fun of them, it will be because of their inability to arrive at work on time regularly.

Given the undoubted effectiveness of this direct form of leadership in the workplace, why are companies so reluctant to give this kind of authority to FLMs? I think that the answer is to be found in the fact that, over the years, companies, and in particular their personnel functions, have become increasingly obsessed with a concept of *fairness* based on the consistent treatment of all individuals within the organisation. Naturally this development has worked hand-in-hand with the development of remote control management. For *professionals* working in the central personnel function and imbued with this way of thinking, there is nothing that goes against the grain more than the notion that different individuals within the company may be treated differently. There is a fear that any attempt to take the personal characteristics and circumstances of individual employees into account would damage a homogeneous response and a uniform set of company standards for all. However, with the management of people, as Kenneth Blanchard and others have pointed out, 'there is nothing more unequal than the equal treatment of unequals'.[4]

Cold, antiseptic and unyielding 'disciplinary' standards, imposed and monitored from the centre, are simple and straightforward. They require no effort to manage. They are a perfect example of the sedentary attractions of remote control management. There are no good or bad performers among employees, no good or bad attitudes, no negative or positive qualities of any sort. There are only those who adhere to the rules and regulations and those who are in breach of them; and, in the case of the latter, there is a simple and automatic counter-response from the centre.

When it is suggested that FLMs ought to manage in accordance with their own knowledge of their people, then this homogeneity, this enforced simplicity, is immediately threatened and stoutly defended by those who have grown accustomed to holding it dear, in spite of its tendency to reduce all individual performance to the lowest common denominator. At this point a mythical character is usually brought out of the closet. He is talked about in hushed voices, much like the 'bogeymen' and 'long-legged scissormen' of childhood. This is the Apollonine spectre of the 'blue-eyed boy'. He resembles the other hobgoblins in that no one seems to know much about him or be able to give an accurate description of him. Yet some protagonists even talk as if his presence is so real that it is possible to attribute to him some kind of medical or neurological condition. 'We mustn't create the conditions for "blue-eyed boy syndrome", must we!', warn the defenders of remote and centrally imposed 'consistency'.

I have often wondered about the identity of the 'blue-eyed boy'. What is being implied here? Who is the 'blue-eyed boy' and why should he be favoured? It seems that this is simply expressing the view that, unlike their more 'professional'

HRD colleagues, production FLMs are incapable of making considered judgements about the relative calibre of their staff – so much so that they are prone to distributing favour in accordance with the most absurd and bizarre of subjective considerations. However, nobody seems to want to be very clear about what these considerations are.

Let us look at the situation of FLMs in a GK company, a lean company. They face perpetual and relentless demands for achievement and improvement of every aspect of their small businesses. They have a powerful and complementary package of responsibilities which make it very difficult for them to pass the buck. What qualities therefore do they demand of team members? They will value skill, flexibility, honesty, reliability, concentration, conscientiousness, punctuality, a good attendance record, an ability to work well with colleagues; perhaps, in addition, some spark of ingenuity in terms of finding and exploiting opportunities for improved team performance or perhaps some indication of potential to move on to positions of higher responsibility. If we call an employee or team member with several or all of these characteristics a 'blue-eyed boy' or 'girl' then what can possibly be wrong with recognising and reinforcing these behaviours in the work environment?

Of course there is no end to the paraphernalia of giraffe-scaring. Time sheets, 'pass-outs' ... consign them to a bonfire, reduce administrative costs and let FLMs manage their businesses and lead their teams.

EMPHASIS ON INTERNAL DEVELOPMENT AND APPOINTMENT

Affected, it seems, by the principle that 'familiarity breeds contempt', companies always seem to undervalue their own people. We tend to be able to think of them only in terms of the positions they currently fill or the jobs they presently perform. It seems that the approach we generally adopt when needing to fill a managerial position is that of an enthusiastic amateur card player. We look at the nines and tens in our hand and cast them into the pack in the forlorn hope that we might later draw out a Jack or a King – and we enter into the game of external recruitment with youthful enthusiasm and relish.

There is a common argument put forward by individuals who find some merit as such in this approach. This is the 'new-blood argument', so called because it is almost invariably put in those terms. 'The organisation needs new blood ... fresh blood in order to keep it healthy and vibrant.' Occasionally this argument is put in the negative sense. 'If the organisation does not receive regular infusions of new blood, then it will stagnate.' Analogies with incest and the congenital defects associated with inbreeding are also common. I am always deeply suspicious of arguments which appear to rely on stark imagery alone. Seldom, it seems, is anyone prepared to put forward any logic to indicate that external hires are somehow more invigorating and useful to a company than its existing loyal and experienced employees doing a new and invigorating job. Empirically, this argument would also appear to be invalid since it is not borne out by what we know of the practices of companies in Japan, whose performance does not seem to have been blunted by their marked reluctance to hire outwith their own ranks.

Many organisations seem to have a peculiar affection for gauging and setting limits on people's capabilities. People, we are told, commonly 'reach a plateau' in their development; find themselves in positions where they are 'square pegs in square holes'. However, it is not so much the concept of the individual plateau that I find difficult to accept. Rather it is that, even having been closely involved with the activity in a company which took its responsibilities for career planning very seriously indeed, I nevertheless remain acutely sceptical of the ability of senior managers or specialists to determine when these plateaux have been reached. So many of our best companies are headed by talented individuals who, in a previous company and in a much more junior position, had been judged as having 'reached a plateau' in their career development.

By contrast, in GK companies there is a presumption in favour of *internal promotion*. Managers of GK companies are most reluctant to recruit externally. In GK companies managers and the organisation as a whole tend to regard the need to recruit beyond their existing ranks as *failure* (to identify and develop people with potential), except in the pursuit of certain specialist knowledge of new products, processes or skills related to them. They recognise that this approach is the most powerful motivational tool available to them and to the company, and they will not discard it lightly.

This contrasts with the approach of one multinational company. In order to further the worthy pursuit of enhancing and upgrading the capabilities of its supervisors, it has made it clear, to the whole organisation, that it will expect its future supervisors to be graduates in a technical discipline. It has succeeded, therefore, in giving its whole workforce the distinct perception that there will be very little promotional opportunity for production workers. I have to admit that, were I a production worker in such a company, I would not exert myself nor put myself out one inch for its sake – beyond that required to keep my job and until such time as I was able to find another.

Of course, not everyone wants more responsibility. Many are quite content to come to work and perform a low-key task conscientiously and well: such is their own choice. In any healthy organisation, however, there will always be a surplus of ambition over opportunity. Our task, therefore, is to manage the expectations of people and to maximise our opportunities for fulfilling them. A GK organisation does not put barriers in the way of its employees who have the ability and the desire to occupy more senior positions, to perform new tasks and take on greater responsibilities. Above all, it must be recognised that every management position filled by internal appointment pays a tribute to *everyone* in the organisation, *regardless* of their ambitions and expectations. By contrast, every resort to external hire is a slur on the workforce. As an employee carrying out production operations on the shop floor, I may be perfectly content to remain gainfully employed in this situation for the rest of my working life, perhaps finding fulfilment outside work. But in manifestly setting before us all a gulf that we may not cross, my company contemns me just as much as it does my more ambitious colleagues.

COMMON TERMS AND CONDITIONS OF EMPLOYMENT

My old boss Peter Wickens used to sum up the importance of this item most succinctly: 'You can't get first-class performance from people who are treated like second-class citizens.' The subject of hourly-paid status, and how its combination with work quotas erects hard and tangible barriers to improved productivity, has been explored in previous chapters. That status has, of course, much broader implications. As we enter the new millenium, though they may achieve ISO 9000, a Queen's Award to Industry, a knighthood for the chairman or even an 'Investors in People' award, companies that nevertheless retain the distinction between 'staff' and 'hourly paid', each with their respective separate mutual obligations and standards of treatment, may as well erect a sign over the factory gates proclaiming: 'Welcome to Jurassic Park'. 'Our workforce is our strength', says our mission statement, but when I am ill my family and I still benefit from my full salary whereas those in the workforce only get what the state insists we provide. 'People are our most valuable resource', but, whereas I drive through the gates to my designated parking space by the door, most people walk 300 yards in the rain.

Are these observations not perhaps rather petty and irrational? After all, if I were to park outside and get wet like everyone else, would that make them any drier? Over two centuries ago, as the age of reason and enlightenment reached its zenith, Edmund Burke reminded us that in our dealings with people we should be guided not so much by the cause of human reason as by an appreciation of human nature. There is little point in questioning why people *should* become irritated by discriminatory terms and conditions of employment in organisations. Perception is reality. It is enough in itself that they do. It has ever been so in every country and in every culture. A common (though in fact mistaken) Western assumption about the Japanese is that they are inherently more loyal and supportive of their organisations. Thus if Japanese companies put so much value on harmonised working conditions, how much more important are they for us?[5]

There can be few of us unfamiliar with the Genesis story of Joseph and his brothers: how his immodesty earned their dislike and how his fate was finally sealed when his father, Jacob, showed him favour by giving him a coat 'of many colours'. We learned how his brothers, after contemplating his murder and leaving him in a deep pit in the middle of the desert, merely relented inasmuch as they sold him into a lifetime of slavery and told their father that he had been devoured by wild beasts.

I always found this tale a little difficult to swallow. It does, on the face of it, seem to be a rather extreme reaction to a relatively minor display of paternal favouritism. Surely throwing the lad, coat and all, into the nearest muddy pond or gorse bush would have been a more proportionate expression of sibling jealousy. However 1960s research, made in preparation for the *New English Bible*, revealed that Jacob did not give his son a coat 'of many colours' at all. A more accurate description of his gift was a coat 'with long sleeves'. Now we begin to understand. The significance of a coat with long sleeves in a primitive agricultural society and in a hot climate is immediately apparent. Jacob was making his intentions for his son very clear to the whole tribe: *he would not be expected to do physical work*. By this simple act, Jacob was marking out his son as being *separate* from his brothers, conferring on him the authority of management by issuing him with the business suit of the ancient world. Thus we have one of the earliest recorded examples of antipathy between those designated *manager* and *managed*; the first chapter in the saga of 'them and us' attitudes in which the very outward trappings of management themselves provide the catalyst for a vicious and destructive form of enmity and distrust.

'Professionalism' is the reason so often given for the survival of the business suit in the factory. 'You have to look professional ... You have to look the part.' If I go into a men's outfitters to buy a suit, then I expect the sartorial style of those working in the shop to reflect that of the goods on offer. That would constitute professional dress. I have different expectations in a grocery store, or in a bank, or in a gymnasium, or when I meet my son's teacher to discuss his progress.

If we are to judge the 'professionalism' or otherwise of wearing a business suit on the shop floor of a factory, then it can only be from the standpoint of those people who are actually there to see it. If we truly believe that by wearing such apparel we increase our stature in the eyes of the workforce in terms of our projected competence or authority, then we may well be justified in requiring our production managers and specialist personnel to do so. We must ask ourselves whether the wearing of clothing so radically different from that of those who are expected to do a physical job of work is a help or a hindrance when it comes to managing their activity. If these outward and visible manifestations of managerial authority are merely a sham to conceal limited leadership ability and lack of knowledge and competence, then we would be far better off without them.

Not long ago I had a discussion with an FLM from a motor manufacturing company which has clung more tenaciously than any other motor manufacturer I know to the professional standard of the lounge suit. The FLM was proud of his ability to build a very harmonious relationship with both his workforce and with the local union representatives on his shift, who still maintain some considerable influence within his organisation. He intimated that he never encountered any problems in introducing improvements to the activities carried out in his section. But he told of an immediate hardening of attitudes whenever 'a manager in a suit' walked on to the factory floor. 'We'll do it for you but not for *those bastards!*' was the prevailing attitude. He went on to explain how 'a whole morning's work' of patient perseverance could be nullified in an instant by the untimely appearance and involvement of 'a suit'.[6]

THE POWER OF GESTURE

We should never underestimate the power of gesture. What sticks most in the mind of every high-school pupil taught about Peter the Great of Russia and his struggle to bring his country 'kicking and screaming' into the modern world? Not the building of a navy; not the importation of Western technology; not the Battle of Poltava or the creation of a central bureaucracy. Rather it is the story that he summoned his medieval princes and boyars to court, stood them in a long line and, with a pair of shears, snipped off their cherished full beards: to them the very symbols of their manhood and their religion; to him a symbol only of backwardness and literal barbarity.

Newcastle United Football Club is the main focus of supporting affection in the North-Eastern region of England. The performance of its soccer team during the 1950s was the pinnacle of a glorious history. The three subsequent decades, however, were lacklustre in comparison, not only in terms of performance on the field but also financially. More recently, however, its fortunes have been transformed. By 1995 it had become one of the most successful and powerful two or three clubs in England. There was an unprecedented amount of investment in ground improvements and in 1996 it broke all records by paying £15 million for one player.

Most people date this transformation from the involvement of Sir John Hall, a coalminer's son and entrepreneur, who gradually assumed control of the club in the early 1990s. Quite recently I had an interesting conversation in my local pub with one of the club's most passionate *aficionados*. I had never met this man before and have never met him since; but he was keen to impress on me the achievements which he thought Sir John had gained for the club without showing any great insight about how he had brought them about.

Eventually, though, he told me a story: how he had heard that, after the meeting at which Sir John secured the chairmanship and effective control of the club, he walked into the members' bar and ordered a round. The drinks were promptly poured and presented and Sir John drew out his wallet. The barman, with a smile and a dismissive wave, sought to remind Sir John that, as a director of the club, his drinks were complimentary.

'I *pay* for my drinks', Sir John responded quietly, 'and, from now on', he added, raising his voice slightly for the benefit of the assembled company, '*everybody else does too!*'

Events may have happened exactly in the way that they were described to me. On the other hand, like all our favourite legends, the story may simply be a considerable embellishment on a related episode, changed with each subsequent retelling – or else a complete fiction. But the amount of truth in the story is wholly irrelevant. In the perceptions of people who are employees, members or affiliates of any organisation, gestures of commitment from the top, however small and insignificant they might appear, have a major role to play.

When making my farewells on my last day at Nissan, I found Ian Gibson, CBE, chief executive of one of Britain's biggest exporters of manufactured product, sitting at his undistinguished desk in a large open-plan area populated in the main by engineers and quality assurance personnel.[7]

But is it of any significance that the MD at Nissan or at Sony's plant in Wales does not have his own private office? Does it *matter* that some people in the organisation have their own designated car parking space? Does it *matter* if some members of our organisation wear working clothes and others wear lounge suits? Does it *matter* that we have about five different designs of office chair, ranging in opulence from swivel chairs without arms, through swivel chairs *with* arms to something which looks like the captain's chair on the bridge of the starship *Enterprise*? (Senior managers clearly have more tender backsides than other people.)

Yes, it does. These differences matter not in spite of but *because of* their triviality. We need our organisations to be such that our core operating principles and disciplines are the characteristics that stand proud and tall in the organisation; that are uppermost in the minds of everyone. To achieve this we need to strip away the nonsense which obscures and detracts from them.

We remember the people of ancient Sparta for three reasons: their military prowess, their rigorous discipline and their austerity. The very word 'spartan' survives in our language to mean any of these three things, depending on the context in which we use it. This is no mere coincidence; the three aspects naturally hang together. Exemplary performance in any organised activity, be it war, team sport or production, is largely a function of discipline and adherence to and respect for axiomatic principles of conduct. For these principles to stand in high regard in an organisation there will be invariably a corresponding *dis*regard for anything which is not associated with them – anything shallow or superficial, trivial or vainglorious.

NOTES

1. Akio Morita (1987), *Made in Japan* (p. 130), London: Collins.
2. It is merely by chance that these observations are recorded at a time when the actions of some of Britain's newly privatised utilities have raised these issues to the level of such national prominence and controversy. No political commentary is intended. The most damning indictment that could be made from the perspective of belief in both *Genba Kanri* and market liberalism is neither social injustice nor corporate avarice, but lack of managerial foresight, understanding and courage.
3. Maintenance technicians are usually paid a higher salary in recognition of the market value of

their skills and of the time and qualifications involved in acquiring them. Labourers are rarely found in GK companies. All employees are expected to keep the workplace and equipment clean, tidy and in good order. Floor cleaning and waste disposal are usually subcontracted.

4. K. Blanchard and P. Zigarmi (1986), *Leadership and the One Minute Manager*, London: Collins.

5. Examples of what is meant by 'common terms and conditions of employment' are:

   common method of payment – monthly salary;
   common provision of company benefits (healthcare, pensions and so on);
   common policy on sickness absence payment and holiday provision;
   common hours of work (day shift start and finish times the same);
   undifferentiated dining facilities, car parking, washrooms, desks, chairs;
   no ostentatious differences in dress.

6. What is advocated here is not simply a relaxation of company management dress codes. Recent years have witnessed the growth of a strange ritual, especially common to American corporations. Friday has become 'go as you please' day. There is a similar arrangement at my son's primary school. Every once in a while he and his classmates are excused uniform as a special treat in exchange for a modest charity donation. But it matters not at all to those in the *genba* whether managers and office employees wear lounge suits or designer sweaters, chinos and expensive loafers. The impression given is still the same: 'Please don't get me dirty; I'd hate anyone to think I work in the factory.'

7. One of the reasons that this made a lasting impression on me was that, only days afterwards, British newspapers carried the story that the country's state-owned, loss-making rail network was spending a five-figure sum on refurbishing its chairman's office. The news broke not long before the start of what proved to be a particularly difficult round of annual pay negotiations.

17 Establishing GK

Till a voice, as bad as Conscience, rang interminable changes
On one everlasting Whisper day and night repeated – so:
'Something hidden. Go and find it. Go and look behind the ranges –
Something lost behind the Ranges. Lost and waiting for you. Go!'

Rudyard Kipling, *The Explorer*

Since my first encounter with them, as a young production manager many years ago, I have despised consultants. I can hardly complain, therefore, about the degree of suspicion which attaches itself to the profession in which I now find myself. However, there is one pairing of accusations which has always struck me as rather unfair, since the avoidance of one almost always invites the other. When consultants propound detailed strategies and approaches, they are accused of dogma and insensitivity to the unique needs of specific organisations. When they refuse to prescribe *anything* until a full diagnosis of requirements has been carried out, this just goes to prove that the mercenary bastards will cough up nothing of value until the meter is actually running.

On this chapter rest my ambitions to avoid both accusations. I am not disposed to let everyone savour the soup and then only give them six-foot long chopsticks for eating it. Yet it should be acknowledged that what follows cannot aspire to address all possible teething problems of GK introduction, much less contend with the particular circumstances of individual companies. Nevertheless, I hope that useful pointers follow for those with the confidence to proceed under their own steam and who can supplement them with their own solutions to their own unique problems. The main criterion for the inclusion of these key points is that they bear on the hazards which, experience tells us, companies are most likely to encounter when attempting the all important shift to Hyperdrive.

STRATEGY

DO IT DURING THE GOOD TIMES

Do it when demand is buoyant and volumes are increasing. That way the benefits of GK can come straight off the bottom line without causing lay-offs. Employee insecurity is pure poison for productivity-related improvements and for the identification of waste. Once we have decided to make the jump, or even if we are just seriously considering it, we should suspend all recruitment *immediately*, if only for a week or two to take stock of the implications. We should not lift the embargo until expectations of improved productivity have been factored into revised budgets. The same goes for machines. In both cases we should expect enhanced *manufacturing capability* to fund a portion of required additional capacity. We need to think about how much this portion might be and allow for it. We should not be overcautious – we either believe in what we are doing or we don't. Experience suggests improvements in every aspect of input cost (man, machine, materials) of at least 25 per cent in the first year and 10 per cent in subsequent years. We must do our best to avoid a situation where, because of reduced breakdowns and set-up times, two machines need not have been bought or an additional shift need not have been launched; where, because of improved methods and/or better product quality, ten recently hired people are soon surplus to requirements.[1]

EDUCATE ALL SENIOR MANAGERS IN THE PRINCIPLES AND BENEFITS OF GK

Secure their commitment and involvement. Without this the initiative will fail. This means directors and the heads of all departments, including purchasing, marketing, sales and finance. For though GK is principally a manufacturing doctrine, real and tangible changes affecting the *whole* company will be needed to make it work.

AVOID LONG-TERM SERIAL AND PIECEMEAL CHANGES

All organisations hanker for a 'greenfield' opportunity – a chance to start completely afresh. But the benefits of a 'greenfield site' are often exaggerated and misunderstood; too many companies use the absence of such an opportunity as an excuse for apathy and inertia. A completely fresh start is neither a necessary nor sufficient condition for success – many 'greenfield' enterprises fail, while established, traditional companies in 'brownfield' situations have achieved remarkable results.[2] There is no such thing as a perfectly fresh start, for there are no 'greenfield' people – they all bring their established attitudes and expectations with them. The main advantage of the 'greenfield' is not *cultural*, but *practical*. It gives us quality *time*. It affords a unique, never-to-be-repeated opportunity to put the right things in place *before production begins*. For, once the inexorable and unforgiving flywheel starts to turn, once there are schedules to meet and customers to satisfy, the time, effort and money that can be devoted to making changes is severely curtailed – even for the biggest and most resourceful of companies.

Faced with these constraints, most of us have a simple choice to make. We can either do *something everywhere* or *everything somewhere*. Many companies opt for the former, though it is rarely effective and always expensive. Carrying out a comprehensive, root-and-branch transformation in one small corner of the operation, and then cascading it onwards, is a far more profitable exercise. I am grateful to Jack Zenger for a most helpful analogy.[3] You cannot bake a cake *serially*, one ingredient at a time. There is only one way to bake a cake and that is to mix together all the ingredients, in their due proportions, and put them in the oven together. This is especially true of GK because of the extent to which each of the elements is mutually supportive of the others. This is why separate 'team briefing' programmes always fail, why visual management displays so often turn into wallpaper, why so much sophisticated and expensive training is squandered for lack of the mechanisms which need to be in place for it to bear fruit. If we cannot lavish the time and resources needed for a whole cake without jamming the flywheel, then we must make a succession of rock buns or cup cakes.

BE AMBITIOUS AND ADVENTUROUS

Boldness and thoroughness are the safest bet. The first lesson on the school football field is that it is usually the faint-hearted tackler who gets hurt. This does not mean that we should be reckless or blind to possible pitfalls. We need to use the PDCA cycle *ourselves* to plan our strategy, check progress and take corrective actions as we go. But we should not back off before we even begin by real or often imagined factors of resistance. We must especially be prepared to abandon any cherished business practices which are restrictive or distracting (payment systems, working agreements, inappropriate and unhelpful measures of performance and the like). 'Productivity'-related pay, as only one example, *must go*. There can be no fudging the issue.

Fortunately the 'cup cake' approach helps us. The practice of lighting small fires, making radical and comprehensive changes in a small area, is easy to justify in the name of experimentation and is unlikely to precipitate hard opposition. Any organisation can create its own patch of green. All it takes is a blank sheet of paper and an undertaking by all parties not to be bound by existing assumptions about organisation structures, rules, regulations and procedures, roles and responsibilities and conditions of employment.

COMMIT TO PROGRESS TOWARDS COMMON TERMS AND CONDITIONS OF EMPLOYMENT

Modern competitive business and working practices, which make greater demands on people, are not compatible with employment practices which are disrespectful and demeaning. The key words here are 'progress' and 'commit'. It is obviously a tall order to expect many small companies or those which operate on the narrowest of profit margins immediately to extend private medical cover from the few to all, for example. But we need to start somewhere. Often the most galling and unnecessary distinctions are those which cost little or nothing to remedy. Progress on many of the others can accompany the cumulative yield of GK benefits. The commitment must be genuine: mere words are not enough to allay the cynicism of a workforce always accustomed to second-class treatment. There should be an early, tangible and impacting gesture made *right at the start* – something that will capture everybody's attention. In this way, people can see that we mean business and that the proposed changes will be good for everyone. Top management must lead by example; other managers will surely follow.

DON'T BEGIN BY SETTING UP A 'STEERING COMMITTEE'

If the introduction of GK principles is important for the business then it should be *managed* like any other business project. An out-of-character overindulgence in consensus building should be avoided. Yes, communicate. Tell everyone what is happening and why. There need be no hidden agenda; nor must there be. Get people involved. By all means conduct whatever discussions or negotiations are required by the company's existing agreements with unions and employee representatives. Listen to opinions and accommodate them where you can. But the trouble with 'steering committees' is that they always want something to steer. With GK, the only hands we seek to place on the wheel, right from the start, are those of our FLMs and their team members. *Navigation*, not steering, is what we need from management. Navigation is best undertaken by an executive body, not a representative one. A small team of three or four committed and influential managers, who fully understand GK principles, is best suited to the task.

SPURN THE USE OF FACILITATORS, COORDINATORS AND 'CHAMPIONS'

For the reasons given in Chapter 4, and following the same rationale of the previous point. If the only way to make progress or to 'kick-start' the initiative is to free someone from the duties of operations management and give them the task of leading the project, make it clear that this is a temporary secondment with a specific, timetabled end to their involvement. The person chosen should be one of the most valued and capable executives or line managers in the organisation – ideally a senior and respected production manager. We should not use such a role as a means of occupying or 'developing' management trainees or as a sinecure for any likeable square peg who has difficulty fitting into any of our managerial round holes.

PROTECT AND ENCOURAGE FLMS AND PRODUCTION TEAMS

Much hangs on the outcome of the critical period when FLMs and their teams start to expand their activity beyond that traditionally assigned to them, begin to exercise their newly defined roles and fulfil the demands of their broadened responsibilities. In many companies this will mean that they must cross into territory which was once the exclusive preserve of specialists in other departments. Moreover, though they may be confident and assertive (and we need them to be), they will make mistakes. It is the responsibility of higher production management to watch their backs, to 'ride shotgun' on their endeavours for a while, to make sure that nobody permanently damages their confidence and that they get the response and respect that they need from support functions. Pursue the introduction of customer-focused, visual performance measures for these functions to ensure that support is forthcoming.

COMBINE GK WITH THE INTRODUCTION OF NEW PROJECTS

Let us begin by considering the options afforded to us in our business plan. The next best opportunity to a complete 'greenfield' situation is any upcoming business project which will, in any case, have a significant impact on the factory and on the manufacturing organisation: the development and launch of a new product, the installation of new facilities or a significant uplift in volume or a reconfiguration of the product mix. These all constitute ideal opportunities for introducing GK principles, for creating a framework for the uptake of new roles and responsibilities and for implementing new business and working practices. If there is such an opportunity then the following key points apply.

NEW PRODUCTS AND FACILITIES

FULLY EXPLOIT THE OPPORTUNITY

New products and facilities provide our best chance to start afresh and prove to ourselves what can be achieved. We must not contaminate it with business and working practices which are no longer appropriate. We must leave all old debilitating habits behind.

PROVIDE THE MANPOWER FOR THE PROJECT FROM AMONG EXISTING EMPLOYEES

This is particularly important for the Second Line Manager (if the project is big enough to warrant one), the FLM and Team Leader positions. The ideal people for this undertaking are already working for us somewhere in the organisation: there is no need to look outside. Yes, people will require training. In all probability this will involve a completely different way of working. But this will be the case for outsiders too. When the experiment succeeds it will have to be cascaded on to the rest of the organisation eventually. Let us begin as we mean to go on. Let us send out a positive signal to the whole company by maximising the opportunities for recognising and developing our most capable people.[4] Ideally, any Second Line Manager should appoint his or her own FLMs. The FLMs should in turn select their Team Leaders and team members. (However, guidelines might have to be established to avoid simply creaming off the best from the existing organisation. Not only might this prove to be dysfunctional for existing operations, but it would be self-defeating in the long run since eventually GK will be spread across the whole plant.)

APPOINT FIRST AND SECOND LINE MANAGERS EARLY

Our aims are twofold: to make them the drivers of all operational aspects of the project; and to use the opportunity to cast a new mould for the roles, responsibilities and daily activities of production managers. This requires time, not only so that they can be fully involved from the earliest stages, but also so that they can receive training, guidance and practice in the new tasks with which they must be familiar before the product is launched or the facility becomes operational. How early? Companies must establish this for themselves, depending on their base technologies and the specific nature of the new project. It might be worth recalling that the first production supervisors at Nissan's British plant were *in situ* while their factory was just a sea of mud and girders, a year before the first production trials and 14 months before the start of production. Our chosen project may be less ambitious but a similar set of preparatory activities must be encompassed. Of prime importance is exploiting the opportunity to provide the new FLMs with the process knowledge they will need both to draft a full initial set of Standard Operations and to ensure that, when their team members finally join them in the new facility, they are already in the assured position of being able, with confidence, to give instruction and guidance and to demonstrate true leadership.

LINK GK INTRODUCTION CLOSELY WITH THE COMMERCIAL PROJECT

Develop a *master schedule* (a Gantt chart[5] or something equally user-friendly) of key and dependent events. This can be drafted and monitored by the Second Line

Manager, if there is to be one, or by the small navigational group of managers referred to previously, but the FLMs should take collective and individual responsibility for carrying out many of the following items (the list is not exhaustive):

- Establish a viable and realistic rate of climb for initial production volumes.
- Manpower/hiring plan profiled against volume ramp up and allowing for pre-hire and training.
- Appoint and train Team Leaders.
- Identify and train team members.
- Become familiar with all processes (by performing the work), all product specifications and all quality procedures.
- Devise Standard Operations for all processes.
- Identify (with maintenance) suitable activities for TPM and draft Standard Operations accordingly.
- Determine (with engineering) layout for all fixed and large-scale facilities.
- Install and commission equipment; establish training packages for operation and maintenance.
- Establish and prepare team meeting area.
- Identify requirements and budget for hand tools, ancillary equipment and consumables.
- Establish training facility, materials and other resources to enable preliminary training to be carried out before commercial production begins.
- Plan and continually revise floor layout for benches, racking, tools and materials.
- Plan and continually revise work allocation.
- Establish training plan for all team members; develop and monitor job skills matrix.
- Establish subjects, format, content and eventually *targets* for all visual displays of team performance.

STRUCTURE AND SCHEDULE ALL TRAINING ACTIVITY ACCORDING TO THE PROJECT PLAN

The most effective training for new and unfamiliar methods and techniques happens *just-in-time*, that is, no more than one or two weeks before the skills are required. Any longer than that and, without an early opportunity to practise, the learning becomes stale and the knowledge begins to fade. Therefore the training programme should march in step with the items on the project plan; it should become a line on the master schedule. This is, of course, where we begin to cash in on the benefits of our small-scale 'greenfield' opportunity. By dedicating our designated production management team to the new project at an early stage, we ensure that our scope for tailoring the training delivery to the key events is fairly generous: release of the chosen from production operations is not an issue.

ESTABLISHED OPERATIONS

All right, suppose we do not have such an opportunity. We are not introducing any new products or machines. We are not occupying a new building. We are not planning a new configuration of our facilities or a radically different deployment of our people in response to a shift in market demand. We expect things to continue pretty much as they are for the foreseeable future. We still want *Genba Kanri*, by whatever name we choose to call it, but we cannot afford to stop the world on its axis while we make the transition. We must do it on the hoof, continuing to carry out production activities and maintain supply to commercial clients. What then? Where do we start and how do we proceed?

Taking the questions in order, we must first uphold all the strategic key points mentioned earlier.

Second, we can start wherever we like. The very beginning of the production process is a good place; so is the very end. Somewhere in between can be reasonably good too. Some companies like to start where they feel they will be most assured of success – where they feel they have the best people or where they feel they will encounter the least resistance or apathy. That is fine, understandable and their privilege. This aspect does not concern me much, but then I am a GK devotee. I do not need to be convinced. If I lacked belief in what GK principles could achieve then I should not and could not have written this book. Yes, we should begin where we can secure the most successful outcome. My own view is that this will be where there are most opportunities for improvement. Where are the quality problems? Where is the waste? Where do we need more capacity? Which product lines cannot make schedule? Which is the area that we try to steer visitors away from when we show them around the patch? Let us grab some major improvements; and save some money as we go. That is, after all, the object of the whole exercise.

Third, how to proceed? Figure 17.1 suggests a schema for what experience indicates to be the most logical and effective sequence for the introduction of GK elements to established operations.[6] It also demonstrates how each phase brings about its own benefits, to the extent that, if properly managed, GK transition can be a self-financing exercise in terms of improved quality, delivery and costs. This is not a slow-burn 'cultural change programme'. The early phases in particular can be reckoned in weeks rather than months, assuming due desire and determination on the part of management to make progress. Each phase inducts its successor in a natural progression. Indeed, ensuring continued momentum is vital. If progress is interrupted or impeded at any stage, then we run the risk of losing the very benefits we have already achieved; we suffer the penalties of trying to bake a cake one ingredient at a time. The following set of key points applies. The first three are preconditions for starting the initiative.

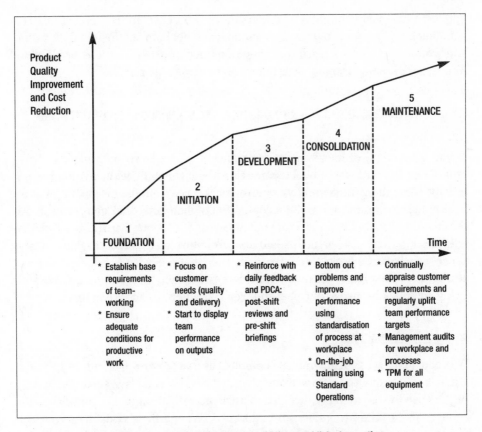

Figure 17.1 Phased introduction of GK to established operations

ENSURE THAT THE TARGET GROUP IS PRACTICALLY AND REALISTICALLY DEPLOYED IN TEAMS

At this stage, this means that groups of no more than 25 production workers (with no restrictions on their flexibility, such as grading structures, piecework or bonus) should report to an FLM who works together with them on the same shift pattern and who has no other demands on his or her time other than the management and leadership of the team. (Any manpower allowances for holiday cover, a modest but realistic amount of absence or other contingencies should be allocated to the team and held as the resource and responsibility of the FLM.)

ENSURE THAT FACTORY CONDITIONS ARE ALREADY TO A REASONABLE STANDARD

Usually they will be; but it has been my experience that, in about 20 to 30 per cent of cases, there is sufficient congestion in the workplace (excess materials, redundant equipment and fixtures, general clutter) to make progress difficult without first engaging in a modest application of JIT and/or 'Five C' activity (see

Appendix II) – just enough to enable us to see where we are and provide a firm foundation for further progress. You cannot even begin to lay the foundations for improvement or for standardised conditions and processes where production workers are literally tripping over debris and excess materials.

ENSURE THAT THERE ARE CLEAR AND UNEQUIVOCAL STANDARDS FOR QUALITY AND DELIVERY

These aspects are of inestimable importance in themselves and, moreover, we cannot develop real operational teamwork without them. As with any other team activity, the spur towards greater achievement comes from the disappointment of failure and the gratification of success. Quality standards that consist in mere opinion, that cannot be numerically quantified or which vary according to who is interpreting them are of no use to us. We must also establish that quality performance can be broken down to team level; that every fault or demerit can be attributed to its origins. We must make sure that quality data can be quickly and easily compiled for use at our post-shift reviews when we introduce them.

PROVIDE A TEAM AREA

We need not begin with anything so complete as that portrayed in Figure 11.4 and it may be that, until some improvements are made, we shall lack sufficient space. All we need to start with is a designated area, on or adjacent to the workplace, big enough for the team to gather around their FLM and their visual management displays at the start of every shift. (About 25 square metres should be adequate for most teams.)

VISUAL MANAGEMENT DISPLAYS

These concentrate only on *outputs* (quality and delivery) to begin with because:

- they are the most important, they concern the customer and are also the key to leanness;
- they are relatively non-contentious and unthreatening (as opposed to, say, attendance or productivity);
- in the early stages of GK introduction they tend to be the ripest opportunities for improvement;
- once the FLM and the team focus on their ability to provide the needs of the downstream, they will naturally and inevitably be drawn to tackle other aspects of their performance without much prompting.

DISPLAY THE TEAMS' OUTPUT PERFORMANCE DATA FOR SOME THREE TO FOUR WEEKS BEFORE INTRODUCING POST-SHIFT REVIEWS

This period is enough to test and establish the displays and enable the FLM to become familiar with the measures and the task of maintaining them. It is usually the case that considerable improvements, particularly relating to product quality and associated costs, accrue during this period alone as team members begin to take an interest in them and become keenly aware of what is expected. After this we must follow promptly with the next step to maintain momentum and avoid losing the initiative.

RUN POST-SHIFT REVIEWS FOR A FULL WEEK BEFORE THE INTRODUCTION OF PRE-SHIFT BRIEFINGS

Post-shift reviews must come first. They provide the substance of the pre-shift briefings and prevent them from being empty exercises in cultural noise. This week allows all attendees – Second Line Manager, FLMs and key support representatives – to develop and become familiar with a format and agenda which are easy to handle and concise and yet meet their own operational objectives and priorities. FLMs also learn how their performance affects and contributes to that of the production unit and develop an understanding of what they need to improve on for the benefit of their downstream colleagues.

ONCE POST-SHIFT REVIEWS AND PRE-SHIFT BRIEFINGS BEGIN THEY MUST BE SACROSANCT

They must happen religiously, without fail; there are *no* exceptions. They must become a normal, accepted and indispensable part of the business. Companies unwilling to make this commitment would do better not to introduce them at all.

DO NOT BE OVEREAGER TO GRASP THE FRUITS OF EFFICIENCY-RELATED IMPROVEMENTS

We need improvements now, but we also want to keep on getting them in six months' time, next year, ten years from now. Redundancies are an unacceptable consequence of production-team-generated improvements. But we need to go a stage further than that, especially in the early days when we have just taken great pains to build strong, determined, well motivated production teams. Let us suppose that a team of 15 makes sufficient improvements to enable it to run with only 14 people. If we rush in immediately and shanghai the surplus person to redeploy them elsewhere, then this damages the integrity and morale of the team. It is best to leave the team alone in the short to medium term. It is much more effective to draw productive work *into* the FLM's domain, by introducing

243

additional products or by pulling operations from upstream or downstream processes, rather than to ship people out. If this is not immediately possible, the FLM may well be able to use the person effectively to facilitate cross-training or identify further improvements.[7] If we are patient, we shall see the team reduce required manning still further to 14 people, 13 people. The most important thing is to *identify* and to *execute* the improvement. Realising the full benefits in costing terms really is a lesser problem. In the very worst case (if we have ignored the first of our strategic key points and have minimal employee turnover) we are still better off than we were. We have already made waste visible and removed it from the operation; we have already improved our *manufacturing capability* and, by our patience, we have retained the commitment and enthusiasm of our people to *go on* improving that capability.

One final point ...

Before committing your company to the principles of *Genba Kanri* under whatever banner you choose to fly, think carefully about the consequences for you and for your organisation, for it can be no lighthearted undertaking. Even if it proves successful you will perpetually reap a mixed harvest of both achievement and frustration. I want to end by sharing the observations of two manufacturing directors of medium-sized companies now well advanced in their efforts to incorporate GK disciplines. 'What we have found', observes one, 'is that the more we achieve the more dissatisfied we are with our achievements; the more we recognise that there is so much more that could be done.'

The other has a number of Japanese companies among his key suppliers and makes regular visits to Japan. 'Before introducing GK practices I used to feel at first intimidated and afterwards humbled and a bit depressed by what I saw in their factories. I don't feel that now. I'm not saying we don't have a little way still to go. But they don't overawe me any more. I know now that it's nothing special and that we can do it – *are* doing it. They don't have anything more to teach us. I honestly feel that in a year, maybe two, we'll match them in every respect.'

It seems to me that these observations are all the more heartening by their realism and sobriety. Realism and sobriety *should* characterise our perspective on the performance of Japanese companies. We should not be complacent about it, but neither should we be cowed. Yes, their swords are sharp: we should not be in any doubt about that. But there is another blade available to us which has long been embedded in the anvil of a proud industrial past, on which were once wrought the very principles contained in this book. Unlike the sword of legend it will yield itself to all and any who are prepared to clear away the weeds and briars by which it has so long been obscured.

NOTES

1. What if there are *no good times*? What if there is stagnant or decreasing demand? What if there is historical overmanning which really must be resolved by compulsory lay-offs in the relatively near future to avoid corporate collapse? Then the dirty work must be done first, before any attempt is made to introduce GK, *kaizen* or any other initiative aimed at continuous improvement.
2. The best-known British example of GK transformation at a 'brownfield site' is probably Rover cars. In less than five years, it managed to move from the status of national embarrassment to that of an organisation worthy of international respect.
3. Drawn at a conference in London's Barbican Centre in 1989.
4. Consider the example of Nissan's UK plant in the autumn of 1985. Eight months after the core management team had been appointed and eight months before the start of production, when the whole population of the company was still less than 200, it had to contend with an unexpected vacancy for a final assembly manager. With many of the existing managers and supervisors still undergoing training, Nissan could easily have justified recruiting an experienced production manager from elsewhere in the motor industry. Instead it chose to demonstrate its commitment to developing and growing its own staff at the earliest opportunity. The position was filled by laterally transferring the paint shop manager. The resulting vacancy was filled by the diagonal promotion of the paint shop's senior engineer. That vacancy was filled by another diagonal promotion for a paint shop supervisor who had engineering experience. A Team Leader was promoted to supervisor and his place in turn was filled by promoting one of Nissan's newly hired paint sprayers. One vacancy led to five seized opportunities to recognise and reinforce the calibre and commitment of an organisation's personnel.
5. Named after its inventor, Henry Gantt, this is the simplest of project planning tools – a diagrammatic representation of grouped and related project activities using horizontal bars to indicate timescale.
6. There may be a degree of interchange between some of the items listed under Phases 4 and 5 in Figure 17.1. In a capital-intensive plant, for example, it may prove appropriate to bring TPM activity forward into Phase 4.
7. What *is* imperative is that, once the improvements have made it possible to operate with a lesser number of people, the FLM must carry out direct production operations with only that lesser number; otherwise the surplus will be reabsorbed and lost.

Appendix I: The Four Principles of Motion Economy

BASIC PRINCIPLE	USE OF THE HUMAN BODY	ARRANGEMENT OF PARTS AND MATERIALS	TOOLS AND EQUIPMENT
1. REDUCE THE NUMBER OF MOTIONS Example: Professional thieves always rifle desk drawers from the bottom up	Reduce eye movements Eliminate searching, selecting, switching hands Pick up more than one item together where possible Consider combining two or more motions	Use containers and tools that make parts and materials easy to handle Use fixed positions for tooling and parts to allow habits to form easily Arrange in order of use during operation Place so that they are easy to use, pick up and set down Present parts in the same and most suitable orientation every time	Put controls within easy reach Make the movement and operating direction of machines the same Combine two or more tools into one (e.g. back-to-back wrenches) Use mechanisms that require fewer motions to mount on jigs Find sequence which minimises slinging and lifting
2. PERFORM MOTIONS SIMULTANEOUSLY Example: Playing the drums in a rock band or driving a car	Employ both hands (and feet) whenever possible Both hands should start moving and finish at the same time Hands and arms should move symmetrically and in opposite directions	Position for simultaneous movement of both hands	If objects must be held steady for a long time, use a holding tool Exploit foot pedals for operating machines, jigs or fixtures Design jigs that allow simultaneous use of both hands
3. SHORTEN MOTION DISTANCES Example: Remote controls for TVs and stereos	Reduce the number of strides required to perform the work Motions should be done using optimum and minimal no. of parts of human body Eliminate bending and stretching Motions should be done in the shortest distance	Make the work area as small as possible without hindering the work Make it easy to dispose of empty boxes or stillages	Operate machines using optimum and minimal no. of parts of human body Exploit gravity: provide chutes and rollers to feed parts and components in/out of the workplace
4. MAKE MOTIONS EASIER Can the number of work factors be reduced? i.e. • Weight • Adjustment • Caution • Change of direction • Stop	Make motions as unrestricted and easy as possible Make changes in direction smooth: curved motions are best	Optimise the heights of parts to avoid awkward lifting Benches and chairs should be at the correct working height to avoid interrupted motions Make it difficult to fit or pick up the wrong part Raise large boxes and containers on platforms. Give containers drop sides	Make handles, levers etc. on tools and equipment easy to grip Use jigs and guides to control a set movement, e.g. locating pins Use counter-balances on heavy tooling Design jigs so that their position can be easily adjusted, e.g. bevel for a better fit

Appendix II: The Five Cs

Steps 1–5 are provided for establishing and maintaining an ordered and productive workplace.

STEP	ACTIVITY	BENEFITS
1. Clear out *Seiri* (neatness)	**Get rid of all unnecessary items** • Identify all items not required in the area • Set stock levels required and return the excess • List all remaining required items, parts and materials	• No clutter • Less chance to use wrong part, gauge or tool • Improved safety and comfort
2. Configure *Seiton* (order)	**Locate all necessary items in their own visually marked place** • Each required item should have a set location or 'address' • Visually identify locations and appropriate stock levels (max./min.) • Clear obstructions to improve safety, access and motion • Specify and clarify appropriate and acceptable limits on gauges	• Items are easier to find • Faster operations, machine settings and maintenance actions • The area is safer to work in • Easy to see when items are missing or misplaced • Reduces damage to parts and equipment
3. Clean and check *Seiso* (cleanliness)	**Clean the area and its equipment, assess its condition and identify problems and irregularities** • Clean and check the area and equipment • Produce a list of problems found • Use paint or tape to mark machine positions, storage locations, walkways etc. clearly • Make it easier to keep things clean – improve inherently 'messy' machines and processes	• Easy to see and address equipment faults • Tools and equipment work when required • Reduced breakdowns • A cleaner, safer more comfortable workplace • Increases team morale and customer confidence
4. Conformity *Seiketsu* (purity)	**Introduce standards, routines and training** • Set standards for what is acceptable • Communicate the purpose and standards • Set times for routine cleaning (shift/week/month) • Ensure 5C requirements for each job are captured by the Standard Operation	• Everyone understands the standards and their purpose • Generates pride in the workplace and team spirit
5. Custom and habit *Shitsuke* (discipline)	**Introduce procedures and systems which maintain and improve these practices** • Be disciplined in maintaining standards • Conduct regular (e.g. monthly) audits • Show results on display boards • Set targets for improvement	• The new standards are maintained • Further improvements are encouraged

Select Bibliography

For those yet to be convinced that Japanese manufacturing performance has little to do with investment in technology, work ethics or culture: John Lorriman and Takashi Kenjo (1994), *Japan's Winning Margins*, Oxford: Oxford University Press.

The seminal work on *kaizen* is written in a style of clear and intelligent English that puts many native English writers on business and management to shame: Masaaki Imai (1986), *Kaizen, The Key to Japan's Competitive Success*, New York: McGraw-Hill.

On motivation and for a brief guided tour through the various manifestations of cultural noise: Frederick Herzberg (1968), 'One more time: how do you motivate employees?' *Harvard Business Review*, Jan/Feb.

On teamwork and leadership: John Adair (1984), *The Skills of Leadership* and (1986), *Effective Teambuilding*, Aldershot, Hants: Gower.

On the concept and benefits of focusing the organisation on the needs of the downstream customer: Richard J. Schonberger (1990), *Building a Chain of Customers*, New York: Free Press and London: Hutchinson Business Books.

For numerous illustrated examples of visual management: Michel Greif (1991), *The Visual Factory: Building Participation Through Shared Information*, Portland, Ore.: Productivity Press.

For some unique, personal insights on lean manufacturing from an individual who, one way or another, has probably converted more waste into productive work than any other: Taiichi Ohno (1988), *Workplace Management*, Cambridge, Mass.: Productivity Press. Originally (1982), *Genba Keiei*, Tokyo: Japan Management Association.

For methods and formats of job standardisation for a range of processes and activities: Shigehiro Nakamura (1993), *The New Standardization*, Portland, Ore.: Productivity Press. Originally (1991), *QCD Kakushin no tameno genba no hyojunka gijutsu*, Tokyo: JMA.

On personnel management practices compatible with GK principles in Western countries: Peter D. Wickens (1987), *The Road to Nissan: Flexibility, Quality, Teamwork*, Basingstoke, Hants: Macmillan.

For those still seeking practical examples of GK tools and techniques there are

251

innumerable options but, as compendia of the most important applications, Richard J. Schonberger's contributions have never been surpassed: (1982), *Japanese Manufacturing Techniques: Nine Hidden Lessons in Simplicity* and (1986), *World Class Manufacturing: The Lessons of Simplicity Applied*, New York: Free Press and London: Hutchinson Business Books.

Finally, a classic from a man whose philosophy, characterised by clear reason and profound humanity, remains as valid for Western business now as it was in 1982 and (despite a few disingenuous whisperings to the contrary) is valued as much in Japan today as it was in 1950: W. Edwards Deming (1986), *Out of the Crisis*, Cambridge, Mass.: MIT and Cambridge, England: Cambridge University Press.

Index

ISO 9000 Quality Systems Auditing

Dennis Green

This book addresses every aspect of ISO 9000 Quality Systems Auditing. Any organization preparing for ISO certification will need to carry out Internal Audits to confirm that its Quality System has been implemented and is effective in achieving the organization's objectives. Such auditing also provides opportunities for everyone to make changes to the Quality System so that it can become more efficient.

Dr Green addresses 'evaluation' of suppliers through second party audits, but he also shows how these can be kept to an absolute minimum by the introduction of a systematic method for getting on to an Approved List.

The mystique surrounding third party audits is removed by detailed explanations of pre-audits, pre-assessments and assessments. The attributes of good auditors and important facets of good auditing are discussed. Inexperienced and experienced auditors could also benefit from studying the set of 'core questions' prepared for their use.

No other book attempts to deal with quality systems auditing in such a comprehensive and authoritative manner.

Gower

ISO 14000 and ISO 9000

Brian Rothery

This is a practical 'hands-on' description of how companies can
implement a comprehensive system to meet the requirements of
the ISO 14000 Environmental Management Standard and the ISO
9000 Quality Management Standard, in addition to the Health and
Safety regulations, and other public and product safety and general
liability requirements. Written by the leading authority in this
field, it anticipates the Phase Two revisions of ISO 9000 and
provides complete sets of generic documentation including a
Quality Manual and all the environmental registers and manuals.

The author also takes account of the 'backlash' against the ISO
9000 certification process which uses checklists of documents to
please inspectors rather than implementing real quality
improvement schemes. Throughout the book, advice is given on
introducing good, comprehensive systems rather than producing
sets of bureaucratic documents.

By presenting an integrated approach to the standards covering
quality, health and safety and environmental issues, Brian Rothery
has once again provided managers with an important
reference and guide.

Gower

Process Improvement

A Handbook for Managers

Sarah Cook

Sarah Cook's book offers a systematic, customer-focused approach to improving the way we work. The methods it describes can be applied equally to a specific area or function and to the organization as a whole.

The author outlines a four-stage approach and shows what is involved at each stage and how to use the relevant techniques. The text is supplemented by case studies drawn from a variety of businesses and notes on sources of further information.

For managers, team leaders, trainers and consultants looking for practical ways to enhance organizational performance, here is a powerful new tool.

Gower

Re-Engineering at Work
Second Edition

Michael Loh

Business process re-engineering has been hailed as the answer to
the challenges faced by businesses in the late 1990s, yet many
re-engineering programmes have fallen short of expectations, or
have failed altogether. Several years on, where is it going now?
What benefits does it have to offer today?

Dr Michael Loh is a long-time believer in the benefits of
re-engineering, and believes that when it fails, it's because
insufficient attention has been paid to the human element.
Changing an organization means changing the behaviour of its
people. And unless those people are enthusiastic, no lasting change
can take place. He sets out a simple four stage framework for
introducing a successful re-engineering programme. Using
examples from a wide range of organizations in many different
cultures, he explains what is involved at each stage, and shows
how to align the aspirations of the individual with the goals of the
organization to secure genuine commitment.

This new edition of *Re-Engineering at Work* has been fully updated.
Several completely new chapters include: information technology
as an enabler, the way ahead, and the Asian experience.

Gower

DATE DUE

GAYLORD			PRINTED IN U.S.A.